CW01304857

Italian

Learn Italian For Beginners Including Italian Grammar, Italian Short Stories and 1000+ Italian Phrases

© Copyright 2018

All rights reserved. No part of this book may be reproduced in any form without permission in writing from the author. Reviewers may quote brief passages in reviews.

Disclaimer: No part of this publication may be reproduced or transmitted in any form or by any means, mechanical or electronic, including photocopying or recording, or by any information storage and retrieval system, or transmitted by email without permission in writing from the publisher.

While all attempts have been made to verify the information provided in this publication, neither the author nor the publisher assumes any responsibility for errors, omissions or contrary interpretations of the subject matter herein.

This book is for entertainment purposes only. The views expressed are those of the author alone, and should not be taken as expert instruction or commands. The reader is responsible for his or her own actions.

Adherence to all applicable laws and regulations, including international, federal, state and local laws governing professional licensing, business practices, advertising and all other aspects of doing business in the US, Canada, UK or any other jurisdiction is the sole responsibility of the purchaser or reader.

Neither the author nor the publisher assumes any responsibility or liability whatsoever on the behalf of the purchaser or reader of these materials. Any perceived slight of any individual or organization is purely unintentional.

Contents

INTRODUCTION 1

CHAPTER 1 – PRONUNCIATION 2
   1.1 THE ITALIAN ALPHABET 2
      1.1.1 Vowels 2
      1.1.2 Consonants and their combinations 4
   1.2 ACCENTS 7
      1.2.1 Grave accent 7
      1.2.2 Acute accent 7

CHAPTER 2 – BASIC GRAMMAR RULES 9
   2.1 GENDER FORMS 9
   2.2 ARTICLES 11
      2.2.1 Definite article 11
      2.2.2 Indefinite article 13
   2.3 QUANTIFIERS 14
   2.4 NOUNS AND THEIR PLURAL 14

CHAPTER 3 – ADJECTIVES 16
   3.1 COMPARATIVE ADJECTIVES 16
   3.2 POSSESSIVE ADJECTIVES 17
   3.3 INTERROGATIVE ADJECTIVES 18
   3.4 DEMONSTRATIVE ADJECTIVES 18
   3.5 INDEFINITE ADJECTIVES 20

CHAPTER 4 – PRONOUNS 22
   4.1 PERSONAL PRONOUNS 22
      4.1.1 Subject pronouns 22
      4.1.2 Object pronouns 23
      4.1.2.1 Direct object pronouns 23
      4.1.2.2 Indirect object pronouns 24
   4.2 POSSESSIVE PRONOUNS 25
   4.3 INTERROGATIVE PRONOUNS 25
   4.4 RELATIVE PRONOUNS 26
   4.5 DEMONSTRATIVE PRONOUNS 28
   4.6 INDEFINITE PRONOUNS 29

CHAPTER 5 – PREPOSITIONS 31
5.1 SIMPLE PREPOSITIONS 31
5.2 ARTICULATED PREPOSITIONS 32

CHAPTER 6 – VERBS 35
6.1 TRANSITIVE AND INTRANSITIVE VERBS 35
6.2 VERBAL MODES 35
6.2.1 Finite modes 35
6.2.2 Indefinite modes 36
6.3 VERBAL TENSES 36
6.4 AUXILIARY VERBS 37
6.4.1 Essere – to be 37
6.4.1.1 Simple tenses 37
6.4.1.2 Compound tenses 39
6.4.2 Avere – to have 41
6.4.2.1 Simple tenses 41
6.4.2.2 Compound tenses 42
6.5 MODAL VERBS 45
6.5.1 Potere – to can, to may 45
6.5.1.1 Simple tenses 45
6.5.1.2 Compound tenses 46
6.5.2 Volere – to want 48
6.5.2.1 Simple tenses 48
6.5.2.2 Compound times 50
6.5.3 Dovere – to must, to have to 52
6.5.3.1 Simple times 52
6.5.3.2 Compound tenses 53
6.6 REGULAR VERBS CONJUGATION 55
6.6.1 First conjugation in –are 55
6.6.1.1 Simple tenses 56
6.6.1.2 Compound tenses 58
6.6.2 Second conjugation in –ere 59
6.6.2.1 Simple tenses 60
6.6.2.2 Compound tenses 62
6.6.3 Third conjugation in –ire 63
6.6.3.1 Simple tenses 64
6.6.3.2 Compound tenses 68

6.7 Irregular verbs conjugations 71
    6.7.1 Irregular verbs in –are *71*
    6.7.2 Irregular verbs in –ere *73*
    6.7.3 Irregular verbs in –ire *76*
    6.7.4 Irregular verbs in –arre, -orre, -urre *79*
6.8 Reflexive verbs 81
6.9 Pronominal verbs 82

CHAPTER 7 – PROPOSITIONS 84
7.1 Types of propositions 84
    7.1.1 Principal propositions *84*
    7.1.2 Subordinated propositions *85*
    7.2.1 Hypotetical period *88*
    7.1.3 Coordinated propositions *89*

CHAPTER 8 – COMPLEMENTS 91
8.1 Direct complements 91
8.2 Indirect complements 92
    8.2.1 Complement of comparison *94*
8.3 Circumstantial complements 95
    8.3.1 Complements of place *96*
    8.3.2 Complements of time *97*

CHAPTER 9 – HOW TO… 98
9.1 … make the passive form of a verb? 98
9.2 … build the negative form of a sentence? 98
9.3 … compose the courtesy form? 99
9.4 … tell the time? 99
9.5 … tell the date? 100

CHAPTER 10 – USEFUL VOCABULARY 101
10.1 Numbers 101
    10.1.1 Cardinal numbers *101*
    10.1.2 Ordinal numbers *102*
10.2 Days, months, seasons, festivities 103
10.3 The weather 105
10.4 Greeting, introduction, basic expressions 105
10.5 Countries, nationalities 107
10.6 Colors 109
10.7 Pets and animals 110

- 10.8 Food and eating 111
  - *10.8.1 Fruits 111*
  - *10.8.2 Vegetables 111*
  - *10.8.3 Other foods and dishes 112*
- 10.9 Places 113
- 10.10 Occupations 114

CONCLUSION **117**

PART 2: ITALIAN SHORT STORIES **118**

9 SIMPLE AND CAPTIVATING STORIES FOR EFFECTIVE ITALIAN LEARNING FOR BEGINNERS **118**

INTRODUCTION **119**

CHAPTER 1: LA STORIA DEL SIGNOR TEMPO – THE STORY OF MR. TIME **120**
- 1.1 – Summary 121
- 1.2 – Vocabulary 122
- 1.3 – Questions 122
- 1.4 – Answers 123

CHAPTER 2: IL SINGHIOZZO DELLA VOLPE – THE SOB OF THE FOX **124**
- 2.1 – Summary 126
- 2.2 – Vocabulary 126
- 2.3 – Questions 127
- 2.4 – Answers 127

CHAPTER 3: LE ZUPPE MAGICHE – THE MAGICAL SOUPS **128**
- 3.1 – Summary 129
- 3.2 – Vocabulary 130
- 3.3 – Questions 130
- 3.4 - Answers 131

CHAPTER 4: TRISTE E ALLEGRA – SAD AND HAPPY **132**
- 4.1 – Summary 135
- 4.2 – Vocabulary 135
- 4.3 – Questions 136
- 4.4 – Answers 137

CHAPTER 5: C'È UNA LUCERTOLA NEL CAMINO – THERE'S A LIZARD IN THE…..138
- 5.1 – Summary 142
- 5.2 – Vocabulary 142
- 5.3 – Questions 143
- 5.4 – Answers 144

CHAPTER 6: BOLLE DI SAPONE – SOAP BUBBLES **145**

- 6.1 – Summary 148
- 6.2 – Vocabulary 148
- 6.3 – Questions 149
- 6.4 – Answers 150

CHAPTER 7: IL PACCHETTO VERDE – THE GREEN PACKAGE **152**
- 7.1 – Summary 155
- 7.2 – Vocabulary 156
- 7.3 – Questions 157
- 7.4 – Answers 158

CHAPTER 8 - IL PETTIROSSO DI CARTA – THE PAPER ROBIN **159**
- 8.1 – Summary 163
- 8.2 – Vocabulary 163
- 8.3 – Questions 164
- 8.4 – Answers 166

CHAPTER 9: UN ROSETO SOTTO TERRA – A ROSE GARDEN UNDER THE GROUND **167**
- 9.1 – Summary 169
- 9.2 – Vocabulary 170
- 9.3 – Questions 170
- 9.4 – Answers 171

CONCLUSION **173**

PART 3: ITALIAN PHRASE BOOK **174**

INTRODUCTION **175**

CHAPTER 1 – BASIS **176**
- 1.1 Single letters pronunciation 176
- 1.2 Combinations pronunciation 177
- 1.3 Numbers 177
  - *1.3.1 Cardinal numbers* *177*
  - *1.3.2 Ordinal numbers* *178*
- 1.4 Time 180
  - *1.4.1 Useful words about time* *182*
- 1.5 Date 182
  - *1.5.1 Useful words about date* *183*
- 1.6 Colors 185

CHAPTER 2 - **187**

TRAVELLING IN ITALY **187**
- 2.1 At the airport 187

2.2 AT THE ACCOMMODATION 190

2.3 MONEY 195

 2.3.1 AT THE BANK 196

CHAPTER 3 - EVERYDAY LIFE 199

3.1 GREETINGS, THANKING, SAYING YES OR NO 199

3.2 TALKING ABOUT THE WEATHER 202

3.3 GOING AROUND 204

 3.3.1 Useful vocabulary to go around 207

3.4 (DOING THE) SHOPPING 209

 3.4.1 Shops names 213

 3.4.2 Food vocabulary 214

 3.4.3 Other articles 216

3.5 AT THE HAIR SALOON 217

3.6 EATING OUT 219

 3.6.1 What's on the menu? 224

3.7 (ON THE) PHONE 225

3.8 MAKING PLANS 228

 3.8.1 Some ideas 230

3.9 SPARE TIME 231

 3.9.1 At the museum 231

 3.9.2 At the cinema 232

 3.9.3 At the club 234

 3.9.4 Useful words about spare time 237

3.10 EMERGENCIES 241

3.11 ASKING FOR INTERNET AND WIFI 243

3.12 MAKING COMPLIMENTS 244

 3.12.1 AND GOING DEEPER… 244

CHAPTER 4 - TALKING ABOUT YOU 247

4.1 INTRODUCING YOURSELF 247

 4.1.1 I come from… 250

 4.1.2 So I am… 253

4.2 WHAT'S YOUR WORK? 256

 4.2.1 Professions names 257

4.3 WHAT'S YOUR RELIGION? 259

 4.3.1 I am… 259

 4.3.2 Religious places 260

 4.4 Likes, dislikes, feelings 260

 4.5 Talking about your daily routine 264

  4.5.1 Adverbs of time 266

CHAPTER 5 - HEALTH **268**

 5.1 Going to the doctor 268

  5.1.1 Body parts 271

  5.1.2 Symptoms 272

  5.1.3 Other words about health 272

 5.2 Buying medications 274

CHAPTER 6 – EDUCATION, POLITICS, ACTUALITY **276**

 6.1 Approaching to a course 276

  6.1.1 Subjects 277

 6.2 Talking about politics 278

  6.2.1 Useful vocabulary about politics 279

 6.3 Talking about actuality 280

  6.3.1 Useful vocabulary about actuality 281

CHAPTER 7 – INTO THE REAL ITALIAN SPIRIT **283**

 7.1 Some ways of saying 283

 7.2 Italian regions and towns 285

 7.3 What are the public holidays? 288

  7.3.1 Holidays greetings 290

CHAPTER 8 – USEFUL TERMS **292**

CONCLUSION **306**

Part 1: Italian
An Essential Guide to Italian Language Learning

Introduction

The Italian language gets its origins from Latin. Starting from this elaborated jargon, the so-called Neo-Latin languages were born: French, Spanish, Portoguese, Romanian, Ladin – an Italian dialect – and, of course, Italian.

In Italy, the official spoken language is Italian, but there many different dialects, too. These are real local languages which are still in use, even if not as often, in everyday life.

When learning the Italian language, you will have the opportunity to shape your knowledge about it in various fields: in literature, culture, eclectic and full of facets, and in food, maybe one of the topics at the top places of the Italian heritage.

Dictionary at hand and step by step, you will approach learning the basics to speak Italian at its, and your, best.

"All the people of Earth listen to the Italian language with pleasure, but no one writes it, no one had the courage to take it out from its delicious geographical domains."

[Pedro Felipe Monlau]

What about you?

Chapter 1 – Pronunciation

1.1 The Italian alphabet

The Italian alphabet involves 21 letters: 5 vowels and 16 consonants. There are a further 5 letters of foreign origins – j, k, w, x, y – which come from other languages words, but are in current usage.

For the letters of the alphabet below, the English pronunciation is in brackets.

A [Ah]

B [Bee]

C [Chee]

D [Dee]

E [Ay]

F [Effay]

G [Gee]

H [Ahkka]

I [Ee]

L [Ellay]

M [Emmay]

N [Ennay]

O [Oh]

P [Pee]

Q [Koo]

R [Erray]

S [Essay]

T [Tee]

U [Oo]

V [Vee]

Z [Zeta]

1.1.1 Vowels

Italian vowels are a, e, i, o and u.

A has always an open sound, like in *casa* or *amare*. Its pronunciation is like the letter "a" in the word "r<u>a</u>ther."

Mor<u>a</u>   Blackberry
B<u>a</u>gno   Bathroom
Giorn<u>a</u>ta   Day
C<u>a</u>stello   Castle
Limon<u>a</u>ta   Lemonade

E may have two variants:

A closed sound like the letter a in the word "d<u>a</u>y."

Fréccia   Arrow
Battésimo   Baptism
Forchétta   Fork
Dolcézza   Sweetness
Moménto   Moment

An open sound pronounced like the e letter in "<u>e</u>gg."

Bandièra   Flag
Erède   Heir
Tredicènne   Thirteen-year-old
Mittènte   Sender
Cèrvo   Deer

I always has a closed sound, as in the words *inverno* and *fila*. It is pronounced like the double e in English words "sh<u>ee</u>p", "d<u>ee</u>p" or "k<u>ee</u>p."

Cap<u>i</u>tano   Capitain
Anz<u>i</u>ano   Old man
C<u>i</u>polla   Onion
Man<u>i</u>polare   To manipulate
M<u>i</u>lle   One thousand

O can be pronounced with an open sound as in the word "ph<u>o</u>ne."

Tuòno   Thunder
Scuòla   School
Suòcera   Mother-in-law
Mentòlo   Menthol
Pròlogo   Prologue

... or with a closed sound as in the word "g<u>o</u>t."

M<u>o</u>ndo   World
Gi<u>o</u>rno   Day

Cast<u>o</u>ro   Beaver
Pescat<u>o</u>re   Fisherman
Corrid<u>oi</u>o   Hallway

U is always pronounced like the double o in the words "sp<u>oo</u>n" or "m<u>oo</u>d."

T<u>u</u>nica   Tunic
L<u>u</u>na   Moon
C<u>u</u>ccia   Kennel
Z<u>u</u>ppa   Soup
Es<u>u</u>ltare   To exult

1.1.2 Consonants and their combinations

Consonants, as you may imagine, are the 16 remaining letters of the alphabet. However, you have to pay attention about the pronunciation of their combinations; these can be made with both vowels and consonants.

C or double C before e and i vowels is pronounced as the English "ch" in the words "<u>ch</u>eese" or "<u>Ch</u>ina."

<u>C</u>ena   Dinner
Ami<u>ci</u>   Friends
<u>C</u>esoia   Shear
Re<u>c</u>into   Fence
Car<u>ce</u>re   Jail

C before a, o or u is pronounced as k sound in the word "<u>c</u>at."

<u>C</u>ane   Dog
<u>C</u>oltello   Knife
<u>C</u>ucina   Kitchen
Mar<u>ca</u>   Brand
Par<u>co</u>   Park

CH before e and i vowels has the hard "k" sound as in the English word "<u>c</u>ar."

<u>Ch</u>ela   Claw
Anar<u>chia</u>   Anarchy
An<u>che</u>   Hips
Ginoc<u>chio</u>   Knee
Zuc<u>ch</u>ero   Sugar

G or double G before e and i is pronounced as the English sound "dg" as in the word "jeans."

<u>Gi</u>ocattolo   Toy
<u>G</u>elato   Ice cream
Ser<u>g</u>ente   Sergeant

Re**gg**ere   To bear

Monta**gg**io   Mounting

G before a, o and u vowels is pronounced as the hard "g" sound in "good."

Gonna   Skirt
La**go**   Lake
Gomma   Gum
Guscio   Shell
Lin**gu**a   Tongue

GH before e and i sounds like the g in the word "gelatin."

Ghepardo   Cheetah
Do**ghe**   Staves
Un**ghi**a   Nail
Ghiro   Dormouse
In**ghi**lterra   England

GL before i is pronounced like the "–lli" sound in "bri**lli**ant."

Fi**gli**o   Son
A**gli**o   Garlic
Detta**gli**o   Detail
Fami**gli**a   Family
Germo**gli**o   Bud

GN, followed by any of the vowels, is pronounced like the –ni sound in "opi**ni**on."

Campa**gn**a   Country
Lasa**gn**e   Lasagna
Si**gn**ificante   Significant
Ra**gn**o   Spider
Pia**gn**ucolare   To whine

GU is pronounced as the "gw" sound in the English proper noun "**Gu**yneth."

Guanti   Gloves
U**gu**ale   Equal
Man**gu**sta   Mangoose
Conse**gu**ire   To achieve
Uru**gu**ay   Uruguay

H is never pronounced, but, as you already learned before, it modifies c and g.

QU sounds as the English "kw" in "**qu**estion."

Quando   When
Liquore   Liquor
Cinque   Five
Colloquio   Interview
Pasqua   Easter

S, when between two vowels, is generally a soft sound as the s in English word "salt."

Rosa   Rose
Viso   Face
Difeso   Defended
Chiesa   Curch
Blusa   Blouse

… but sometimes it has a hard sound as the "z" in "zoo."

Disegnare   To draw
Svelto   Quick
Spalla   Shoulder
Lastra   Plate
Slitta   Sleigh

SC before e and i vowels is pronounced as the sound "sh" in the words "shell" or "shock."

Uscita   Exit
Lasciare   To leave
Cuscino   Pillow
Discesa   Downhill
Vascello   Vessel

SCH followed by e and i is pronounced sk as in "sky."

Schermo   Screen
Scheletro   Skeleton
Schivare   To avoid
Affreschi   Frescos
Maschile   Masculine

Z or double Z is soft when between two vowels. It is pronounced as the "ts" in English word "bits."

Azoto   Nitrogen
Azalea   Azalea
Ozono   Ozone
Sintetizzare   To synthesize
Penalizzare   To penalize

However, there's the hard-sound version, which is similar to the "ds" pronunciation in "roads."

Zodiaco   Zodiac
Zenzero   Ginger
Zanna   Fang

1.2 Accents

1.2.1 Grave accent

There two kinds of accents in Italian. The most common one by far is the so-called *accento grave*, grave accent. It's a little line pointing downwards and can appear above any vowel.

Città   City
Falò   Bonfire
È   (He/she) is

It is obligatory to use the grave accent in these cases:

In monosyllabic words with the form of "consonant + i or u + vowel."

Può   (he/she) can
Già   Already, yet
Ciò   This, that

In some monosyllabic words in order to distinguish two different meanings of a given word:

Da   From, since
Dà   (He/she) gives

Di   Of
Dì   Day

E   And
È   (He/she) is

La   The (f.sing.)
Là   There

Si   It-/him-/herself
Sì   Yes

1.2.2 Acute accent

The *accento acuto*, acute accent, a small upwards-pointing line, is normally used only in connection with the letter "e." As said in chapter 1.1.1, this vowel has two possible pronunciations in the Italian language and this fact is due to the accent type.

The *accento acuto* is used:

In the words ending with –ché.
Affinché   In order that
Poiché   Since, because

In a few monosyllabic words to distinguish two different meanings and pronunciations.
Ne   From there, of it   Né   Neither, not
Se   If   Sé   Self

This accent may be used in dictionaries and in language instruction to help remember the correct pronunciation, but in practice it has to be learnt by heart if it is an open or closed sound.

Chapter 2 – Basic grammar rules

2.1 Gender forms

In the Italian language there are only two gender forms: masculine and feminine. In the case of animated beings, the grammatical genre corresponds to the sex of the indicated man or animal.

In some cases, male or female gender can be predictable on the basis of belonging to certain categories.

In most cases, it is feminine with:

Fruit names.

La pera   Pear
La mela   Apple
La pesca   Peach

Names of sciences, disciplines and abstract concepts.
La chimica   Chemistry
La grammatica   Grammar
La scienza   Science

Names which indicate military activities.
La pattuglia   Patrol
La guardia   Guard
La guida   Guide

Names of cities, islands, regions, states and continents.
La Ferrara estense   The Estes' Ferrara
La Germania   Germany
L'America   America

In most cases, it is masculine with:

Tree names.

Il melo   Apple tree
Il pero   Pear tree
Il cipresso   Cypress

Names of metals and chemical elements.

L'oro   Gold
Lo iodio   Iodine
Il carbonio   Carbon

Names of seas, mountains, lakes, rivers.

Il Tevere   Tiber
Il Mediterraneo   Mediterranean
L'Appennino   Apennines

Names of cardinal points

Il nord   North
Il sud   South
L'ovest   West
L'est   East

In general, the distinction between masculine and feminine is given by termination of words. These are considered, of course, in their singular form.

The masculine form is generally recognizable from:

the ending with –o letter.

Il caval<u>lo</u>   Horse
Il lib<u>ro</u>   Book
Lo sca<u>fo</u>   Boat
Il materas<u>so</u>   Mattress

names, largely of foreign origin, ending in consonant.

Il compute<u>r</u>   Computer
Il route<u>r</u>   Router
Il provide<u>r</u>   Provider
Il rada<u>r</u>   Radar

The feminine form is generally recognizable from:

almost all names with ending in –a

La taz<u>za</u>   Mug
La pian<u>ta</u>   Plant
La sca<u>la</u>   Stair
La por<u>ta</u>   Door

names with endings in –tà and –tù

La vir<u>tù</u>   Goodness
La fatali<u>tà</u>   Fate
La schiavi<u>tù</u>   Slavery
La mortali<u>tà</u>   Mortality

There are also some special cases that concern the genre of names.

Some words (such as *insegnante, giornalista, psichiatra, amante*) have a unique invisible form for male and female and gender may be signaled by the article or by the presence of a previous adjective.

Some words (especially animal names like *tigre, gorilla*) have a single invisible shape for both the male specimen and female specimen. The only way to distinguish male from female is to expose the gender information:

La tigre femmina   The female tiger

Il gorilla maschio   The male gorilla

Some words are subject to a false change of gender and, in the apparent transition from male to female, they actually have a different meaning.

Il busto (m.)   The bust;
la busta (f.)   Envelope

Il palmo (m.)   Hand palm;
la palma (f.)   Palm tree

Il manico (m.)   Handle;
la manica (f.)   Sleeve

Some words have very different shapes for masculine and feminine genders.

Il toro e la vacca   Bull and cow
Il marito e la moglie   Husband and wife
Il genero e la nuora   Son-in-law and daughter-in-law
Il pollo e la gallina   Chicken and hen

2.2 Articles

In Italian language the article agrees with its noun.
It can therefore be masculine or feminine, singular or plural.

<u>La</u> cornice (f./sing.)   The frame
<u>Il</u> lombrico (m./sing.)   The worm
<u>Le</u> ragazze (f./pl.)   The girls
<u>Gli</u> amici (m./pl.)   The friends

2.2.1 Definite article

The definite article is used before nouns to refer to someone or something already mentioned previously and to refer to someone or something specific.

IL it's masculine and singular.

Il tostapane   The toaster
Il mostro   The monster
Il borsello   The man purse
Il quadro   The painting
Il muro   The wall

LO it's masculine and singular; it is used before gn, pn, ps, s followed by consonants and before z.

Lo gnomo   The gnome
Lo pneumatico   The tyre
Lo psicologo   The psychologist
Lo stadio   The stadium
Lo zaino   The backpack

LA is feminine and singular.

La zona   The zone
La nocciola   The hazelnut
La televisione   The television
La camicia   The shirt
La tasca   The pocket

L' is both masculine and feminine. It is used before nouns which begin with a vowel (a, e, i, o, u).

L'asfalto   The asphalt
L'elefante   The elephant
L'intruso   The intruder
L'ospedale   The hospital
L'uccello   The bird

I is masculine and plural.

I ruscelli   The brooks
I bambini   The children
I divani   The sofas
I quaderni   The notebooks
I monaci   The monks

GLI is masculine and plural. It is used before vowels, gn, ps, s followed by consonants and before z.

Gli alleati   The allies
Gli gnomi   The gnomes
Gli psicologi   The psychologists
Gli scarafaggi   The cockroaches
Gli zii   The uncles

LE is feminine and plural.

Le unghie   The nails
Le viti   The screws
Le suore   The nuns
Le nipoti   The nephews
Le spazzole   The brushes

2.2.2 Indefinite article

The indefinite article is used only with singular nouns in order to make general statements.

UN is masculine.

Un lavoro   A job
Un cassetto   A drawer
Un libro   A book
Un forno   An oven
Un manuale   A handbook

UNO is masculine and used before gn, pn, ps, s followed by consonant and before z.

Uno gnomo   A gnome
Uno pneumatico   A tyre
Uno psicologo   A psychologist
Uno slittino   A sleigh
Uno zaino   A backpack

UNA is feminine.

Una casa   A house
Una lavagna   A blackboard
Una bottiglia   A bottle
Una felpa   A sweatshirt
Una mela   An apple

UN' is feminine and used before vowels.

Un'aragosta   A lobster
Un'eclissi   An eclipse
Un'istrice   A porcupine
Un'oasi   An oasis
Un'unghia   A nail

2.3 Quantifiers

In English languages, quantifiers are some and any. They are used to express a certain amount of something.

In Italian language, unlike in English, these quantifiers can be omitted, especially if the sentence is negative.

For example, "I haven't any brothers" can be translated into Italian "Non ho fratelli": "I have no brothers."

DELLO and DELL' are masculine and singular.

<u>Del</u> pane   Some bread
<u>Dello</u> zucchero   Some sugar
<u>Dell'</u>aceto   Some vinegar
<u>Del</u> latte   Some milk

DELLA and DELL' are feminine and singular.

<u>Della</u> salsa   Some sauce
<u>Dell'</u>insalata   Some salad
<u>Della</u> pasta   Some pasta
<u>Dell'</u>acqua   Some water

DEI and DEGLI are masculine and plural.

<u>Dei</u> ragazzi   Some boys
<u>Degli</u> agnelli   Some lambs
<u>Dei</u> fucili   Some rifles
<u>Degli</u> psicopatici   Some psychopaths

DELLE is feminine and plural.

<u>Delle</u> donne   Some women
<u>Delle</u> finestre   Some windows
<u>Delle</u> foglie   Some leaves
<u>Delle</u> caramelle   Some candies

2.4 Nouns and their plural

When wanting to form the plural of Italian words, some rules must be taken into account:

When a noun ends in –o, usually it is masculine. The plural is formed by eliminating the –o and adding –i.

Il letto   I letti   Bed   Beds
Il libro   I libri   Book   Books
Il mulino   I mulini   Mull   Mulls

Some words ending with –o are, however, feminine and remain the same when transformed in plural. Be careful to use the singular article and you won't make a mistake!

L'auto   Le auto   Car   Cars
La mano   Le mani   Hand   Hands
La radio   Le radio   Radio   Radios

Nouns ending with –a are usually feminine. The plural is formed by eliminating –a and adding –e.

La camera   Le camere   Room   Rooms
La data   Le date   Date   Dates
La stagione   Le stagioni   Season   Seasons

Sometimes, the noun may be masculine, too. In that case, just eliminate the –a and add the –i.

L'artista   Gli artisti   Artist   Artists
 L'aroma   Gli aromi   Flavor   Flavors   Il poeta   I poeti   Poet   Poets

Nouns which end with –e may be both masculine and feminine. The plural is formed by eliminating the –e and adding the –i. Words ending with –u and –i remain the same.

Il signore (m.)   I signori   Sir   Sirs
La notte (f.)   Le notti   Night   Nights
L'analisi   Le analisi   Analysis   Analyses

Nouns ending with –co (m.), -ca (f.), -go (m.), -ga (f.) take respectively the –chi (m.), -che (f.), -ghi (m.) and –ghe (f.) endings. They may be both masculine and feminine, so be careful with articles!

Il parco   I parchi   Park   Parks
L'amica   Le amiche   Friend   Friends
Il collega   I colleghi   Colleague(s)

Obviously, it's not all schematic - in fact, in the Italian language there are many examples of irregular plurals, unfortunately.

L'amico   Gli amici   Friend   Friends
Il medico   I medici   Doctor   Doctors
L'uovo   Le uova   Egg   Eggs
Il dito   Le dita   Finger   Fingers
Il ginocchio   Le ginocchia   Knee   Knees

Chapter 3 – Adjectives

In the Italian language, every adjective agrees with the noun it is coupled with. Usually, the adjective comes after it, but there are some exceptions, too.

When considering nouns referring to people and animals which have both feminine and masculine form, adjective agreement follows one of these rules:

The masculine adjective ends with –o; when it's feminine, it ends in –a. In order to transform them into plural, follow the rules in chapter 2.4.

Un uomo alto   A tall man
La donna bassa   The short woman
Il cavallo nero   The black horse
Una luce bianca   A white light

Adjectives which end in –e remain the same both in feminine and masculine form.

Il bambino felice   The happy child
Una bambina intelligente   A smart girl
Un cane vivace   A lively dog
La casa verde   The green house

3.1 Comparative adjectives

In order to form a comparative in Italian language, put più (more) or meno (less/not as) before the adjective.

Il mio cane è più educato del tuo.
My dog is more educated than yours.

La Germania è meno popolata degli Stati Uniti.
Germany is less popolate than United States.

When saying something is equal to something else, use come (the same as/as... as) before the thing compared with the subject.

Questo quadro è come quello là.
This painting is the same as that one.

Paolo gioca bene a calcio come Giuseppe.
Paolo is as good at soccer as Giuseppe.

When forming a superlative in Italian language, put il/la più (the most) or il/la meno (the least) before the adjective.

Questa carne è la meno cara.
This meat is the least expensive.

Il cavallo rosso è il più bello.
The red horse is the most beautiful.

3.2 Possessive adjectives

In Italian languages, unlike in English, the possessive adjective corresponds to the possessive pronoun. This adjective is not always preceded by the article.

Remember: adjectives agree in gender and number with the noun being referred to.

Masculine and singular   Masculine and plural

(Il) mio   My
I miei   My

(Il) tuo   Your
I tuoi   Your

(Il) suo   His/her
I suoi   His/her

(Il) nostro   Our
I nostri   Our

(Il) vostro   Your (pl.)
I vostri   Your (pl.)

(Il) loro   Their
I loro   Their

Feminine and singular   Feminine and plural

(La) mia   My
Le mie   My

(La) tua   Your
Le tue   Your

(La) sua   His/her
Le sue   His/her

(La) nostra   Our
Le nostre   Our

(La) vostra   Your (pl.)
Le vostre   Your (pl.)

(La) loro   Their
Le loro   Their

Mio figlio va a scuola   My son goes to school.

Le loro mogli sono sorelle   Their wives are sisters.

I nostri cavalli sono veloci   Our horses are fast.

La sua casa è rosa   His/her house is pink.

3.3 Interrogative adjectives

Interrogative adjectives in Italian language are quale and che. These two are intended to ask for quality or identity of the noun they refer to. Another interrogative adjective is quanto, which is used to ask for the quantity of referred noun. This one agrees with it, both in number and gender.

QUALE is both feminine and masculine, but singular. It may be translated in English language with "which."

Quale persona (f.)?   Which person?
Quale portiere (m.)?   Which goalkeeper?

QUALI may be of both gender and it's plural. As with singular *quale*, it's translated in English as "which."

Quali fiori (m)?   Which flowers?
Quali sardine (f.)?   Which sardines?

CHE may substitute quale form and it's invariable. It is used in friendly speech and is translated in "what."

Che cosa stai facendo?   What are you doing?
Che lavoro fai?   What's your job?

QUANTO may be translated in English to "how much" or "how many."

Quanto spazio hai...?   How much space...?
Quante zie hai?   How many aunts do you have?

3.4 Demonstrative adjectives

Demonstrative adjectives are used to indicate the identity of what is spoken and its location in space and time, also to indicate the relationship of closeness or distance to whoever speaks or who is listening.

Almost all of them are always placed before the noun with which they agree in gender and number. They are never preceded by the article.

QUESTO (questa, questi, queste) indicates the proximity of the person or person concerned to whoever speaks. It may be translated with English word "this" if singular and "these" if plural.

Questo gioiello è mio   This jewel is mine.
Questa stanza non è blu   This room isn't blue.

Vuoi questi libri?   Do you want these books?
Queste sorelle sono gemelle   These sisters are twins.

QUELLO indicates the distance of the person or person concerned with whoever is speaking and who's listening.

This *aggettivo dimostrativo* has different forms depending on the initials of the name that follows. It behaves in the same way as the determinative article.

Il - QUEL Quel mestolo
That ladle

L' - QUELL' Quell'albero
That tree

Quell'amica (f.)
That friend

Lo - QUELLO Quello zaino
That back pack

La - QUELLA Quella papera
That duck

I - QUEI Quei quaderni
Those notebooks

Gli – QUEGLI Quegli studenti
Those students

Le – QUELLE Quelle guerre
Those wars

CODESTO indicates something far away from the speaker and close to the listener. In the language of common use, written and spoken, this is replaced by *questo* or *quello*.

Codesto luogo   This place
Codesta ragione   This reason
Codesti poliziotti   These polireme
Codeste regole   These rules

3.5 Indefinite adjectives

Indefinite adjectives indicate an unclear amount. They agree with the gender (masculine-feminine) and the number (singular-plural) of the name to which they are linked.

Some of these adjectives have all the forms: masculine, feminine, singular and plural.

ALCUNO, -a, -i, -e (watch out to the plural form!)

Alcune finestre aperte   Some open windows
Alcun libro   No book

ALTRO, -a, -i, -e

Un'altra pizza   Another pizza
L'altro museo   The other museum

ALTRETTANTO, -a, -i, -e

Altrettante persone   As much people
Altrettanta voglia   As much desire…

DIVERSO, -a, -i, -e (watch out to the plural form!)

Una diversa concezione   A different conception   Diversi interessi   Many interests

PARECCHIO, -a, -i, -e

Parecchio sollievo   A lot of relief
Parecchi lavori   A lot of jobs

MOLTO, -a, -i, -e

Molti cappelli   A lot of hats
Molte scuse   Many excuses

POCO, -a, -chi, -che

Pochi giorni   A few days
Poca amicizia   Little friendship

TANTO, -a, -i, -e

Tanti cavalli   A lot of horses
Tanto sonno   A lot of sleep

TROPPO, -a, -i, -e

Troppe case   Too many houses
Troppo casino   Too much noise

TUTTO, -a, -i, -e (watch out to the plural form!)

Tutto il mese   The whole month
Tutte le settimane   Every week

CERTI, -a, -i, -e

Certi esemplari   Certain specimens
Una certa libertà   A certain freedom

Other adjectives have only two forms, masculine and feminine singular.

NESSUNO, -a

Nessun fratello   No brother
Nessuna borsa   No bag

CIASCUNO, -a

Ciascun livello   Each level
Ciascuna matricola   Each freshman

Other indefinite adjectives have only one form that does not change or apply to all people and numbers. This adjective is always used in Italian with the singular.

QUALCHE

Qualche fiore (m.)   Some flowers
Qualche foglia (f.)   Some leale

OGNI

Ogni istante (m.)   Every instant
Ogni lettera (f.)   Every letter

QUALSIASI/QUALUNQUE

Qualsiasi modo (m.)   Any way
Qualsiasi nota (f.)   Any note

Chapter 4 – Pronouns

4.1 Personal pronouns

Personal pronouns are short particles which may replace persons or things. They can be subjects or play a different role.

In Italian languages, types of object pronouns are:

Subject pronouns

Object pronouns

Possessive pronouns

Relative pronouns

4.1.1 Subject pronouns

In Italian language, subject pronouns are often omitted, since the verb form indicates the subject. There are a few exceptions, anyway: when you have to make a clarification, when modified by *anche* (also), or when you have the will to put an emphasis or a contrast.

Io: Io gioco a calcio   I play soccer

Tu: Tu lavori in casa   You work at home

Lui: Lui ascolta   He listens

Egli: Egli osservò   He observed

Lei: Lei studia   She studies

Ella: Ella viaggiò   She travelled

Esso: Esso era blu   It (m.) was blue

Essa: Essa cambiò   It (f.) changed

Noi: Noi cantiamo   We sing

Voi: Voi negate   You (pl.) deny

Essi: Essi litigarono   They (m.) quarreled

Esse: Esse piangono   They (f.) cry

In modern Italian language, people use the most *lei*, *lui* and *loro*, in both feminine and masculine forms.

Personal pronouns are the only part of the sentence in which Italian makes a distinction between masculine, feminine and neutre.

Neutre gender is used for objects, plants and animals except men; but this distinction does not cause any important change, because all other parts of the sentence (nouns, verb inflections, adjectives, etc.) do not have a neutre gender, which is simply handled by using either masculine or feminine.

4.1.2 Object pronouns

Object pronouns are both direct or indirect. They can't stand alone without a verb. The direct object receives the action of the verb directly, while the indirect object is indirectly affected by it.

4.1.2.1 Direct object pronouns

Direct object pronouns stand immediately before the verb or the auxiliary verb in the compound tenses.

Io – Mi Mi ha salutata.
He/she greeted me.

Tu – Ti Ti ho sposato.
I married you.

Lui - Lo/Gli Lo vedo stasera   I'm seeing him tonight.
            Gli hai telefonato?   Did you phone him?

Lei - La/Le Oggi la incontro   Today I'm meeting her.
   Le do un regalo   I give her a gift.

Esso – Lo Lo butto via.
I'm throwing it (m.) away.

Essa – La La coloro di rosso.
I'm coloring it (f.) in red.

Noi – Ci Ci incontriamo là.
We're meeting (us) there.

Voi – Vi Vi aspettiamo qui.
We wait for you (pl.) here.

Essi – Li Lui li paga.
He pays them (m.).

Esse – Le Io le mangio.
I eat them (f.).

When the sentence is negative, the word "non" must come before the object pronoun.

Ecco una carota. Il cavallo <u>non</u> la mangia.
Here's a carrot. The horse doesn't eat it (f.).

Non mi funziona il telefono, quindi <u>non</u> vi telefono.
My telephone doesn't work, so I don't call you (pl.).

When in a sentence there's an infinitive, the object pronoun must be attached to it. The final –e just has to be substituted with the chosen object pronoun.

Ho comprato delle medicine; è importante <u>prender</u>le.
I bought some meds; it's important <u>to take</u> them (f.).

I genitori sono arrabbiati, quindi è meglio non <u>disturbar</u>li.
Parents are angry, so better not <u>to annoy</u> them (m.).

The object pronouns are attached to ecco (here... is), an expression in order to say "Here I am," "Here you are," and so on with any other subject.

Eccovi!   Here you (pl.) are!

Eccolo!   Here he is!

4.1.2.2 Indirect object pronouns

Direct object pronouns answer the question *cosa?* (what?) or *chi?* (whom?), while indirect object pronouns may be an answer to *a chi?* (to whom?) or *per chi?* (for whom?).

Io – Mi   Mi ha dato soldi.
He/she gave me money.

Tu – Ti   Ti regalo una rosa.
I give you a rose.

Lui – Gli   Gli prestano la biro.
They lend him the pen.

Lei – Le   Le facciamo uno scherzo.
We make her a joke.

Esso – Gli   Gli do colore.
I give it (m.) color.

Essa – Le   Le scriviamo un biglietto.
We write her a card.

Noi – Ci   Ci hanno dato un libro.
They gave us a book.

Voi – Vi   Vi diamo ascolto.
We listen to you (pl.).

Essi – loro (m.)

Esse – loro (f.)   Compriamo loro (f. & m.) una casa.
We buy them a house.

4.2 Possessive pronouns

The possessive pronouns correspond to possessive adjectives (chapter 3.2), even if there's a difference: in case of pronouns, it is always preceded by the article.

Remember: as with adjectives, possessive pronouns agree in gender and number with the noun they replace.

Masculine and singular   Masculine and plural

Il mio   Mine   I miei   Mine
Il tuo   Yours   I tuoi   Yours
Il suo   His/hers   I suoi   His/hers
Il nostro   Ours   I nostri   Ours
Il vostro   Yours (pl.)   I vostri   Yours (pl.)
Il loro   Theirs   I loro   Theirs

Feminine and singular   Feminine and plural

La mia   Mine   Le mie   Mine
La tua   Yours   Le tue   Yours
La sua   His/hers   Le sue   His/hers
La nostra   Ours   Le nostre   Ours
La vostra   Yours (pl.)   Le vostre   Yours (pl.)
La loro   Theirs   Le loro   Theirs

Questo animale è il nostro   This pet is ours.

I fiori gialli sono i tuoi   Yellow flowers are yours.

Quest'auto è la vostra?   Is this car yours?

Quelle scarpe sono sue   These shoes are his/hers.

4.3 Interrogative pronouns

Italian interrogative pronouns are chi and che cosa.

CHI refers to people. It may be coupled with a preposition which has to come before the pronoun. *Chi* is invariable (that is always equal to male, female, singular or plural) and wants the verb to the 3rd singular person.

Chi vuole dei biscotti?   Who wants some cookies?

A chi apri la porta?   Who do you open the door to?

Con chi canti?   Who do you sing with?

CHE COSA is referred to things and may be translated to English interrogative "what."

Che cosa usi per cucinare?   What do you use to cook?

A che cosa stai pensando?   What are you thinking of?

Con che cosa ti pettini?   What do you comb with?

4.4 Relative pronouns

The relative pronoun is used in both written and spoken language. It has a dual function:

It replaces a name;

It relates two propositions (sentences) between them

The item replaced by the relative pronoun is called *antecedente*, antecedent; this can be:

A name

A pronoun

A whole proposition

CHE is invariable in gender and number. It can be used both for a subject or for a direct object. When used as a subject, the verbs, the participles, ajd the adjectives of the relative proposition agree with the gender and the number of the antecedent.

Il padre che (sub.) è alto
The father who is tall

Il fiore che (obj.) ho raccolto
The flower that I picked

La signora che (sub.) ha cantato
The woman who sang

Le mostre che (obj.) ho visto
The exhibitions that I saw

For the indirect complements (introduced by the preposition) we use CUI and IL QUALE (and its forms) preceded by a preposition.

CUI is invariable and is used only as an indirect complement, preceded by a preposition. The choice of exposure depends on which preposition the verb wants and, hence, the type of indirect complement.

Il ragazzo di cui sto parlando
The boy I'm talking of

Le persone su cui contare
People you can count on

Il negozio in cui lavoro
The shop I work in

La donna a cui sto pensando
The woman I'm thinking of

CHI may be replaced by DEL QUALE and its forms, but not from the pronoun *che*.

IL QUALE and it forms agree with the genre and the number of the name to which they refer.

IL QUALE is masculine and singular.
LA QUALE is feminine and singular.
I QUALI is masculine and plural.
LE QUALI is feminine and plural.

These pronouns are mainly used with the function of indirect complement (alternatively to *cui*), along with the simple prepositions *di*, *a*, *su*, *in* which, combined with the determinative article, become articulated prepositions.

DI del (m./sin.) – della (f./sing.)
degli (m./pl.) – delle (f./pl.)

A al (m./sin.) – alla (f./sin.)
ai (m./pl.) – alle (f./pl.)

SU sul (m./sin.) – sulla (f./sing.)
sui (m./pl.) – sulle (f./pl.)

IN nel (m./sing.) – nella (f./sing.)
nei (m./pl.) – nelle (f./pl.)

Il ragazzo del quale ti parlo
The boy I tell you about

La bambina alla quale parlo
The little girl I talk to

I balconi sui quali cammino
The balconies I walk on

Le coperte nelle quali dormo
The blankets I sleep in

Unlike other related pronouns, which allow us to specify the gender and number of antecedent, we use the relative one when the use of *che* and *cui* could produce unclear phrases.

4.5 Demonstrative pronouns

In Italian language demonstrative pronouns are used almost exclusively in the formal written register. At their place, in speech and in the less formal written form, pronouns with pronominal function or personal pronouns (chapter 4.1) are used.

The main demonstrative pronouns are following the same rules of demonstrative adjectives (chapter 3.4):

QUESTO and its flex forms.

Il mio gioiello è questo
My jewel is this one.

La stanza blu non è questa
The blue room isn't this one.

I tuoi libri sono questi?
Are these your books?

Le sorelle gemelle sono queste
The twin sisters are these ones.

The flex forms of QUELLO, however, do not coincide with those of the demonstrative adjectives because they do not appear like *quei*, *quegli*. The shapes are *quello*, *quella*, *quelli*, *quelle*.

Il cioccolato che mi hai portato è buono, ma a me piace di più quello con le nocciole.   The chocolate you brought me is tasty, but I prefer the one with nuts.

La novità è quella: ho passato il test!   The piece of news is that one: I passed the test!

I colori che devi usare non sono quelli. Cambiali.   The colours you have to use aren't those ones. Change them.

Ci sono delle torte. Compro quelle?   There are some cakes. Do you buy those ones?

CODESTO and its variations. As you already know, it may substitute *questo* in a more formal way.

Il mio gioiello è codesto
My jewel is this one.

La stanza blu non è codesta
The blue room isn't this one.

I tuoi libri sono codesti?
Are these your books?

Le sorelle gemelle sono codeste
The twin sisters are these ones.

4.6 Indefinite pronouns

Indefinite pronouns are used to replace nouns that indicate people or things in a generic way, without specifying the exact quantity or quality.

Some indefinite pronouns, as indefinite adjectives, are masculine, feminine, singular and plural.

ALCUNO, -a, -i, -e

"Quanti giorni di vacanza hai?" "Ne ho alcuni." "How many days of holidays do you have?" "I have some."

ALTRO, -a, -i, -e

Queste caramelle sono buone. Ne voglio altre!
These candies are tasty. I want some others!

ALTRETTANTO, -a, -i, -e

Io ho molta fame, tu ne hai altrettanta!
I have a lot of hunger, you have the same!

DIVERSO, -a, -i, -e

Io so di non aver coraggio. Paolo ne ha diverso.
I know not to have courage. Paolo has some.

PARECCHIO, -a, -i, -e

Credevo di non aver paura, invece ne ho parecchia!
I thought not to have fear, but I have a lot!

MOLTO, -a, -i, -e

Luciano non ha capelli, io ne ho molti.
Luciano has no hair, I have a lot.

POCO, -a, -chi, -che

Dovrebbero esserci delle bambine. Ne vedo poche.
There should be some baby girls. I see a few.

TANTO, -a, -i, -e

"C'è sporco in questa stanza?" "Sì, ce n'è tanto!"
"Is there dirt in this room?" "Yes, there's a lot!"

TROPPO, -a, -i, -e

Quanta pasta hai cucinato? È troppa!
How much pasta did you cook? It's too much!

TUTTO, -a, -i, -e

Ho accarezzato dei bei cuccioli: li vorrei tutti!
I pet some wonderful puppies: I want them all!

Other pronouns have only two forms: just the singular or just the plural.

UNO, -a – singular

"Hai la bicicletta?" "Sì, ne ho una molto vecchia."
"Do you have a bike?" "Yes, I have a really old one."

QUALCUNO, -a – singular

Vorrei venire alla tua festa. C'è qualcuno che conosco?
I'd like to come to your party. Is there someone I know?

CIASCUNO, -a – singular

Ecco i miei genitori. Regalo un biglietto ciascuno.
Here's my parents. I give each one a card.

OGNUNO, -a – singular

Dato che noi siamo in tanti, ognuno vada per sé.
Since we're a lot, each one have to go for him-/herself.

NESSUNO, -a – singular

Invitai molte donne. Non venne nessuna.
I invited a lot of women. No one came.

CERTI, -e – plural

Conosco alcuni musicisti, certi sono molto bravi.
I know some musicians, some are really good.

Other pronouns have only one form that does not change and applies to all people and numbers.

CHIUNQUE

Il mio cane va d'accordo con chiunque.
My dog gets along with anyone.

QUALCOSA

Tua figlia è maleducata, dovresti dirle qualcosa.
Your daughter misbehaves, you should tell her something.

NIENTE, NULLA

Non voglio nulla/niente dal mercato.
I want nothing from the market.

Chapter 5 – Prepositions

The prepositions are invariable parts of the speech which, put before a name, a pronoun, an adverb or an infinite verb, specifies the syntactic function.

5.1 Simple prepositions

In Italian language simple prepositions are:

DI

Partiremo di lunedì   We will be leaving on Monday.
Questa scatola è di carta   This box is made of paper.
Sono i pastelli di Alice   These are the crayons of Alice.

A

Dalla a me!   Give it to me!
Francesco abita a Venezia   Francesco lives in Venice.

DA

Hans viene da Berlino   Hans comes from Berlin.
Vieni da Anna?   Are you coming to Anna?

CON

Canti con Nicolas?   Are you singing with Nicolas?

SU

Essi contano su di te   They count on you.
Abbiamo parlato di Nicola   We talked about Nicola.

PER

Questo regalo è per Sara   This gift is for Sara.

TRA

Arrivo tra tre ore   I arrive in three hours.
Benvenuto tra noi!   Welcome among us!

FRA

Lei è fra me e te   She's between me and you.
Ci vediamo fra due minuti   See you in two minutes.

SOTTO, SOPRA

La borsa è sotto il tavolo   The bag is under the table.
Il vino è sopra la padella   The wine is on the pan.

PRIMA DI, DOPO

Dopo cena sparecchiamo   After dinner we clear up.
Prima di parlare, pensa!   Before speaking, think!

5.2 Articulated prepositions

When simple prepositions merge with the determinative articles, they give rise to articulated prepositions. They are, in facts, prepositions which contain the article.

DI + IL = DEL – m. sin. consonant

Il pelo del gatto   The fur of the cat

DI + LA = DELLA – f. sin. consonant

Il pettine della moglie   The comb of the wife

DI + I = DEI – m. pl. consonant

La maggior parte dei casi   The major part of cases

DI + GLI = DEGLI – m. pl. vowel

La casa degli zii   The house of uncles

DI + LE = DELLE – f. pl. vowel/consonant

Il colore delle rose   The colour of roses

DELL' – m./f. sin. vowel
It is used in the same cases of *del* and *della*.

Gli abitanti dell'America
The inhabitants of America

A + IL = AL – m. sin. consonant

Andare al lavoro   Going to work

A + I = AI – m. pl. consonant

Chiedere ai nonni   Ask to grandparents

A + GLI = AGLI – m. pl. vowel

Rinunciare agli studi   Renounce to studies

A + LA = ALLA – f. sin. consonant

Contributo alla causa   Contribute to the cause

A + LE = ALLE – f. pl. vowel/consonant

Affluenza alle urne   Affluence to ballot boxes

ALL' – m./f. sin. vowel
It is used in the same cases of *al* and *alla*.

Rivolgersi all'agenzia   Apply to the agency

DA + IL = DAL – m. sin. consonant

Andare dal dentista   Going to the dentist

DA + I = DAI – m. pl. consonant

Togliersi dai guai   Get away from troubles

DA + GLI = DAGLI – m. pl. vowel

La terapia formulata dagli psicologi
Therapy formulated by psychologists

DA + LA = DALLA – f. sin. consonant

Esco dalla casa   I exit (from) the house

DA + LE = DALLE – f. pl. vowel/consonant

Ritornare dalle vacanze   Return from holidays

DALL' – m./f. sin. vowel
It is used in the same cases of *dal* and *dalla*.

Visita dall'endocrinologo
Visit to the endocrinologist

IN + IL = NEL – m. sin. consonant

Camminare nel prato   Walk in the meadow

IN + LA = NELLA – f. sin. consonant

Rimanere nella norma   Stay in the standard

IN + I = NEI – m. pl. consonant

Nei casi di smarrimento   In cases of loss

IN + GLI = NEGLI – m. pl. vowel

Shampoo negli occhi   Shampoo in the eyes

IN + LE = NELLE – f. pl. consonant

Acqua nelle scarpe   Water in the shoes

NELL' – m./f. sin. vowel
It is used in the same cases of *nella* and *nel*.

Lavorare nell'editoria   Work in the publishing

SU + IL = SUL – m. sin. consonant

Salire sul palco   Climb on the stage

SU + I = SUI – m. pl. consonant

Sui colli circostanti   On the surrounding hills

SU + GLI = SUGLI – m. pl. consonant

I gatti sugli armadi   Cats on the wardrobes

SU + LA = SULLA – f. sin. consonant

Il quadro sulla parete   The painting on the wall

SU + LE = SULLE – f. pl. vowel/consonant

Camminare sulle braccia   Walk on the arms

SULL' – m./f. sin. vowel
It is used in the same cases of *sul* and *sulla*.

L'uccello sull'albero   The bird on the tree

Chapter 6 – Verbs

Verbs are maybe the most difficult part to learn when studying the Italian language. Let's explain every rule of them in order to not make errors in the course of learning.

6.1 Transitive and intransitive verbs

Let's begin by saying that Italian verbs may be of two different types: transitive and intransitive. This is important to understand their function when in a sentence.

A verb is transitive when a verb accepts a direct object, expressed or tacit, without a preposition.

Mangiare la pasta   To eat pasta
Ascoltare la musica   To listen to music

In these cases *mangiare* and *ascoltare* are transitive verbs because, in Italian language, they're followed by direct objects, *pasta* and *music*.

It is intransitive when, at the contrary, a verb does not allow a direct object.

Passeggiare in casa   To walk in the house
Lavorare di lunedì   To work on Monday

In these cases *passeggiare* and *lavorare* are intransitive because *in casa* and *di lunedì* are respectively a place complement and a time complement, not direct objects.

6.2 Verbal modes

In Italian, verbs have seven verbal modes. These are usually grouped into two categories: finite modes and indefinite modes.

6.2.1 Finite modes

Finite modes define the type and number of the subject: masculine, feminine, singular or plural. These are four.

INDICATIVO is the most often used mode, especially in spoken language. It is the mode of certainty, objectivity, reality. Therefore, it is used both in the main propositions and in the employed propositions to indicate a true and certain fact or a way to indicate what is perceived by whomever speaks or writes.

CONGIUNTIVO is mainly used in two cases: after verbs expressing opinions, thoughts or feelings, such as *pensare*, *credere*, *ritenere*; and in the hypothetical period.

CONDIZIONALE is the verbal mode which indicates that an action occurs if it occurs another way. It may be used in order to express a desire or a gentle request.

IMPERATIVO is used to give orders, instructions, invite and even pray. It is not difficult, and in Italy it is frequently used.

6.2.2 Indefinite modes

In Italian, indefinite modes do not define the type and number of the subject, at the contrary of finite modes.

INFINITO expresses the action of the verb in a generic and indeterminate manner.

PARTICIPIO may have a nominal value, so it can be used as an adjective. The use of the *participio* with verbal value is very rare, we find it mainly in the juridical-bureaucratic language. When used with verbal value, it may substitute for a relative proposition introduced by –che.

GERUNDIO is used in subordinate propositions and establishes a close relationship with the verb of the principal one. Simple *gerundio* does not express the time of an action but a relationship of contemporaneity with the action of the verb of the main proposition.

6.3 Verbal tenses

Composing the verbal conjugation system, there are also the verbal tenses, which consist in timing the action. These are the Italian presente (present), passato (past) and futuro (future). They have two subcategories:

Tempo semplice (simple tense), consisting of one word.

Io sono   I am
Lui mangia   He eats

This *tempo semplice* joins presente, imperfetto, futuro semplice, passato remoto, condizionale, imperativo, participio and gerundio.

Tempo composto (compound time), consisting of the combination of verbal forms of auxiliaries essere and avere with the participle of the verbs.

Io sono stato   I have been
Lei ebbe giocato   She had played

The words underlined with a line are the auxiliary verbs conjugated to the choosen person and time. Those underlined with dashes are the concurring participles.

This *tempo composto* joins passato prossimo, trapassato prossimo, trapassato remoto and futuro anteriore.

Finite and indefinite modes have their own verbal tense. They may be resumed in this way:

Indicativo has eight times.

Simple times are *presente, imperfetto, passato remoto, futuro semplice*. Compound times are *passato prossimo, trapassato prossimo, trapassato remoto* and *futuro anteriore*.

Congiuntivo has four times.

Simple times are *presente*, *passato* and *imperfetto*. There's only one compound time, which is *trapassato*.

Condizionale has two times.
The simple time is *presente*.
The compound time is *passato*.

Imperativo has only a simple time: the *presente*.

Infinito has two times: the simple *presente* and the compound *passato*.

Participio has two simple times: *presente* and *passato*.

Gerundio has a simple and a compound time: *presente* and *passato*.

6.4 Auxiliary verbs

In Italian, conjugation of verbs at their compound tenses requires the use of auxiliary verbs *essere* (to be) and *avere* (to have). With these and the past participle of the verb the compound times are formed. However, the auxiliary verbs must be conjugated.

6.4.1 Essere – to be

6.4.1.1 Simple tenses

Indicativo presente – Simple present

Io sono   I am
Tu sei   You are
Lui/lei è He/she is
Noi siamo We are
Voi siete You are (pl.)
Loro sono They are

Imperfetto – Imperfect

Io ero   I was
Tu eri   You were
Lui/lei era He/she was
Noi eravamo We were
Voi eravate You were (pl.)
Loro erano   They were

Futuro semplice – Simple future

Io sarò   I will be
Tu sarai   You will be
Lui/lei sarà He/she will be
Noi saremo   We will be

Voi sarete   You will be (pl.)
Loro saranno   They will be

Passato remoto – Simple past

Io fui   I was
Tu fosti   You were
Lui/lei fu   He/she was
Noi fummo   We were
Voi foste   You were (pl.)
Loro furono   They were

Condizionale – Simple conditional

Io sarei   I would be
Tu saresti   You would be
Lui/lei sarebbe   He/she would be
Noi saremmo   We would be
Voi sareste   You would be (pl.)
Loro sarebbero   They would be

Congiuntivo presente

(che) io sia
(che) tu sia
(che) lui/lei sia
(che) noi siamo
(che) voi siate
(che) loro siano

Congiuntivo imperfetto

(che) io fossi
(che) tu fossi
(che) lui/lei fosse
(che) noi fossimo
(che) voi foste
(che) loro fossero

Imperativo – Imperative

Sii!   Be! (you, sin.)
Sia!   Be! (he/she)
Siamo!   Let's be! (we)
Siate!   Be! (you, pl.)
Siano!   Be! (they)

Participio - Participle

Essente

Participio passato – Past participle

Stato

Gerundio – Gerund

Essendo   Being

6.4.1.2 Compound tenses

Subject + simple tense + participio passato declined as an adjective depending on gender and number of the subject.

Passato prossimo – Present perfect
Indicativo presente + participio passato

Io sono stato/a   I have been
Tu sei stato/a   You have been
Lui/lei è stato/a   He/she has been
Noi siamo stati/e   We have been
Voi siete stati/e   You have been (pl.)
Loro sono stati/e   They have been

Trapassato prossimo – Past perfect
Imperfetto + participio passato

Io ero stato/a   I had been
Tu eri stato/a   You had been
Lui/lei era stato/a   He/she had been
Noi eravamo stati/e   We had been
Voi eravate stati/e   You had been (pl.)
Loro erano stati/e   They had been

Trapassato remoto
Passato remoto + participio passato

Io fui stato/a   I was
Tu fosti stato/a   You were
Lui/lei fu stato/a   He/she was
Noi fummo stati/e   We were
Voi foste stati/e   You were (pl.)
Loro furono stati/e   They were

Futuro anteriore
Futuro semplice + participio passato

Io sarò stato/a   I will have been
Tu sarai stato/a   You will have been

Lui/lei sarà stato/a   He/she will have been
Noi saremo stati/e   We will have been
Voi sarete stati/e   You will have been (pl.)
Loro saranno stati/e   They will have been

Condizionale passato – Past conditional
Condizionale presente + condizionale passato

Io sarei stato/a   I would have been
Tu saresti stato/a   You would have been
Lui/lei sarebbe stato/a   He/she would have been
Noi saremmo stati/e   We would have been
Voi sareste stati/e   You would have been (pl.)
Loro sarebbero stati/e   They would have been

Congiuntivo passato – Past subjunctive
Congiuntivo presente + participio passato

(Che) io sia stato/a
(Che) tu sia stato/a
(Che) lui/lei sia stato/a
(Che) noi siamo stati/e
(Che) voi siate stati/e
(Che) loro siano stati/e

Congiuntivo trapassato
Congiuntivo imperfetto + participio passato

(che) io fossi stato/a
(che) tu fossi stato/a
(che) lui/lei fosse stato/a
(che) noi fossimo stati/e
(che) voi foste stati/e
(che) loro fossero stati/e

Infinito passato
Infinito presente + participio passato

Essere stato/a   To have been

Gerundio passato
Gerundio presente + participio passato

Essendo stato/a

6.4.2 Avere – to have
6.4.2.1 Simple tenses

Presente

Io ho   I have
Tu hai   You have
Lui/lei ha   He/she has
Noi abbiamo   We have
Voi avete   You have (pl.)
Loro hanno   They have

Imperfetto

Io avevo   I had
Tu avevi   You had
Lui/lei aveva   He/she had
Noi avevamo   We had
Voi avevate   You had (pl.)
Loro avevano   They had

Passato remoto

Io ebbi   I had
Tu avesti   You had
Lui/lei ebbe   He/she had
Noi avemmo   We had
Voi aveste   You had (pl.)
Loro ebbero   They had

Futuro semplice

Io avrò   I will have
Tu avrai   You will have
Lui/lei avrà   He/she will have
Noi avremo   We will have
Voi avrete   You will have (pl.)
Loro avranno   They will have

Condizionale presente

Io avrei   I would have
Tu avresti   You would have
Lui/lei avrebbe   He/she would have
Noi avremmo   We would have

Voi avreste   You would have (pl.)
Loro avrebbero   They would have

Congiuntivo presente

(Che) io abbia
(Che) tu abbia
(Che) lui/lei abbia
(Che) noi abbiamo
(Che) voi abbiate
(Che) loro abbiano

Congiuntivo imperfetto

(Che) io avessi
(Che) tu avessi
(Che) lui/lei avesse
(Che) noi avessimo
(Che) voi aveste
(Che) loro avessero

Imperativo presente

Abbi   Have! (you, sin.)
Abbia   Have! (he/she)
Abbiamo   Let's have! (we)
Abbiate   Have! (you, pl.)
Abbiano   Have! (they)

Infinito presente

Avere   To have

Participio presente

Avente - declined as an adjective depending on gender and number of the subject.

Participio passato

Avuto

Gerundio presente

Avendo   Having

6.4.2.2 Compound tenses

Subject + simple tense + participio passato

Passato prossimo – Present perfect
Presente + participio passato

Io ho avuto   I had
Tu hai avuto   You had
Lui/lei ha avuto   He/she had
Noi abbiamo avuto   We had
Voi avete avuto   You had (pl.)
Loro hanno avuto   They had

Trapassato prossimo – Past perfect
Imperfetto + participio passato

Io avevo avuto   I had had
Tu avevi avuto   You had had
Lui/lei aveva avuto   He/she had had
Noi avevamo avuto   We had had
Voi avevate avuto   You had had (pl.)
Loro avevano avuto   They had had

Trapassato remoto
Passato remoto + participio passato

Io ebbi avuto   I had had
Tu avesti avuto   I had had
Lui/lei ebbe avuto   He/she had had
Noi avemmo avuto   We had had
Voi aveste avuto   You had (pl.)
Loro ebbero avuto   They had

Futuro anteriore
Futuro semplice + participio passato

Io avrò avuto   I will have had
Tu avrai avuto   You will have had
Lui/lei avrà avuto   He/she will have had
Noi avemo avuto   We will have had
Voi avrete avuto   You will have had (pl.)
Loro avranno avuto   They will have had

Condizionale passato – Past conditional
Condizionale presente + participio passato

Io avrei avuto   I would have had
Tu avresti avuto   You would have had
Lui/lei avrebbe avuto   He/she would have had
Noi avremmo avuto   We would have had

Voi avreste avuto   You would have had (pl.)
Essi avrebbero avuto   They would have had

Congiuntivo passato

Congiuntivo presente + participio passato

(Che) io abbia avuto
(Che) tu abbia avuto
(Che) lui/lei abbia avuto
(Che) noi abbiamo avuto
(Che) voi abbiate avuto
(Che) loro abbiano avuto

Congiuntivo trapassato

Congiuntivo imperfetto + participio passato

(che) io avessi avuto
(che) tu avessi avuto
(che) lui/lei avesse avuto
(che) noi avessimo avuto
(che) voi aveste avuto
(che) loro avessero avuto

Infinito passato

Infinito presente + participio passato

Avere avuto   To have had

Gerundio passato

Gerundio presente + participio passato

Avendo avuto

6.5 Modal verbs

The verbs potere, volere, dovere are considered modal (or servile) verbs because they are followed by an infinite verb, adding an idea of opportunity, will, obligation, or necessity.

6.5.1 Potere – to can, to may

6.5.1.1 Simple tenses

Presente

Io posso   I can/may
Tu puoi   You can/may
Lui/lei può   He/she can/may
Noi possiamo   We can/may
Voi potete   You can/may (pl.)
Loro possono   They can/may

Imperfetto

Io potevo   I could/might
Tu potevi   You could/might
Lui/lei poteva   He/she could/might
Noi potevamo   We could/might
Voi potevate   You could/might (pl.)
Loro potevano   They could/might

Passato remoto

Io potei   I could/might
Tu potesti   You could/might
Lui/lei poté   He/she could/might
Noi potemmo   We could/might
Voi poteste   You could/might (pl.)
Loro poterono   They could/might

Futuro semplice

Io potrò   I will be able to
Tu potrai   You will be able to
Lui/lei potrà   He/she will be able to
Noi potremo   We will be able to
Voi potrete   You will be able to (pl.)
Loro potranno   They will be able to

Condizionale presente

Io potrei   I would be able to
Tu potresti   You would be able to
Lui/lei potrebbe   He/she would be able to
Noi potremmo   We would be able to
Voi potreste   You would be able to (pl.)
Loro potrebbero   They would be able to

Congiuntivo presente

(Che) io possa
(Che) tu possa
(Che) lui/lei possa
(Che) noi possiamo
(Che) voi possiate
(Che) loro possano

Congiuntivo imperfetto

(Che) io potessi
(Che) tu potessi
(Che) lui/lei potesse
(Che) noi potessimo
(Che) voi poteste
(Che) loro potessero

Infinito presente

Potere   To can/may

Participio presente

Potente

Participio passato

Potuto

Gerundio presente

Potendo   Being able to

6.5.1.2 Compound tenses

Subject + simple tense + participio passato

Passato prossimo – Present perfect
Presente + participio passato

Io ho potuto   I could
Tu hai potuto   You could
Lui/lei ha potuto   He/she could

Noi abbiamo potuto   We could
Voi avete potuto   You could (pl.)
Loro hanno potuto   They could

Trapassato prossimo – Past perfect
Imperfetto + participio passato

Io avevo potuto   I could
Tu avevi potuto   You could
Lui/lei aveva potuto   He/she could
Noi avevamo potuto   We could
Voi avevate potuto   You could (pl.)
Loro avevano potuto   They could

Trapassato remoto
Passato remoto + participio passato

Io ebbi potuto   I could
Tu avesti potuto   I could
Lui/lei ebbe potuto   He/she could
Noi avemmo potuto   We could
Voi aveste potuto   You could (pl.)
Loro ebbero potuto   They could

Futuro anteriore
Futuro semplice + participio passato

Io avrò potuto
Tu avrai potuto
Lui/lei avrà potuto
Noi avemo potuto
Voi avrete potuto
Loro avranno potuto

Condizionale passato – Past conditional
Condizionale presente + participio passato

Io avrei potuto
Tu avresti potuto
Lui/lei avrebbe potuto
Noi avremmo potuto
Voi avreste potuto
Loro avrebbero potuto

Congiuntivo passato
Congiuntivo presente + participio passato

(Che) io abbia potuto
(Che) tu abbia potuto
(Che) lui/lei abbia potuto
(Che) noi abbiamo potuto
(Che) voi abbiate potuto
(Che) loro abbiano potuto

Congiuntivo trapassato
Congiuntivo imperfetto + participio passato

(che) io avessi potuto
(che) tu avessi potuto
(che) lui/lei avesse potuto
(che) noi avessimo potuto
(che) voi aveste potuto
(che) loro avessero potuto

Infinito passato
Infinito presente + participio passato

Avere potuto   To have could

Gerundio passato
Gerundio presente + participio passato

Avendo potuto

6.5.2 Volere – to want

6.5.2.1 Simple tenses

Presente

Io voglio   I want
Tu vuoi   You want
Lui/lei vuole   He/she wants
Noi vogliamo   We want
Voi volete   You want (pl.)
Loro vogliono   They want

Imperfetto

Io volevo   I wanted
Tu volevi   You wanted
Lui/lei voleva   He/she wanted
Noi volevamo   We wanted
Voi volevate   You wanted (pl.)
Loro volevano   They wanted

Passato remoto

Io volli   I wanted
Tu volesti   You wanted
Lui/lei volle   He/she wanted
Noi volemmo   We wanted
Voi voleste   You wanted (pl.)
Loro vollero   They wanted

Futuro semplice

Io vorrò   I will want
Tu vorrai   You will want
Lui/lei vorrà   He/she will want
Noi vorremo   We will want
Voi vorrete   You will want (pl.)
Loro vorranno   They will want

Condizionale presente

Io vorrei   I would want
Tu vorresti   You would want
Lui/lei vorrebbe   He/she would want
Noi vorremmo   We would want
Voi vorreste   You would want (pl.)
Loro vorrebbero   They would want

Congiuntivo presente

(Che) io voglia
(Che) tu voglia
(Che) lui/lei voglia
(Che) noi vogliamo
(Che) voi vogliate
(Che) loro vogliano

Congiuntivo imperfetto

(Che) io volessi
(Che) tu volessi
(Che) lui/lei volesse
(Che) noi volessimo
(Che) voi voleste
(Che) loro volessero

Infinito presente

Volere   To want

Participio presente

Volente

Participio passato

Voluto

Gerundio presente

Volendo   Wanting

6.5.2.2 Compound times

Subject + simple tense + participio passato

Passato prossimo – Present perfect
Presente + participio passato

Io ho voluto   I wanted
Tu hai voluto   You wanted
Lui/lei ha voluto   He/she wanted
Noi abbiamo voluto   We wanted
Voi avete voluto   You wanted (pl.)
Loro hanno voluto   They wanted

Trapassato prossimo – Past perfect
Imperfetto + participio passato

Io avevo voluto   I had wanted
Tu avevi voluto   You had wanted
Lui/lei aveva voluto   He/she had wanted
Noi avevamo voluto   We had wanted
Voi avevate voluto   You had wanted (pl.)
Loro avevano voluto   They had wanted

Trapassato remote
Passato remoto + participio passato

Io ebbi voluto   I had wanted
Tu avesti voluto   I had wanted
Lui/lei ebbe voluto   He/she had wanted
Noi avemmo voluto   We had wanted
Voi aveste voluto   You had wanted (pl.)
Loro ebbero voluto   They had wanted

Futuro anteriore
Futuro semplice + participio passato

Io avrò voluto   I will have wanted
Tu avrai voluto   You will have wanted
Lui/lei avrà voluto   He/she will have wanted
Noi avemo voluto   We will have wanted
Voi avrete voluto   You will have wanted (pl.)
Loro avranno voluto   They will have wanted

Condizionale passato – Past conditional
Condizionale presente + participio passato

Io avrei voluto   I would have wanted
Tu avresti voluto   You would have wanted
Lui/lei avrebbe voluto   He/she would have wanted
Noi avremmo voluto   We would have wanted
Voi avreste voluto   You would have wanted (pl.)
Essi avrebbero voluto   They would have wanted

Congiuntivo passato
Congiuntivo presente + participio passato

(Che) io abbia voluto
(Che) tu abbia voluto
(Che) lui/lei abbia voluto
(Che) noi abbiamo voluto
(Che) voi abbiate voluto
(Che) loro abbiano voluto

Congiuntivo trapassato
Congiuntivo imperfetto + participio passato

(che) io avessi voluto
(che) tu avessi voluto
(che) lui/lei avesse voluto
(che) noi avessimo voluto
(che) voi aveste voluto
(che) loro avessero voluto

Infinito passato
Infinito presente + participio passato

Avere voluto   To have wanted

Gerundio passato
Gerundio presente + participio passato

Avendo volute

6.5.3 Dovere – to must, to have to
6.5.3.1 Simple times

Presente

Io devo   I must
Tu devi   You must
Lui/lei deve   He/she must
Noi dobbiamo   We must
Voi dovete   You must (pl.)
Loro devono   They must

Imperfetto

Io dovevo   I had to
Tu dovevi   You had to
Lui/lei doveva   He/she had to
Noi dovevamo   We had to
Voi dovevate   You had to (pl.)
Loro dovevano   They had to

Passato remoto

Io dovetti   I had to
Tu dovesti   You had to
Lui/lei dovette   He/she had to
Noi dovemmo   We had to
Voi doveste   You had to (pl.)
Loro dovettero   They had to

Futuro semplice

Io dovrò   I will have to
Tu dovrai   You will have to
Lui/lei dovrà   He/she will have to
Noi dovremo   We will have to
Voi dovrete   You will have to (pl.)
Loro dovranno   They will have to

Condizionale presente

Io dovrei   I would have to
Tu dovresti   You would have to
Lui/lei dovrebbe   He/she would have to
Noi dovremmo   We would have to

Voi dovreste   You would have to (pl.)
Loro dovrebbero   They would have to

Congiuntivo presente

(Che) io debba
(Che) tu debba
(Che) lui/lei debba
(Che) noi dobbiamo
(Che) voi dobbiate
(Che) loro debbano

Congiuntivo imperfetto

(Che) io dovessi
(Che) tu dovessi
(Che) lui/lei dovesse
(Che) noi dovessimo
(Che) voi doveste
(Che) loro dovessero

Infinito presente

Volere   To have to

Participio presente

Dovente

Participio passato

Dovuto

Gerundio presente

Dovendo   Having to

6.5.3.2 Compound tenses

Subject + simple tense + participio passato

Passato prossimo – Present perfect
Presente + participio passato

Io ho dovuto   I had to
Tu hai dovuto   You had to
Lui/lei ha dovuto   He/she had to
Noi abbiamo dovuto   We had to
Voi avete dovuto   You had to (pl.)
Loro hanno dovuto   They had to

Trapassato prossimo – Past perfect
Imperfetto + participio passato

Io avevo dovuto   I had to
Tu avevi dovuto   You had to
Lui/lei aveva dovuto   He/she had to
Noi avevamo dovuto   We had to
Voi avevate dovuto   You had to (pl.)
Loro avevano dovuto   They had to

Trapassato remoto
Passato remoto + participio passato

Io ebbi dovuto   I had to
Tu avesti dovuto   I had to
Lui/lei ebbe dovuto   He/she had to
Noi avemmo dovuto   We had to
Voi aveste dovuto   You had to (pl.)
Loro ebbero dovuto   They had to

Futuro anteriore
Futuro semplice + participio passato

Io avrò dovuto   I will have to
Tu avrai dovuto   You will have to
Lui/lei avrà dovuto   He/she will have to
Noi avremo dovuto   We will have to
Voi avrete dovuto   You will have to (pl.)
Loro avranno dovuto   They will have to

Condizionale passato – Past conditional
Condizionale presente + participio passato

Io avrei dovuto   I had to
Tu avresti dovuto   You had to
Lui/lei avrebbe dovuto   He/she had to
Noi avremmo dovuto   We had to
Voi avreste dovuto   You had to (pl.)
Loro avrebbero dovuto   They had to

Congiuntivo passato
Congiuntivo presente + participio passato

(Che) io abbia dovuto
(Che) tu abbia dovuto
(Che) lui/lei abbia dovuto

(Che) noi abbiamo dovuto
(Che) voi abbiate dovuto
(Che) loro abbiano dovuto

Congiuntivo trapassato
Congiuntivo imperfetto + participio passato

(che) io avessi dovuto
(che) tu avessi dovuto
(che) lui/lei avesse dovuto
(che) noi avessimo dovuto
(che) voi aveste dovuto
(che) loro avessero dovuto

Infinito passato
Infinito presente + participio passato

Avere dovuto   To have had to

Gerundio passato
Gerundio presente + participio passato

Avendo dovuto

6.6 Regular verbs conjugation

In the Italian language, we speak about first, second and third conjugation to indicate the infinite verbs ending with –are (first), -ere (second) and –ire (third). Often, the conjugated forms of the three conjugations are distinguished by a single vocal, called the thematic.

6.6.1 First conjugation in –are

Among the three conjugations, the first one (the one in -are) is the most frequent and is still the only productive one: in fact, the neologisms that introduce new verbs only suffice in –are.

Formattare   To format
Twittare   To twit
Linkare   To link
Taggare   To tag

Regular verbs ending with -are, such as *lottare* (to fight), *ascoltare* (to listen), *illuminare* (to light up) or *camminare* (to walk), in order to be conjugated must be removed from their ending and joined to another one common to all verbs in –are.

In order to list these ending replacements, it is better to make examples. These will be highlighted in bold and capitalized.

The verb is *cantare*   to sing

6.6.1.1 Simple tenses

Presente

Io cantO   I sing
Tu cantI   You sing
Lui/lei cantA   He/she sings
Noi cantIAMO   We sing
Voi cantATE   You sing (pl.)
Loro cantANO   They sing

Imperfetto

Io cantAVO   I sang
Tu cantAVI   You sang
Lui/lei cantAVA   He/she sang
Noi cantAVAMO   We sang
Voi cantAVATE   You sang (pl.)
Loro cantAVANO   They sang

Passato remoto

Io cantAI   I sang
Tu cantASTI   You sang
Lui/lei cantÒ   He/she sang
Noi cantAMMO   We sang
Voi cantASTE   You (pl.) sang
Loro cantARONO   They sang

Futuro semplice

Io cantERÒ   I will sing
Tu cantERAI   You will sing
Lui/lei cantERÀ   He/she will sing
Noi cantEREMO   We will sing
Voi cantERETE   You (pl.) will sing
Loro cantERANNO   They will sing

Condizionale presente

Io cantEREI   I would sing
Tu cantERESTI   You would sing
Lui/lei cantEREBBE   He/she would sing
Noi cantEREMMO   We would sing

Voi cantERESTE   You (pl.) would sing
Loro cantEREBBERO   They would sing

Congiuntivo presente

(Che) io cantI
(Che) tu cantASSI
(Che) lui/lei cantI
(Che) noi cantIAMO
(Che) voi cantIATE
(Che) loro cantINO

Congiuntivo imperfetto

(Che) io cantASSI
(Che) tu cantASSI
(Che) lui/lei cantASSE
(Che) noi cantASSIMO
(Che) voi cantASTE
(Che) loro cantASSERO

Imperativo presente

CantA   Sing! (you)
CantI   Sing! (he/she)
CantIAMO   Let's sing! (we)
CantATE   Sing! (you, pl.)
CantINO   Sing! (they)

Infinito presente

CantARE

Participio presente

CantANTE

Participio passato

CantATO

Gerundio presente

CantANDO

6.6.1.2 Compound tenses

Compound tenses with regular verbs are made with subject + conjugated auxiliary verb at simple tense + participio passato.

Passato prossimo
Ausiliare presente + participio passato

Io ho cantato   I sang
Tu hai cantato   You sang
Lui/lei ha cantato   He/she sang
Noi abbiamo cantato   We sang
Voi avete cantato   You (pl.) sang
Loro hanno cantato   They sang

Trapassato prossimo
Ausiliare imperfetto + participio passato

Io avevo cantato   I sang
Tu avevi cantato   You sang
Lui/lei aveva cantato   He/she sang
Noi avevamo cantato   We sang
Voi avevate cantato   You (pl.) sang
Loro avevano cantato   They sang

Trapassato remoto
Ausiliare passato remoto + participio passato

Io ebbi cantato   I had sung
Tu avesti cantato   You had sung
Lui/lei ebbe cantato   He/she had sung
Noi avemmo cantato   We had sung
Voi aveste cantato   You (pl.) had sung
Loro ebbero cantato   They had sung

Futuro anteriore
Ausiliare futuro semplice + participio passato

Io avrò cantato   I will have sung
Tu avrai cantato   You will have sung
Lui/lei avrà cantato   He/she will have sung
Noi avremo cantato   We will have sung
Voi avrete cantato   You (pl.) will have sung
Loro avranno cantato   They will have sung

Condizionale passato
Ausiliare condizionale presente + participio passato

Io avrei cantato   I would have sang
Tu avresti cantato   You would have sang
Lui/lei avrebbe cantato   He/she would have sang
Noi avremmo cantato   We would have sang
Voi avreste cantato   You (pl.) would have sang
Loro avrebbero cantato   They would have sang

Congiuntivo passato
Ausiliare congiuntivo presente + participio passato

(Che) io abbia cantato
(Che) tu abbia cantato
(Che) lui/lei abbia cantato
(Che) noi abbiamo cantato
(Che) voi abbiate cantato
(Che) loro abbiano cantato

Congiuntivo trapassato
Ausiliare congiuntivo imperfetto +
participio passato

(Che) io avessi cantato
(Che) tu avessi cantato
(Che) lui/lei avesse cantato
(Che) noi avessimo cantato
(Che) voi aveste cantato
(Che) loro avessero cantato

Infinito passato
Ausiliare infinito presente + participio passato

Avere cantato

Gerundio passato
Ausiliare gerundio presente + participio passato

Avendo cantato

6.6.2 Second conjugation in –ere

The conjugation -ere is the one richer than irregular shapes. These irregularities are already found in the forms of the present. Again, with regard to the second group, this generally involves the fall of the -e forms of the *futuro semplice* and the *condizionale presente*.

Regular verbs ending with -ere, such as *leggere* (to read), *ridere* (to laugh), *prendere* (to take, to get) or *mettere* (to put), in order to be conjugated must be removed from their ending and joined to another one common to all verbs with –ere.

These endings will be highlighted in bold and capitalized, as with the previous verbal conjugation.

The verb is *temere* to fear

6.6.2.1 Simple tenses

Presente

Io tem**O**   I fear
Tu tem**I**   You fear
Lui/lei tem**E**   He/she fears
Noi tem**IAMO**   We fear
Voi tem**ETE**   You fear (pl.)
Loro tem**ONO**   They fear

Imperfetto

Io tem**EVO**   I feared
Tu tem**EVI**   You feared
Lui/lei tem**EVA**   He/she feared
Noi tem**EVAMO**   We feared
Voi tem**EVATE**   You feared (pl.)
Loro tem**EVANO**   They feared

Passato remoto

Io tem**ETTI**   I feared
Tu tem**ESTI**   You feared
Lui/lei tem**ETTE**   He/she feared
Noi tem**EMMO**   We feared
Voi tem**ESTE**   You (pl.) feared
Loro tem**ETTERO**   They feared

Futuro semplice

Io tem**ERÒ**   I will fear
Tu tem**ERAI**   You will fear
Lui/lei tem**ERÀ**   He/she will fear
Noi tem**EREMO**   We will fear
Voi tem**ERETE**   You (pl.) will fear
Loro tem**ERANNO**   They will fear

Condizionale presente

Io temEREI   I would fear
Tu temERESTI   You would fear
Lui/lei temEREBBE   He/she would fear
Noi temEREMMO   We would fear
Voi temERESTE   You (pl.) would fear
Loro temEREBBERO   They would fear

Congiuntivo presente

(Che) io temA
(Che) tu temA
(Che) lui/lei temA
(Che) noi temIAMO
(Che) voi temIATE
(Che) loro temANO

Congiuntivo imperfetto

(Che) io temESSI
(Che) tu temESSI
(Che) lui/lei temESSE
(Che) noi temESSIMO
(Che) voi temESTE
(Che) loro temESSERO

Imperativo presente

TemI   Fear! (you)
TemA   Fear! (he/she)
TemIAMO   Let's fear! (we)
TemETE   Fear! (you, pl.)
TemANO   Fear! (they)

Infinito presente

TemERE

Participio presente

TemENTE

Participio passato

TemUTO

Gerundio presente

TemENDO

6.6.2.2 Compound tenses

Compound tenses with regular verbs are made with subject + conjugated auxiliary verb at simple tense + participio passato.

Passato prossimo
Ausiliare presente + participio passato

Io ho temuto   I feared
Tu hai temuto   You feared
Lui/lei ha temuto   He/she feared
Noi abbiamo temuto   We feared
Voi avete temuto   You (pl.) feared
Loro hanno temuto   They feared

Trapassato prossimo
Ausiliare imperfetto + participio passato

Io avevo temuto   I feared
Tu avevi temuto   You feared
Lui/lei aveva temuto   He/she feared
Noi avevamo temuto   We feared
Voi avevate temuto   You (pl.) feared
Loro avevano temuto   They feared

Trapassato remoto
Ausiliare passato remoto + participio passato

Io ebbi temuto   I had feared
Tu avesti temuto   You had feared
Lui/lei ebbe temuto   He/she had feared
Noi avemmo temuto   We had feared
Voi aveste temuto   You (pl.) had feared
Loro ebbero temuto   They had feared

Futuro anteriore
Ausiliare futuro semplice + participio passato

Io avrò temuto   I will have feared
Tu avrai temuto   You will have feared
Lui/lei avrà temuto   He/she will have feared
Noi avremo temuto   We will have feared
Voi avrete temuto   You (pl.) will have feared
Loro avranno temuto   They will have feared

Condizionale passato

Ausiliare condizionale presente + participio passato

Io avrei temuto   I would have feared
Tu avresti temuto   You would have feared
Lui/lei avrebbe temuto   He/she would have feared
Noi avremmo temuto   We would have feared
Voi avreste temuto   You (pl.) would have feared
Loro avrebbero temuto   They would have feared

Congiuntivo passato

Ausiliare congiuntivo presente + participio passato

(Che) io abbia temuto
(Che) tu abbia temuto
(Che) lui/lei abbia temuto
(Che) noi abbiamo temuto
(Che) voi abbiate temuto
(Che) loro abbiano temuto

Congiuntivo trapassato

Ausiliare congiuntivo imperfetto +
participio passato

(Che) io avessi temuto
(Che) tu avessi temuto
(Che) lui/lei avesse temuto
(Che) noi avessimo temuto
(Che) voi aveste temuto
(Che) loro avessero temuto

Infinito passato

Ausiliare infinito presente + participio passato

Avere temuto

Gerundio passato

Ausiliare gerundio presente + participio passato

Avendo temuto

6.6.3 Third conjugation in –ire

Regular verbs ending with -ire, such as *partire* (to leave), may follow two different patterns.

The first one follows the pattern of *dormire*   to sleep

These endings will be highlighted in bold and capitalized, as with the previous verbal conjugations.

6.6.3.1 Simple tenses

Presente

Io dormO   I sleep
Tu dormI   You sleep
Lui/lei dormE   He/she sleeps
Noi dormIAMO   We sleep
Voi dormITE   You sleep (pl.)
Loro dormONO   They sleep

Imperfetto

Io dormIVO   I slept
Tu dormIVI   You slept
Lui/lei dormIVA   He/she slept
Noi dormIVAMO   We slept
Voi dormIVATE   You slept (pl.)
Loro dormIVANO   They slept

Passato remoto

Io dormII   I slept
Tu dormISTI   You slept
Lui/lei dormÌ   He/she slept
Noi dormIMMO   We slept
Voi dormISTE   You (pl.) slept
Loro dormIRONO   They slept

Futuro semplice

Io dormIRÒ   I will sleep
Tu dormIRAI   You will sleep
Lui/lei dormIRÀ   He/she will sleep
Noi dormIREMO   We will sleep
Voi dormIRETE   You (pl.) will sleep
Loro dormIRANNO   They will sleep

Condizionale presente

Io dormIREI   I would sleep
Tu dormIRESTI   You would sleep
Lui/lei dormIREBBE   He/she would sleep
Noi dormIREMMO   We would sleep
Voi dormIRESTE   You (pl.) would sleep
Loro dormIREBBERO   They would sleep

Congiuntivo presente

(Che) io dormA
(Che) tu dormA
(Che) lui/lei dormA
(Che) noi dormIAMO
(Che) voi dormIATE
(Che) loro dormANO

Congiuntivo imperfetto

(Che) io dormISSI
(Che) tu dormISSI
(Che) lui/lei dormISSE
(Che) noi dormISSIMO
(Che) voi dormISTE
(Che) loro dormISSERO

Imperativo presente

DormI   Sleep! (you)
DormA   Sleep! (he/she)
DormIAMO Let's sleep! (we)
DormITE   Sleep! (you, pl.)
DormANO   Sleep! (they)

Infinito presente

DormIRE

Participio presente

DormENTE/IENTE

Participio passato

DormITO

Gerundio presente

DormENDO

The second type follows the pattern of *preferire* to prefer. Note the -isc between the stem and the ending!

Presente

Io preferISCO   I prefer
Tu preferISCI   You prefer
Lui/lei preferISCE He/she prefers
Noi preferIAMO   We prefer

Voi preferITE   You prefer (pl.)
Loro preferISCONO   They prefer

Imperfetto

Io preferIVO   I preferred
Tu preferIVI   You preferred
Lui/lei preferIVA   He/she preferred
Noi preferIVAMO   We preferred
Voi preferIVATE   You preferred (pl.)
Loro preferIVANO   They preferred

Passato remoto

Io preferII   I preferred
Tu preferISTI   You preferred
Lui/lei preferÌ   He/she preferred
Noi preferIMMO   We preferred
Voi preferISTE   You (pl.) preferred
Loro preferIRONO   They preferred

Futuro semplice

Io preferIRÒ   I will prefer
Tu preferIRAI   You will prefer
Lui/lei preferIRÀ   He/she will prefer
Noi preferIREMO   We will prefer
Voi preferIRETE   You (pl.) will prefer
Loro preferIRANNO   They will prefer

Condizionale presente

Io preferIREI   I would prefer
Tu preferIRESTI   You would prefer
Lui/lei preferIREBBE   He/she would prefer
Noi preferIREMMO   We would prefer
Voi preferIRESTE   You (pl.) would prefer
Loro preferIREBBERO   They would prefer

Congiuntivo presente

(Che) io preferISCA
(Che) tu preferISCA
(Che) lui/lei preferISCA
(Che) noi preferIAMO
(Che) voi preferIATE
(Che) loro preferISCANO

Congiuntivo imperfetto

(Che) io preferISSI
(Che) tu preferISSI
(Che) lui/lei preferISSE
(Che) noi preferISSIMO
(Che) voi preferISTE
(Che) loro preferISSERO

Imperativo presente

PreferISCI   Prefer! (you)
PreferISCA   Prefer! (he/she)
PreferIAMO   Let's prefer! (we)
PreferITE   Prefer! (you, pl.)
PreferISCANO   Prefer! (they)

Infinito presente

PreferIRE

Participio presente

PreferENTE

Participio passato

PreferITO

Gerundio presente

PreferENDO

When there's doubt about which pattern with -ire a verb uses, it is better to consult a dictionary.

Below is a list of common -isc verbs that follow the same pattern as *preferire*.

Agire   to act
Ambire   to aspire
Ammonire   to admonish
Ardire   to venture
Capire   to understand
Chiarire   to clarify
Colpire   to hit
Costruire   to construct
Demolire   to demolish
Favorire   to favour
Ferire   to wound
Fiorire   to flourish
Fornire   to supply

Finire   to finish
Guarire   to heal
Inserire   to insert
Impedire   to prevent
Obbedire   to obey
Partire   to suffer
Percepire   to become aware of
Proibire   to prohibit
Pulire   to clean
Punire   to punish
Rapire   to kidnap
Restituire   to give back
Riferire   to relate, to refer
Scolpire   to sculpt
Sparire   to disappear
Spedire   to send
Stabilire   to establish
Subire   to suffer
Suggerire   to suggest
Tossire   to cough
Tradire   to betray
Trasferirsi   to move
Unire   to unite

There are some verbs that can follow both patterns:

Aborrire   to abhor
Applaudire   to applaud
Assorbire   to absorb
Inghiottire   to swallow
Mentire   to lie
Nutrire   to nourish
Tossire   to cough

6.6.3.2 Compound tenses

Compound tenses with regular verbs, even there are two forms with verbs in –ire, are made anyway with subject + conjugated auxiliary verb at simple tense + participio passato.

The verb, in this case, is irrelevant.

The used one is the first of chapter 6.6.3.1, *dormire*.

Passato prossimo

Ausiliare presente + participio passato

Io ho dormito   I slept
Tu hai dormito   You slept
Lui/lei ha dormito   He/she slept
Noi abbiamo dormito   We slept
Voi avete dormito   You (pl.) slept
Loro hanno dormito   They slept

Trapassato prossimo

Ausiliare imperfetto + participio passato

Io avevo dormito   I slept
Tu avevi dormito   You slept
Lui/lei aveva dormito   He/she slept
Noi avevamo dormito   We slept
Voi avevate dormito   You (pl.) slept
Loro avevano dormito   They slept

Trapassato remoto

Ausiliare passato remoto + participio passato

Io ebbi dormito   I had slept
Tu avesti dormito   You had slept
Lui/lei ebbe dormito   He/she had slept
Noi avemmo dormito   We had slept
Voi aveste dormito   You (pl.) had slept
Loro ebbero dormito   They had slept

Futuro anteriore

Ausiliare futuro semplice + participio passato

Io avrò dormito   I will have slept
Tu avrai dormito   You will have slept
Lui/lei avrà dormito   He/she will have slept
Noi avremo dormito   We will have slept
Voi avrete dormito   You (pl.) will have slept
Loro avranno dormito   They will have slept

Condizionale passato

Ausiliare condizionale presente + participio passato

Io avrei dormito   I would have slept
Tu avresti dormito   You would have slept
Lui/lei avrebbe dormito   He/she would have slept

Noi avremmo dormito   We would have slept
Voi avreste dormito   You (pl.) would have slept
Loro avrebbero dormito   They would have slept

Congiuntivo passato

Ausiliare congiuntivo presente + participio passato

(Che) io abbia dormito
(Che) tu abbia dormito
(Che) lui/lei abbia dormito
(Che) noi abbiamo dormito
(Che) voi abbiate dormito
(Che) loro abbiano dormito

Congiuntivo trapassato

Ausiliare congiuntivo imperfetto +
participio passato

(Che) io avessi dormito
(Che) tu avessi dormito
(Che) lui/lei avesse dormito
(Che) noi avessimo dormito
(Che) voi aveste dormito
(Che) loro avessero dormito

Infinito passato

Ausiliare infinito presente + participio passato

Avere dormito

Gerundio passato

Ausiliare gerundio presente + participio passato

Avendo dormito

6.7 Irregular verbs conjugations

In Italian, we have to deal with the weird verbs that are irregular. Those are verbs (almost all belong to the second conjugation in -ere) which do not combine by following the same pattern, but change from tense to tense.

While in other languages, such as English, irregular verbs are reduced to a small group and are studied by heart, in Italian they cover a large verbal slice, so the best solution is to study them, repeat them aloud, write them down and try to use them as often as possible.

Irregular verbs are not perceptible at first sight, since their infinite form is always with endings of three conjugations, -are, -ere and –ire.

In this chapter there will be just simple tenses.

As you already know, their compound tenses may be built by conjugating the auxiliary verb in simple tense added with participio passato.

6.7.1 Irregular verbs in –are

The irregular verbs of the first conjugation are mainly four.

Andare   To go

Presente
Vado, vai, va, andiamo, andate, vanno.

Futuro
Andrò, andrai, andrà, andremo, andrete, andranno.

Passato remoto
Andai, andasti, andò, andammo, andaste, andarono.

Congiuntivo presente
Vada, vada, vada, andiamo, andiate, vadano.

Congiuntivo imperfetto
Andassi, andassi, andasse, andassimo, andaste, andassero.

Condizionale presente
Andrei, andresti, andrebbe, andremmo, andreste, andrebbero.

Imperativo
Va'! (you, sin.), vada! (he/she), andiamo! (we), andate! (you, pl.), vadano! (they).

Participio passato
Andato

Dare   To give

Presente
Do, dai, dà, diamo, date, dànno.

Imperfetto
Davo, davi, dava, davamo, davate, davano

Futuro
Darò, darai, darà, daremo, darete, daranno

Passato remoto
Diedi, désti, diede, démmo, déste, diedero.

Congiuntivo presente
Dia, dia, dia, diamo, diate, díano.

Congiuntivo imperfetto
Dessi, dessi, desse, dessimo, déste, dessero.

Condizionale presente
Darei, daresti, darebbe, daremmo, dareste, darebbero.

Imperativo
Da'! (you, sin.), dia! (he/she), diamo! (we), date! (you, pl.), diano! (you, pl.).

Participio presente
Dante

Participio passato
Dato

Stare   To stay

Presente
Sto, stai, sta, stiamo, state, stanno

Imperfetto
Stavo, stavi, stava, stavamo, stavate, stavano

Futuro
Starò, starai, starà, staremo, starete, staranno

Passato remoto
Stetti, stesti, stette, stemmo, steste, stettero

Congiuntivo presente
Stia, stia, stia, stiamo, stiate, stiano

Congiuntivo imperfetto
Stessi, stessi, stesse, stessimo, steste, stessero

Condizionale presente
Starei, staresti, starebbe, staremmo, stareste, starebbero

Imperativo
Sta! (you, sin.), stia! (he/she), stiamo! (we), state! (you, pl.), stiano! (they)

Participio presente
Stante

Participio passato
Stato

Gerundio semplice
Stando

Fare   To do, to make

Presente
Faccio, fai, fa, facciamo, fate, fanno

Imperfetto
Facevo, facevi, faceva, facevamo, facevate, facevano

Futuro
Farò, farai, farà, faremo, farete, faranno

Passato remoto
Feci, facesti, fece, facemmo, faceste, fecero

Congiuntivo presente
Faccia, faccia, faccia, facciamo, facciate, facciano

Congiuntivo imperfetto
Facessi, facessi, facessi, facessimo, faceste, facessero

Condizionale presente
Farei, faresti, farebbe, faremmo, fareste, farebbero

Imperativo
Fa'! (you, sin.), faccia! (he/she), facciamo! (we), fate! (you, pl.), facciano!

Participio presente
Facente

Participio passato
Fatto

6.7.2 Irregular verbs in –ere

Among Italian verbs, the ones of second conjugation ending in –ere and irregular are the most numerous.

Here there are the most used ones.

Bere   To drink

Presente
Bevo, bevi, beve, beviamo, bevete, bevono

Imperfetto
Bevevo, bevevi, beveva, bevevamo, bevevate, bevevano

Futuro
Berrò, berrai, berrà, berremo, berrete, berranno

Passato remoto
Bevetti, bevetti, bevette, bevemmo, beveste, bevettero

Congiuntivo presente
Beva, beva, beva, beviamo, beviate, bevano

Congiuntivo imperfetto
Bevessi, bevessi, bevesse, bevessimo, beveste, bevessero

Condizionale presente
Berrei, berresti, berrebbe, berremmo, berreste, berrebbero

Imperativo
Bevi! (you, sin.), beva! (he/she), beviamo! (we), bevete! (you, pl.), bevano! (they)

Participio presente
Bevente

Participio passato
Bevuto

Scegliere   To choose

Presente
Scelgo, scegli, sceglie, scegliamo, scegliete, scelgono

Imperfetto
Sceglievo, sceglievi, sceglieva, sceglievamo, sceglievate, sceglievano

Futuro
Sceglierò, sceglierai, sceglierà, sceglieremo, sceglierete, sceglieranno

Passato remoto
Scelsi, scegliesti, scelse, scegliemmo, sceglieste, scelsero

Congiuntivo presente
Scelga, scelga, scelga, scegliamo, scegliate, scelgano

Congiuntivo imperfetto
Scegliessi, scegliessi, scegliesse, scegliessimo, sceglieste, scegliessero

Condizionale presente
Sceglierei, sceglieresti, sceglierebbe, sceglieremmo, scegliereste, sceglierebbero

Imperativo
Scegli! (you, sin.), scelga! (he/she), scegliamo! (we), scegliete! (you, pl.), scelgano! (they)

Participio presente
Scegliente

Participio passato
Scelto

Tenere   To keep

Presente
Tengo, tieni, tiene, teniamo, tenete, tengono

Imperfetto
Tenevo, tenevi, teneva, tenevamo, tenevate, tenevano

Futuro
Terrò, terrai, terrà, terremo, terrete, terranno

Passato remoto
Tenni, tenesti, tenne, tenemmo, teneste, tennero

Congiuntivo presente
Tenga, tenga, tenga, teniamo, teniate, tengano

Congiuntivo imperfetto
Tenessi, tenessi, tenesse, tenessimo, teneste, tenessero

Condizionale presente
Terrei, terresti, terrebbe, terremmo, terreste, terrebbero

Imperativo
Tieni! (you, sin.), tenga! (he/she), teniamo! (we), tenete! (you, pl.), tengano! (they)

Participio presente
Tenente

Participio passato
Tenuto

Sedere   To sit

Presente
Siedo, siedi, siede, sediamo, sedete, siedono

Imperfetto
Sedevo, sedevi, sedeva, sedevamo, sedevate, sedevano

Futuro
Siederò, siederai, siederà, siederemo, siederete, siederanno

Passato remoto
Sedei, sedesti, sedé, sedemmo, sedeste, sederono

Congiuntivo presente
Sieda, sieda, sieda, siedano, sediamo, sediate, siedano

Congiuntivo imperfetto
Sedessi, sedessi, sedesse, sedessimo, sedeste, sedessero

Condizionale presente
Siederei, siederesti, siederebbe, siederemmo, siedereste, siederebbero

Imperativo
Siedi! (you, sin.), sieda! (he/she), sediamo! (we), sedete! (you, pl.), siedano! (they)

Participio presente
Sedente

Participio passato
Seduto

6.7.3 Irregular verbs in –ire

Venire   To come

Presente
Vengo, vieni, viene, veniamo, venite, vengono

Imperfetto
Venivo, venivi, veniva, venivamo, venivate, venivano

Futuro
Verrò, verrai, verrà, verremo, verrete, verranno

Passato remoto
Venni, venisti, venne, venimmo, veniste, vennero

Congiuntivo presente
Venga, venga, venga, veniamo, veniate, vengano

Congiuntivo imperfetto
Venissi, venissi, venisse, venissimo, veniste, venissero

Condizionale presente
Verrei, verresti, verrebbe, verremmo, verreste, verrebbero

Imperativo
Vieni! (you, sin.), venga! (he/she), veniamo! (we), venite! (you, pl.), vengano! (they)

Participio presente
Veniente

Participio passato
Venuto

Auxiliary verb of *venire* is *essere*.
In this case, *venuto* is conjugated as an adjective depending on subject (masculine, feminine, singular, plural).

Dire   To say, to tell

Presente
Dico, dici, dice, diciamo, dite, dicono

Imperfetto
Dicevo, dicevi, diceva, dicevamo, dicevate, dicevano

Futuro
Dirò, dirai, dirà, diremo, direte, diranno

Passato remoto
Dissi, dicesti, disse, dicemmo, diceste, dissero

Congiuntivo presente
Dica, dica, dica, diciamo, diciate, dicano

Congiuntivo imperfetto
Dicessi, dicessi, dicesse, dicessimo, diceste, dicessero

Condizionale presente
Direi, diresti, direbbe, diremmo, direste, direbbero

Imperativo
Di'! (you, sin.), dica! (he/she), diciamo! (we), dite! (you, pl.), dicano! (they)

Participio presente
Dicente

Participio passato
Detto

Auxiliary verb of *dire* is *avere*.

Uscire   To get out, to go out

Presente
Esco, esci, esce, usciamo, uscite, escono

Imperfetto
Uscivo, uscivi, usciva, uscivamo, uscivate, uscivano

Futuro
Uscirò, uscirai, uscirà, usciremo, uscirete, usciranno

Passato remoto
Uscii, uscisti, uscì, uscimmo, usciste, uscirono

Congiuntivo presente
Esca, esca, esca, usciamo, usciate, escano

Congiuntivo imperfetto
Uscissi, uscissi, uscisse, uscissimo, usciste, uscissero

Condizionale presente
Uscirei, usciresti, uscirebbe, usciremmo, uscireste, uscirebbero

Imperativo
Esci! (you, sin.), esca! (he/she), usciamo! (we), uscite! (you, pl.), escano! (they)

Participio presente
Uscente

Participio passato
Uscito

Auxiliary verb of *uscire* is *essere*.
In this case, *uscito* is conjugated as an adjective depending on subject (masculine, feminine, singular, plural).

Salire   To climb, to go up, to rise

Presente
Salgo, sali, sale, saliamo, salite, salgono

Imperfetto
Salivo, salivi, saliva, salivamo, salivate, salivano

Futuro
Salirò, salirai, salirà, saliremo, salirete, saliranno

Passato remoto
Salii, salisti, salì, salimmo, saliste, salirono

Congiuntivo presente
Salga, salga, salga, saliamo, saliate, salgano

Congiuntivo imperfetto
Salissi, salissi, salisse, salissimo, saliste, salissero

Condizionale presente
Salirei, saliresti, salirebbe, saliremmo, salireste, salirebbero

Imperativo
Sali! (you, sin.), salga! (he/she), saliamo! (we), salite! (you, pl.), salgano! (they)

Participio presente
Saliente

Participio passato
Salito

Auxiliary verb of *salire* is *essere*.
In this case, *uscito* is conjugated as an adjective depending on subject (masculine, feminine, singular, plural).

6.7.4 Irregular verbs in –arre, -orre, -urre

As we learned before, Italian verbs are divided into three conjugations. Some, however, have a particular termination in which they differ from those of those three: they're the verbs whose infinite ends in –arre, -orre or –urre. How to classify them, then? Which conjugation do they belong to? All three belong to the second conjugation because they are the contracted forms of the Latin "tràhere" (to get, to obtain), "pònere" (to put) and "condúcere" (to lead).

Let's see how they are conjugated.

Trarre   To get, to obtain

Presente
Traggo, trai, trae, traiamo, traete, traggono

Imperfetto
Traevo, traevi, traeva, traevamo, traevate, traevano

Futuro
Trarrò, trarrai, trarrà, trarremo, trarrete, trarranno

Passato remoto
Trassi, traesti, trasse, traemmo, traeste, trassero

Congiuntivo presente
Tragga, tragga, tragga, traiamo, traiate, traggano

Congiuntivo imperfetto
Traessi, traessi, traesse, traessimo, traeste, traessero

Condizionale presente
Trarrei, trarresti, trarrebbe, trarremmo, trarreste, trarrebbero

Imperativo
Trai! (you, sin.), tragga! (he/she), traiamo! (we), traete! (you, pl.), traggano! (they)

Participio presente
Traente

Participio passato
Tratto

Auxiliary verb of *trarre* is *avere*.

Porre   To put

Presente
Pongo, poni, pone, poniamo, ponete, pongono

Imperfetto
Ponevo, ponevi, poneva, ponevamo, ponevate, ponevano

Futuro
Porrò, porrai, porrà, porremo, porrete, porranno

Passato remoto
Posi, ponesti, pose, ponemmo, poneste, posero

Congiuntivo presente
Ponga, ponga, ponga, poniamo, poniate, pongano

Congiuntivo imperfetto
Ponessi, ponessi, ponesse, ponessimo, poneste, ponessero

Condizionale presente
Porrei, porresti, porrebbe, porremmo, porreste, porrebbero

Imperativo
Poni! (you, sin.), ponga! (he/she), poniamo! (we), ponete! (you, pl.), pongano! (they)

Participio presente
Ponente

Participio passato
Posto

Auxiliary verb of *porre* is *avere*.

Condurre   To lead

Presente
Conduco, conduci, conduce, conduciamo, conducete, conducono

Imperfetto
Conducevo, conducevi, conduceva, conducevamo, conducevate, conducevano

Futuro
Condurrò, condurrai, condurrà, condurremo, condurrete, condurranno

Passato remoto
Condussi, conducesti, condusse, conducemmo, conduceste, condussero

Congiuntivo presente
Conduca, conduca, conduca, conduciamo, conduciate, conducano

Congiuntivo imperfetto
Conducessi, conducessi, conducesse, conducessimo, conduceste, conducessero

Condizionale presente
Condurrei, condurresti, condurrebbe, condurremmo, condurreste, condurrebbero

Imperativo
Conduci! (you, sin.), conduca! (he/she), conduciamo! (we), conducete! (you, pl.), conducano! (they)

Participio presente
Conducente

Participio passato
Condotto

Auxiliary verb of *condurre* is *avere*.

6.8 Reflexive verbs

Reflexive verbs are verbs that, for several reasons, are accompanied by a pronounced pronoun which agrees with the subject. Generally, they are used in order to indicate that the action expressed by the verb directly concerns the subject who does it.

Reflexive verbs are formed with reflexive pronoun + verb.

Reflexive pronouns in Italian are:

Io   - Mi

Tu   - Ti

Lui/lei - Si

Noi - Ci

Voi - Vi

Loro - Si

Reflexive verbs can be transitive verbs such as *lavare* (to wash) or *vestire* (to dress). These verbs can be used both in a transitive or reflexive way.

Io lavo una mela   I wash an apple.

Io mi lavo   I wash myself.

Some reflexives may have a mutual value.

Ci vediamo domani!   See you tomorrow!
which literally means "We are seeing us tomorrow."

It can often happen that Italians transform verbs that are not reflexive in reflexive verbs.

Mi mangio una pizza!
I eat myself a pizza!

Ci fumiamo una sigaretta
We smoke ourselves a cigarette.

Vi fate un piatto di pasta?
Do you make yourself a pasta dish?

6.9 Pronominal verbs

From a formal point of view, this conjugation is identical to the reflexive one because these verbs are constantly accompanied by pronominal particles, but, unlike what happens in reflexive verbs, in this case the pronoun plays a syntactic role. This means it is neither direct object or term complement.

Part of pronominal verbs are a group of intransitive verbs that are used predominantly just the way they are:

Accorgersi   To perceive
Arrabbiarsi   To get angry
Pentirsi   To repent
Ribellarsi   To rebel
Vergognarsi   To be ashamed

Then there's group of transitive verbs that, accompanied by the pronominal particle, change meaning and assume an intransitive value.

Abbandonare   To abandon
Abbandonarsi   To indulge

Alzare   To raise
Alzarsi   To get up

Commuovere   To move
Commuoversi   To get emotional

Decidere   To decide
Decidersi   To come to a decision

Let's see how reflexive verbs are conjugated. Let's take the example of *chiamare*: its reflexive form is *chiamarsi*.

Io mi chiamo
Tu ti chiami
Lui/lei si chiama
Noi ci chiamiamo

Voi vi chiamate

Loro si chiamano

In order to form the infinite form of a reflexive verb, the reflexive pronoun is united with the infinite verb.

Lavare (to wash) – Lavarsi (to wash oneself)

Incontrare (to meet) – Incontrarsi (to meet each other)

With verbs which hold the infinite, the infinite of reflexive verbs is formed by joining the possessive pronoun for the subject of the infinite verb.

Devo lavarmi in fretta   I have to wash myself quickly.

Dovrebbe alzarsi presto   He/she should wake up early.

With modal verbs (dovere, potere, volere) the reflexive pronoun can be found before the verb.

Mi devo alzare presto   I have to wake up early.

Ti devi alzare presto   You have to wake up early.

Chapter 7 – Propositions

The proposition is a speech unit with an accomplished meaning without having the contribution of a situational context or other verbal contexts. It is better known as "sentence," *frase*.

7.1 Types of propositions

In Italian language, there are numerous types of propositions. Those may be divided into two big categories: principal propositions and subordinated propositions.

7.1.1 Principal propositions

In Italian principal propositions are called ordinate. Those are grammatically independent and meaningful sentences. They do not occupy a fixed position in the period and they do not depend on any other proposition present in the period. However, they may hold subordinate propositions and can be coordinated with other main propositions (coordinated propositions, chapter 7.1.3).

The principal propositions can have these verb tenses: *indicativo, congiuntivo, condizionale* and *imperativo*.

With indicativo (*presente, imperfetto, passato remoto, futuro*) a *proposizione* may be:

Informativa, which is the most common phrase type. The statement has the function of informing; it is therefore a sentence used to communicate a fact, report an event or express a judgment or an opinion.

Ieri sono andato a scuola
Yesterday I went to school

Interrogativa diretta, corresponding to a question. It may be posed by a pronoun, an interrogative adjective or a question to which you can answer with *sì* or *no*, yes or no.

Dove hai incontrato Maria?
Where did you meet Maria?

"Hai assaggiato le fragole?" "Sì, erano buone."
"Did you try the strawberries?" "Yes, they were good."

Esclamativa, expressing a statement rich of emphasis.

Che fortuna abbiamo avuto!
What a fortune we had!

With congiuntivo a *proposizione* may be:

Desiderativa, which expresses a desire.

Voglio che tu venga alla mia festa di compleanno
I want you to come to my birthday party

Esortativa, expressing an exhortation. It is often characterized by the use of modes *imperativo* and *congiuntivo*.

Teniamoci in contatto!
Let's keep in contact!

Concessiva, which expresses a concession.

Che mangino brioche!
Let them eat brioches!

With condizionale a *proposizione* may be of two types:

Potenziale, when expresses an intention.

Domani potreste andare al mare.
Tomorrow you (pl.) could go to the sea.

Dubitativa, when used to express an action that should be accomplished.

Mia sorella dovrebbe studiare di più.
My sister should study more.

With imperativo there is the iussiva proposition. It simply expresses an order.

Metti la salsa nel panino!
Put the sauce in the sandwich!

7.1.2 Subordinated propositions

A subordinated (*subordinata*) proposition is a sentence which depends on another proposition. It does not have a syntactic autonomy if considered alone, and is governed by prepositions, adverbial statements, or conjunctions. It can be explicit (verb conjugated in a finite mode) or implicit (the verb is conjugated in an indefinite mode).

Depending on their function, therefore, subordinate propositions may be classified as:

Aggiuntiva, when it adds an information concerning the principal proposition. It is introduced by *oltre a* and and *oltre che*. In contemporary Italian language there's only the implicit form with the verb at the infinite form.

Oltre che essere un calciatore, Paolo è uno studente.
More than being a soccer player, Paolo is a student.

Avversativa, when it dismounts and affirms the opposite meaning of the principal proposition. It is introduced by *ma, invece, però, tuttavia, eppure, mentre, anziché, invece di, in luogo di*.

Invece che urlare, potremmo fare silenzio.
Instead of screaming, we could be silent.

Causale, explaining any motivation for the action taken in the main proposition, is introduced by conjunctions like *perché, siccome, poiché, giacché, come, che* or conjunctival expressions like *per il fatto che, per il motivo che, dal momento che, dato che, visto che, in quanto*.

Mio figlio non va a scuola perché nevica.
My son doesn't go to school because it snows.

Comparativa, when in the subordinate there is a degree of comparison which refers to something affirmed in the main proposition. It is explicit when introduced by conjunction *che, come, quanto, quale*; when implicit, the verb is at its infinite form introduced by *che, piuttosto che, piuttosto di*.

L'albergo era peggio di quello che avrei pensato.
The hotel was worse than I would have thought.

Concessiva, which expresses a fact or situation that occurs despite what is expressed in the main proposition. They may be introduced by *seppure, benché, ancorché, anche se, quand'anche, con tutto che, chiunque, qualunque, comunque, come che*.

Pur essendo molto timido, è un uomo piacevole.
Though he is very shy, he is a nice man.

Consecutiva, which indicates the consequence or the effect of an action expressed in the main proposition. It is introduced by expression *che*.

Maria ha corso così tanto che ora ha il fiatone.
Maria ran so much that she's out of puff now.

Dichiarativa, which are useful to explain or clarify the main content of the principal proposition. This proposition may be introduced by *cioè, ossia, ovvero, ovverosia, infatti, difatti, vale a dire, per essere precisi, in altre parole, in altri termini*.

Vado in piscina, cioè vado a prendere il sole.
I go to the pool, that is, I'm going to sunbathe.

Eccettuativa, which indicates a circumstance excepting for what is true in the main proposition. It may be recognized by its beginning in *sennonché, tranne che, eccetto che, salvo che, a meno che, se non che* and they are build with *indicativo* or *congiuntivo*.

Accetterei volentieri, a meno che tu non abbia qualcosa in contrario.
I would gladly agree, unless you have something in contrary.

Esclusiva, which has the role of replacing the exclusion complement in the main proposition. This kind of propositions may be introduced by *senza* or *senza che*.

Devi buttarti in acqua senza aver paura.
You have to get in the water without having fear.

Finale, that indicates the end or the purpose to which the action expressed in the regent proposition is directed. This proposition, used more in a implicit form than an explicit one, is introduced by *per, a, di, onde, allo scopo di, al fine di, pur di* and has its verb at the infinito.

Te l'ha comunicato affinché tu possa decidere.
He/she communicated that to you, so you can decide.

Incidentale, which is a proposition consisting of a sentence placed in another sentence. It is usually enclosed between two commas, two hyphens, or two round parentheses. This proposition may also be between the end of another sentence and a strong or intermediate punctuation mark. In these cases, the beginning of the incised can only be reported by the comma.

Il treno è arrivato, <u>sembra</u>: non vuoi salire?
The train arrived, <u>it seems</u>: don't you want to go up?

Interrogativa indiretta, which is meant to expound a question, a doubt or a question already present in the main proposition in the form of verb or adjective. These propositions are introduced by conjunctions *se, come, perché, quando, quanto* and <u>question pronouns</u> *chi, che cosa, cosa, quale, quanto*.

Mi chiedo <u>quale sia la soluzione migliore.</u>
I ask myself <u>which solution is the best.</u>

Limitativa, which specifies the narrow scope within which is valid what is said in the principal proposition. An explicit *limitativa* is introduced by *a quanto, per quanto, per quel(lo) che, secondo quanto, secondo che*, an implicit one by *per* and *in quanto*.

<u>In quanto a lavorare</u>, Marco non si stanca mai.
<u>As for working</u>, Marco never gets tired.

Modale, which explain the way in which an action of the principal proposition is made. A modal proposition is constructed only in implicit form; it presents the verb in *gerundio* or *infinito* form and may be introduced by the preposition *con*, too.

<u>Ascoltando l'insegnante</u>, potresti imparare francese.
<u>By listening to the teacher</u>, you could learn French.

Oggettiva, which is a complete proposition which carries the function of the direct object.

Lei è consapevole <u>di stare bene.</u>
She's conscious <u>about feeling good.</u>

Soggettiva, which is a subordinate proposition which has to carry the subject function for the regent proposition. Explicitly, it is introduced by the conjunction *che* and has the verb at *indicativo, congiuntivo* or *condizionale*. In an implicit form it presents the verb to the infinite form and can be introduced by the preposition *di* or not preceded by any preposition.

Dalla lista risulta <u>che Luca è arrivato primo.</u>
From the list it results <u>that Luca arrived first.</u>

Relativa, which is introduced by a pronoun or relative adverb that expresses a quality related to an element contained in the main proposition. When it is explicit, it is introduced by relative pronouns such as *che, cui* and *chi* and related conjunctions *dove* and *onde*; it has the verb at the *indicativo* when it indicates a certain fact, *congiuntivo* or *condizionale* when it indicates a possible fact.

Questo è il parco <u>dove mi alleno tutti i giorni.</u>
This is the park <u>where I work out every day.</u>

Temporale, which indicates the moment in which takes place what is said in the main proposition. Explicit one may be introduced by prima che when expresses anteriority; when it expresses contemporaneity it's introduced by *mentre, quando, allorché, nel momento che, al tempo in cui, finché*; when there's a posteriority intent, it is introduced by *dopo che*. Whnn this proposition is implicit, it may be introduced by *prima di* (anteriority), *al, col, nel, sul* (contemporaneity), *dopo* and *una volta*.

<u>Nel salutare i parenti</u>, a volte confondo i loro nomi.
<u>Greeting relatives</u>, sometimes I confuse their names.

7.2.1 Hypotetical period

A hypothetical period is that period which contains a principal proposition and a subordinated *condizionale* proposition.

In the analysis of the period, a *condizionale* proposition is a subordinate proposition which expresses a fact or situation (a condition or a hypothesis) from which depends the possibility of whether or not what is expressed in the principal one.

It is common to classify three types of hypothetical period:

1st type of reality, where the hypothesis is presented as real or true. The principal proposition can have all the forms of its type of propositions, while the subordinated one has to keep the *indicativo* form.

<u>Se mangi delle verdure</u>, sarai più sano.
<u>If you eat some vegetable</u>, you'll be healtier.

<u>Se studiamo oggi</u>, domani sapremo matematica.
<u>If we study today</u>, tomorrow we'll know maths.

2nd type of possibility, where the hypothesis is presented as possible. The principal proposition has *condizionale*, while the subordinated has the *congiuntivo imperfetto*.

<u>Se facesse bel tempo</u>, andrei in bicicletta.
<u>If there was a good weather</u>, I would ride my bicycle.

<u>Se il negozio fosse aperto</u>, comprerei delle cose.
<u>If the shop was open</u>, I'd buy some stuff.

3rd type of irreality, where the hypothesis is presented as impossible or unreal because it's known that it can not be verified or because it's known as unoccurred in the past. The main proposition is in *condizionale presente* or *condizionale passato*, while the subordinated has *congiuntivo imperfetto* or *congiuntivo trapassato*.

<u>Se io fossi un cavallo</u>, mangerei tante carote.
<u>If I were a horse</u>, I'd eat a lot of carrots.

Se lui avesse avuto tempo, ti avrebbe chiamato.

If he had time, he would have called you.

7.1.3 Coordinated propositions

A coordinated proposition is, within the period, a proposition linked to the main proposition or a subordinate proposition through a coordinating conjunction *e*, *ma*, *però*, *dunque*. It may have its own meaning or contain more information than the previous sentence, without necessarily relying on it.

As subordinated propositions, also the coordinated ones have their categories:

Copulative, when they are introduced by the copulative conjunctions *e*, affirmative, and *né*, negative. These latter put the propositions on the same semantic plane as almost to sum up their content.

Mangio la banana e anche la mela.
I eat the banana and also the apple.

Non capisco aritmetica, né geometria.
I do not understand arithmetic, nor geometry.

Avversative, when they are introduced by adverse conjunctions *ma*, *bensì*, *però*, *tuttavia*, *peraltro*, *nondimeno*, *pure*, *eppure*, *sennonché*, which put two or more opposites against each other.

Chiamalo, però non disturbarlo!
Call him, but don't bother him!

Clara non è austriaca, bensì è tedesca.
Clara isn't Austrian, but she's German.

Disgiuntive, when they are introduced by disjunctive conjunctions *o*, *oppure*, *altrimenti*, indicating a mutually exclusive relationship between the propositions.

Devono studiare, altrimenti falliranno il test.
They have to study, otherwise they'll fail the test.

Corriamo, oppure perdiamo il treno!
Let's run, or we lose the train!

Esplicative, when they are introduced by explicative conjunctions *infatti*, *cioè*, *ossia*, which are used to indicate that this proposition explains, clarifies or reformates what has been stated previously in the main proposition.

Comprate dodici uova, cioè una dozzina.
Buy twelve eggs, that is a dozen.

Ci amiamo molto, infatti a breve ci sposeremo.
We are a lot in love, in fact we will get married soon.

Conclusive, when they are introduced by conclusive conjugations *dunque, quindi, perciò, pertanto*, which establish a relationship as a result between propositions. The coordinated proposition is presented as a logical deduction or as a concluding synthesis of what has been said in the main one.

Luigi non ha soldi, <u>quindi non può andare al cinema.</u>
Luigi has no money, <u>so he can't go to the cinema.</u>

L'autobus è in ritardo, <u>pertanto aspetteremo.</u>
The bus is late, <u>so we'll wait.</u>

Correlative, when they are introduced by correlative links that can be formally formed by various parts of the speech which bind the propositions so strictly that the one directly invokes the other. Correlative propositions are introduced by expressions *sia... sia, ora... ora, né... né, o... o, e... e* or *nonché... non, tanto... quanto*.

<u>Sia che tu vada al mare, sia che tu vada in montagna,</u> non dimenticarti di preparare la valigia!
<u>Whether you go to the sea, whether you go to the mountains,</u> do not forget to prepare your suitcase!

Non fidarti del tempo: <u>ora fa caldo, ora fa freddo.</u>
Don't trust weather: <u>now it's hot, now it's cold.</u>

Chapter 8 – Complements

In Italian, complements are those names or other parts of speech that carry the name function, which are meant to give a sense to a sentence, giving it a sense of accomplishment. They can complete the meaning of the subject, of the predicate or of the attribute.

These complements are of three types:

Direct, directly completing the meaning expressed by the predicate; this complement defines the meaning without any preposition, uniting it to the same predicate.

Indirect, complementing indirectly the meaning expressed by the predicate; this complement defines its meaning through a preposition.

Circumstantial, complementing the meaning expressed by the subject, by the predicate, by the attribute, by the appendix or by any other complement, giving ideas of place, time, cause, matter or other circumstances not strictly necessary for the sense of the sentence. However, this gives more precision.

8.1 Direct complements

Direct complements are three:

Complemento oggetto

It is only used with active transitive verbs and joins directly to the verb without preposition, answering the questions *che cosa?* or *cosa?*, which may be translated into English "what?"

Giovanni legge un libro.
Giovanni reads a book.

Mia mamma ha incontrato mio cugino al mercato.
My mom met my cousin at the market.

Complemento predicativo del soggetto

It is a name or an adjective which refers to the subject and completes the meaning of the verb. Both the name and the adjective agree in genre and number with the subject they refer to.

This complement may be introduced by copulative verbs like *sembrare, parere, diventare, apparire, rimanere, riuscire, risultare, nascere, morire*.

Tuo fratello sembra simpatico.
Your brother looks nice.

Il problema è risultato <u>difficile.</u>
The problem risulted <u>difficult.</u>

Or by appellative (*essere chiamato, essere detto, essere soprannominato*), elective (*essere eletto, essere nominato, essere proclamato*), estimative (*essere stimato, essere giudicato, essere ritenuto*) or effective (ESSERE FATTO, ESSERE RESO) VERBS.

IL SIGNOR ROSSI FU ELETTO SINDACO.
MISTER ROSSI WAS ELECTED AS MAYOR.

Jim Morrison è soprannominato il Re Lucertola.
Jim Morrison is nicknamed <u>the Lizard King.</u>

Complemento predicativo dell'oggetto

This is an adjective or noun that completes the meaning of the verb and refers to the *complemento oggetto*. The same categories of verbs which hold the subject predicative complement, hold the object predicative complement.

Noi abbiamo eletto il signor Rossi <u>sindaco.</u>
We elected Mister Rossi as <u>mayor.</u>

Jim Morrison soprannominò sé stesso <u>il Re Lucertola.</u>
Jim Morrison nicknamed himself <u>the Lizard King.</u>

8.2 Indirect complements

The most common indirect complements are:

Complemento di specificazione

This complement specifies the meaning of a given term by expressing different relationships. It is always introduced by simple or articulated <u>preposition</u> and answers questions *di chi?*, *di che cosa?*.

Barack Obama era Presidente <u>degli Stati Uniti.</u>
Barack Obama was President <u>of United States.</u>

La chitarra blu è <u>di mio zio Nicola.</u>
The blue guitar is <u>my uncle Nicola's.</u>

Complemento di termine

It indicates the term on which the action is expressed by a transitive verb. It is straightforward from simple or articulated preposition *a* and answers the questions *a chi?*, *a che cosa?*.

Andiamo in vacanza; lasciamo il cane <u>a Giada.</u>
We go on holiday; we leave the dog <u>to Giada.</u>

Stasera Daniele e Fabio vanno <u>ad una cena.</u>
Tonight Daniele and Fabio go <u>to a dinner.</u>

Complemento d'agente

This complement indicates the animation from which an action is expressed by a passive transitive verb and which the subject undergoes. It is governed by the preposition *da* or by the phrase *da parte di* and answers the question *da chi?*.

Romolo e Remo furono adottati da una lupa.
Romulus and Remus were adopted by a wolf.

Alessandro ha ricevuto regali da parte di tutti gli amici.
Alessandro received gifts by all his friends.

Complemento di origine o provenienza

It indicates the real or figurative origin, descendency, of a person or thing. It is introduced by verbs, nouns or adjectives which indicate origin or provenance and is held by the Italian preposition *da*.

Luigi proviene da una famiglia povera del Sud Italia.
Luigi comes from a poor family in Southern Italy.

Ho ricevuto alcune lettere dalla mia fidanzata.
I received some letters by my girlfriend.

Complemento di qualità

This complement usually indicates the qualities of a person, an animal, or the properties of a thing. It is usually formed by a noun accompanied by an attribute and introduced by prepositions *di* and *da*.

Carlo è innamorato di una ragazza dagli occhi blu.
Carlo is in love with a blue-eyed girl.

Freeda è una donna di una creatività incredibile.
Freeda is a woman of incredible creativity.

Complemento di materia

It indicates the material of which the subject is made; this answers the question *di che cosa?* and is introduced by preposition *di*.

Nel museo hai visto una statua di bronzo.
In the museum you saw a bronze statue.

Il neonato ruppe un vaso di cristallo.
The infant broke a glass jar.

Complemento di argomento

Complemento di argomento indicates the person or the thing that is told about; it answers questions *di chi?*, *di che cosa?*, *intorno a chi?* or *riguardo a chi/che cosa?*. It is introduced by prepositions *di, su, circa, riguardo a, intorno a*.

Ogni mattina al bar parliamo di calcio.
Every morning at the bar we speak about soccer.

Domani faremo un test su Napoleone.
Tomorrow we're doing a test about Napoleon.

8.2.1 Complement of comparison

The complemento di paragone indicates the second term of a comparison, in which the first term is represented by the person or thing compared.

This complement may be of three types:

Of maggioranza, in which the complement of comparison is expressed by an adjective preceded by the adverb *più*, and the second term of comparison by a name or an adjective preceded by the preposition *di* or conjunction *che*.

La pizza è più buona del sushi.
Pizza is tastier than sushi.

Il libro che mi hai regalato è più bello che divertente.
The book you gave me is nicer than funny.

Of minoranza, where the complement of comparison is expressed by an adjective preceded by the adverb *meno*, and the second term of comparison by a name or an adjective preceded by the preposition *di* or conjunction *che*.

La mia scrivania è meno ordinata della tua.
My desk is less tidy than yours.

Il cavallo è meno veloce che il ghepardo.
The horse is less fast than the cheetah.

Of uguaglianza, in which the complement is expressed by an adjective preceded by the adverd *tanto*, *così*, *non meno*, and the second term of comparison by a name or an adjective preceded by the preposition *di* or conjunction *che*, or the adverbs *come*, *quanto*.

Tu sei tanto studioso quanto intelligente.
You are so scholarly and intelligent.

Luciano è non meno divertente di Andrea.
Luciano isn't less funny than Andrea.

8.3 Circumstantial complements

The most common circumstantial complements are those that indicate place, time, company, cause, end, way, manner, quantity.

Complemento di compagnia

This complement indicates the animated being with whom the subject is accompagned; it is governed by the preposition *con* or from the expressions *insieme con* or *in compagnia di*.

Davide viene alla festa di compleanno con Chiara.
Davide comes to the birthday party with Chiara.

Andrò al cinema in compagnia di mio cugino.
I'll go to the cinema in company of my cousin.

Complemento di causa

Complemento di causa indicates the reason, the cause of an action; answers the question *perché?*, *per quale motivo?*. It is introduced by prepositions *a, di, da, per* or expressions *a causa di, a modo di, per motivi di*.

Ieri Paolo è stato a letto per motivi di salute.
Yesterday Paolo stayed in bed for health reasons.

In montagna tremavamo dal freddo.
In the mountains we shivered because of cold.

Complemento di fine o scopo

This complement indicates the end for which the action is performed or the destination of an object; it answers the questions *a quale fine?*, *per quale scopo?*. It is introduced by prepositions *a, da, per, in*, which precede the noun indicating the purpose or the locutions *al fine di, essere di, dare in, lasciare in, riuscire di*.

Questa è la mia sala da pranzo.
This is my lunchroom.

Al fine di prendere un bel voto, studia molto!
In order to take a good vote, study a lot!

Complemento di mezzo o strumento

It indicates the way or instrument with which the action is expressed by the predicate; it answers the questions *per mezzo di* chi? or *per mezzo di che cosa?*. Its prepositions are *con, per, di, a, in, mediante* and locutions are *per mezzo di, per opera di*.

Elisa andò al concerto con la macchina.
Elisa went to the concert with the car.

Giulio Cesare morì per opera di un gruppo di senatori.
Giulio Cesare died because of a group of senators.

Complemento di modo o maniera

Complemento di modo o maniera indicates the way in which a circumstance is realized; it answers the questions *come?*, *in che modo?*, *in che maniera?* and is introduced by prepositions *con*, *a*, *di*, *da*, *in*, *per* or expressions *come*, *a modo di*, *alla maniera di*.

Anna è in ritardo, quindi cammina di fretta.
Anna is late, so she walks in a hurry.

Mia nonna procedeva a modo di tartaruga.
My grandmother proceeded as a turtle.

8.3.1 Complements of place

Complemento di luogo indicates where the action takes place. In the distinction of the various place complements, one must always take care of the meaning more than the syntactic structure, which can often mislead.

This complement may be of four types:

Complemento di stato in luogo, which indicates where the subject is and the action is done. It is introduced by prepositions *in*, *a*, *su*, *sopra*, *sotto*, *dentro*, *davanti*, *presso*.

Fabrizio è stato dentro casa durante la tempesta.
Fabrizio was inside the house during the storm.

Il gatto di nostro zio è nel letto.
Our uncle's cat is on the bed.

Complemento di moto a luogo depends on a verb of movement and indicates where the subject or the place to which is directed the action. Its prepositions are *a*, *da*, *su*, *per*, *sotto*, *verso*.

Dopo le lezioni, cammino verso casa da solo.
After class, I walk home alone.

Gli alunni andarono dal maestro per ringraziarlo.
The pupils went to the teacher to thank him.

Complemento di moto da luogo, which indicates the place where the action comes from. It is introduced by prepositions *di* and *da*.

Nel 1302 Dante fu esiliato da Firenze.
In 1302 Dante was exiled from Florence.

Domani esco di casa a mezzanotte.
Tomorrow I leave home at midnight.

Complemento di moto per luogo indicates the place through which passes the action. Its prepositions are *per* and *attraverso*.

Il ladro fuggì attraverso i campi.
The thief fled through the fields.

Per andare a Roma, passiamo per Firenze.
In order to go to Rome, we pass through Florence.

8.3.2 Complements of time

Complemento di tempo indicates in what temporal circumstances occurs the action expressed by the verb.

Two basic types of time complements are distinguished:

Complemento di tempo determinato, which indicates the exact time when the action is happening or will take place. It is introduced by prepositions and expressions *a, in, di, su, verso, circa, durante*.

Questa sera andremo a cena verso le otto.
Tonight we'll have dinner about at eight o'clock.

Carolina va a sciare in inverno.
Carolina goes skiing in Winter.

Complemento di tempo continuato indicates how long takes the action expressed by the predicate. The prepositions and expressions which introduced it are *per, durante, circa, su, intorno, verso*.

Ieri pomeriggio Alessandro studiò per molto tempo.
Yesterday afternoon Alessandro studied for a long time.

Anna Frank visse durante la Seconda Guerra Mondiale.
Anna Frank lived during the Second World War.

Chapter 9 – How to...

9.1 ... make the passive form of a verb?

Transitive verbs, the ones with *complemento oggetto* (see chapter 8.1), can have active form and passive form. In this case the subject is no longer the one who performs the action, but undergoes it.

The passive form of any verb is given by the *verbo essere* (chapter 6.4.1) united to the *participio passato*. The person or thing which performs the action is preceded by the Italian preposition *da*, which, in this case, may be translated into English "by."

I ladri sono stati presi dai poliziotti ieri notte.
The thieves were caught by the cops last night.

Questi libri mi sono stati regalati da Federica.
These books were given to me by Federica.

We can find the passive form with the modal verbs *andare* and *venire* (chapter 6.7.1, 6.7.3), too. They substitute the *verbo essere*, but they're always followed by the *participio passato*.

La tassa di iscrizione viene pagata in anticipo.
The registration fee is paid in advance.

Il ragazzo va seguito da un docente responsabile.
The boy should be followed by a responsible teacher.

Remember that the *participio passato* must follow in gender and number to the subject it refers to!

9.2 ... build the negative form of a sentence?

The negative sentence is used to deny an affirmation, not to accept or in order to answer by refusing what has been positively expressed.

The rule is simple; when making the negative form of a sentence, one must put "non" before the verb.

Massimo non gioca a basket, ma a golf.
Massimo does not play basketball, but golf.

Quest'estate loro non vanno in vacanza.
This summer they do not go on vacation.

Negative questioning sentence forms with negation *non* before the verb. Just the intonation changes, not the order of the words.

Non hai mangiato la pizza ieri sera?
Don't you have eat pizza last night?

Perché non andiamo al cinema?
Why don't we go to the cinema?

9.3 ... compose the courtesy form?

When creating the courtesy form in Italian, the rule requires the use of the third person singular to the female gender, *lei*, which substitutes the *tu* personal pronoun.

Lei sa per caso a che ora arriva il treno?
Do you maybe know when the train arrives?

Che cosa (lei) desidera?
What do you desire?

Though *lei* is a female pronoun, the adjective or past participle agrees with the person to whom it is addressed.

Signore, lei è contento del viaggio?
Sir, are you happy about the trip?

Signora, è andata al supermercato?
Miss, did you go to the supermarket?

The possessive pronoun is the one belonging to the third person of the singular form: *il suo, la sua, i suoi, le sue*.

I suoi occhi sono davvero belli, signora!
Your eyes are really beautiful, miss!

La sua cravatta è storta, signore.
Your tie is crooked, sir.

9.4 ... tell the time?

In order to tell what time is it in Italian language, usually the form is plural. It is singular only in three cases:

È l'una   It's one o'clock
È mezzanotte   It's midnight
È mezzogiorno   It's noon

With these times the singular is always used, although after hours there are minutes.

È mezzanotte e tre   It's midnight and three minutes
È l'una e venti   It's one and twenty minutes

You must always put the determinative article before the number which indicates the time.

Sono le otto   It's eight o'clock

Sono <u>le</u> sei e mezza   It's six and a half

The article is always feminine and plural as it refers to hours, except in one case: è l'una (it's one o'clock). In this example the article is feminine but singular.

Only at mezzogiorno and mezzanotte the article isn't used.

Minutes are indicated after the hour.

Sono le due <u>e</u> <u>cinque</u>   It's two and five minutes

When the minutes are 15 you can say:

Sono le nove <u>e</u> <u>un</u> <u>quarto</u>   It's nine and a quarter

When the minutes are 30, it can be said:

Sono le cinque <u>e</u> <u>mezza/o</u>   It's five and a half

When the minutes reach 40, you can normally say the minutes or how many minutes are missing at the next hour.

Sono <u>dieci alle nove</u>   It's ten to nine

When there are no minutes, for example at 17:00, one can say: sono le cinque <u>in</u> <u>punto</u>   it's five o'clock

9.5 ... tell the date?

In order to tell the date, the Italian language uses always the definite article *il* before the number of the day.

Oggi è <u>il</u> 7 ottobre.
Today is October 7[th.]

Domani sarà <u>il</u> 10 settembre.
Tomorrow will be September 10[th.]

The prepositions *a* and *in* are used when a month is precisied.

Andrò in Francia <u>a</u> giugno.
I'm going to France <u>in</u> June.

<u>In</u> luglio 2009 ho comprato un gatto.
<u>In</u> July 2009 I bought a cat.

Before the specification of the year, the used article is the definite *il* or *in*, with every its compound form.

Il mio anno preferito fu <u>il</u> 2005.
My favourite year was 2005.

Luca si trasferirà in Italia <u>nel</u> 2018.
Luca is going to move to Italy <u>in</u> 2018.

Chapter 10 – Useful vocabulary

10.1 Numbers

Numbers are used to provide information on numerical quantities. When accompanied by names, they can have the function of adjective.

10.1.1 Cardinal numbers

1 Uno
2 Due
3 Tre
4 Quattro
5 Cinque
6 Sei
7 Sette
8 Otto
9 Nove
10 Dieci
11 Undici
12 Dodici
13 Tredici
14 Quattordici
15 Quindici
16 Sedici
17 Diciassette
18 Diciotto
19 Diciannove
20 Venti
21 Ventuno
22 Ventidue
23 Ventitré

30 Trenta

40 Quaranta

50 Cinquanta

60 Sessanta

70 Settanta

80 Ottanta

90 Novanta

100 Cento

101 Centouno

102 Centodue

200 Duecento

300 Trecento

1000 Mille

2000 Duemila

10.000 Diecimila

300.000 Trecentomila

1.000.000 Un milione

1.000.009 Un milione e nove

1.500.000 Un milione e cinquecento mila

10.1.2 Ordinal numbers

To get an ordinal number, just remove the last letter of the cardinal number and add:

-esimo for singular and masculine nouns

-esima for singular and feminine nouns

-esimi for plural and masculine nouns

-esime for plural and feminine nouns

Traiano fu il quattordic*esimo* Imperatore romano.
Trajan was the fourteenth Roman emperor.

Arrivammo vent*esimi* alla gara di corsa.
We arrived twentieth to the running race.

The first 10 numbers do not follow this rule. These have their own numbering.

1° Primo/a/i/e

2° Secondo/a/i/e

3° Terzo/a/i/e
4° Quarto/a/i/e
5° Quinto/a/i/e
6° Sesto/a/i/e
7° Settimo/a/i/e
8° Ottavo/a/i/e
9° Nono/a/i/e
10° Decimo/a/i/e

10.2 Days, months, seasons, festivities

Lunedì	Monday
Martedì	Tuesday
Mercoledì	Wednesday
Giovedì	Thursday
Venerdì	Friday
Sabato	Saturday
Domenica	Sunday
Gennaio	January
Febbraio	February
Marzo	March
Aprile	April
Maggio	May
Giugno	June
Luglio	July
Agosto	August
Settembre	September
Ottobre	October
Novembre	November
Dicembre	December
Inverno	Winter
Primavera	Spring
Estate	Summer

Autunno   Fall

Auguri!   Best wishes!

Capodanno   New year

Buon anno!   Happy new year!

Epifania   Ephipany

Pasqua   Easter

Ferragosto   (Feast of assumption)

Tutti i santi   All Saints

Natale   Christmas

Santo Stefano   Saint Stephen

Compleanno   Birthday

Buon compleanno!   Happy birthday!

10.3 The weather

Pioggia   Rain

Piove   It rains

è piovoso   It rains

Pioviggina   It rains slowly

Neve   Snow

Nevica   It snows

Sole   Sun

C'è il sole   It's sunny

È soleggiato   It's sunny

È sereno   It's clear

È nuvoloso   It's cloudy

È ventoso   It's windy

C'è vento   It's windy

È umido   It's wet

È secco   It's dry

È afoso   It's stuffy

Temporale   Thunderstorm

Tempesta   Storm

Grandine   Hailstorm

Lampo   Lightning

Fulmine   Lightning

Tuono   Thunder

Fa caldo   It's hot

Fa freddo   It's cold

Che tempo fa?   How's the weather like?

To tell about weather, verbs are usually used impersonal to the <u>third</u> <u>singular</u> <u>person</u> form.

10.4 Greeting, introduction, basic expressions

Buongiorno   Good morning

Buon pomeriggio   Good afternoon

Buonasera   Good evening

Buonanotte   Goodnight

Ciao   Hello/bye bye

Arrivederci   Goodbye

A più tardi!   See you soon!

Addio   Goodbye (farewell)

Salve   Hello (in a more formal way)

Come ti chiami?   What's your name?

Qual è il tuo nome?   What's your name?

Io mi chiamo…   My name is...

Il mio nome è...   My name is...

Quanti anni hai?   How old are you?

Ho ... anni   I'm ... years-old

Dove vivi?   Where do you live?

Vivo a...   I live in...

Abito a...   I live in...

Da dove vieni?   Where do you come from?

Vengo da...   I come from...

Dov'è il bagno?   Where's the toilet?

Parla inglese?   Do you speak English?

Sì   Yes

Certamente!   Of course!

Certo!   Of course!

No   No

Grazie   Thanks/thank you

Grazie mille   Thank you very much

Mi dispiace   I'm sorry

Scusa!   Sorry

Mi scusi,…   Excuse me

Per favore   Please

Per cortesia   Please

Congratulazioni!   Congrats!

10.5 Countries, nationalities

Italia   Italy
Italiano/a/i/e   Italian

Inghilterra   England
Inglese/i   English

Germania   Germany
Tedesco/a/chi/che   German

Francia   France
Francese/i   French

Austria   Austria
Austriaco/a/i/che   Austrian

Spagna   Spain
Spagnolo/a/i/e   Spanish

Portogallo   Portugal
Portoghese/i   Portuguese

Lussemburgo   Luxembourg

Svizzera   Switzerland
Svizzero/a/i/e   Swiss

Repubblica Ceca   Czech Republic
Ceco/a/chi/che   Czech

Don't confuse with the adjective cieco/a/chi/che   blind!

Slovenia   Slovenia
Sloveno/a/i/e   Slovenian

Slovacchia   Slovakia
Slovacco/a/chi/che   Slovak

Finlandia   Finland
Finlandese/i   Finnish

Norvegia   Norway
Norvegese/i   Norwegian

Irlanda   Ireland
Irlandese/i   Irish

Danimarca   Denmark
Danese/i   Danish

Svezia   Sweden
Svedese/i   Swedish

Olanda   Holland
Olandese/i   Dutch

Polonia   Poland
Polacco/a/chi/che   Polish

Ungheria   Ungary
Ungherese/i   Hungarian

Croazia   Croatia
Croato/a/i/e   Croatian

Serbia   Serbia
Serbo/a/i/e   Serbian

Belgio   Belgium
Belga   Belgian

Bulgaria   Bulgary
Bulgaro/a/i/e   Bulgarian

Albania   Albania
Albanese/i   Albanian

Romania   Romania
Rumeno/a/i/e   Romanian

Turchia   Turkey
Turco/a/chi/che   Turkish

Stati Uniti   United States
Statunitense/i   (from United States)

Cina   China
Cinese/i   Chinese

Giappone   Japan
Giapponese/i   Japanese

Vietnam   Vietnam
Vietnamita/i   Vietnamese

Corea   Korea
Coreano/a/i/e   Korean

India   India
Indiano/a/i/e   Indian

Marocco   Morocco
Marocchino/a/i/e   Moroccan

Africa   Africa
Africano/a/i/e   African

Asia   Asia
Asiatico/a/i/che   Asian

America   America
Americano/a/i/e   American

Canada   Canada
Canadese/i   Canadian

Europa   Europe
Europeo/a/i/e   European

Russia   Russia
Russo/a/i/e   Russian

10.6 Colors

Rosso   Red

Arancio   Orange
Arancione   Orange

Oro   Gold

Giallo   Yellow

Verde   Green

Grigio   Gray

Azzurro   Light blue
Turchese   Light blue

Blu   Blue

Viola   Purple

Rosa   Pink

Fucsia   Fuchsia

Marrone   Brown

Nero   Black

Bianco   White

10.7 Pets and animals

Cane — Dog
Gatto — Cat
Mucca — Cow
Capra — Goat
Gallo — Rooster
Gallina — Hen
Maiale — Pig
Pecora — Sheep
Cavallo — Horse
Toro — Bull
Pappagallo — Parrot
Farfalla — Butterfly
Ape — Bee
Aquila — Eagle
Tacchino — Turkey
Coniglio — Rabbit
Topo — Mouse
Lupo — Wolf
Volpe — Fox
Tigre — Tiger
Rana — Frog
Tartaruga — Turtle
Serpente — Snake
Elefante — Elephant
Giraffa — Giraffe
Rinoceronte — Rhino
Zebra — Zebra
Leone — Lion
Leonessa — Lioness
Ghepardo — Cheetah

Leopardo   Leopard

Scimmia   Monkey

Pesce   Fish

Delfino   Dolphin

Balena   Whale

Foca   Seal

10.8 Food and eating

10.8.1 Fruits

Frutta, frutti   Fruits

Fragola   Strawberry

Mirtillo   Blueberry

Mela   Apple

Pera   Pear

Arancia   Orange

Limone   Lemon

Mandarino   Tangerine

Albicocca   Apricot

Pesca   Peach

Ciliegia   Cherry

Anguria   Watermelon

Zucca   Pumpkin

Uva   Grapes

Pomodoro   Tomato

Ananas   Pineapple

Cocco   Coconut

Castagna   Chestnut

Noce   Nut

Arachide   Peanut

10.8.2 Vegetables

Verdure   Vegetables

Patata   Potato

Insalata   Salad

Zucchina   Zucchini

Melanzana   Aubergine

Carota   Carrot

Cipolla   Onion

Aglio   Garlic

Fungo   Mushroom

Broccolo   Broccoli

Cavolo   Cabbage

Fagiolo   Bean

Pisello   Pea

Legumi   Legumes

10.8.3 Other foods and dishes

Acqua   Water
Bicchiere d'acqua   Glass of water
Acqua naturale   Flat water
Acqua frizzante   Sparkly water

Tè   Tea
Tisana   Tisane
Infuso   Brew

Caffè   Coffee
Tazza di caffè   Cup of coffee
Caffè liscio   Normal coffee
Caffè macchiato   Macchiato
Caffè corretto   Coffee with alchol

Vino   Wine

Birra   Beer
Birra bionda   Blonde beer
Birra scura   Dark beer

Bibita   Flat drink
Bibita gassata   Sparkly drink

Pizza   Pizza
Pizza bianca   Pizza without tomato

Pizza rossa   Pizza without mozzarella

Calzone   Pizza turnover

Pasta   Pasta

Piatto di pasta   Pasta dish

Succo   Juice

Succo di frutta   Fruit juice

Succo d'arancia   Orange juice

Salsiccia   Sausage

Gelato   Ice cream

Panino   Sandwich

Prosciutto   Ham

Pancetta   Bacon

Colazione   Breakfast

Pranzo   Lunch

Cena   Dinner

Merenda   Snack

Pane   Bread

Olio   Oil

Formaggio   Cheese

Carne   Meat

Pesce   Fish

Pollo   Chicken

Maiale   Pork

Di stagione   In season

Fuori stagione   Out of season

Andato a male   Gone bad

Il conto   The check

Avere fame   Being hungry

10.9 Places

Ristorante   Restaurant

Osteria   Inn

Trattoria   Trattoria

Bar   Café
Libreria   Bookshop
Biblioteca   Library
Scuola   School
Asilo   Nursery school
Scuole elementari   Elementary schools
Scuola media   Middle school
Scuole superiori   High school
Università   University
Stazione   Station
Aeroporto   Airport
Municipio   Town hall
Supermercato   Supermercato
Chiesa   Church
Farmacia   Pharmacy
Ospedale   Hospital
Fattoria   Farm
Casa   House, home
Ufficio   Office
Mare   Sea
Montagna   Mountains
Città   City
Campagna   Country
Lago   Lake
Fiume   River

10.10 Occupations

Banchiere/a   Banker
Economista   Economist
Commercialista   Business consultant
Assicuratore   Insurance broker
Dirigente   Manager
Impiegato/a   Office worker

Receptionist — Receptionist
Commesso/a — Salesman/woman
Segretario/a — Segretary
Panettiere/a — Baker
Barbiere — Barber
Parruchiere/a — Hairdresser
Estetista — Beautician
Macellaio/a — Butcher
Pescivendolo/a — Fishmonger
Fiorista — Florist
Fruttivendolo/a — Greengrocer
Dentista — Dentist
Medico, dottore — Doctor
Infermiere/a — Nurse
Veterinario — Vet
Giardiniere — Gardner
Muratore — Builder
Meccanico — Mechanic
Idraulico — Plumber
Barista — Barman/maid
Cuoco/a — Cooker
Cameriere/a — Waiter/waitress
Autista — Driver
Pilota — Pilot
Artista — Artist
Scrittore/trice — Writer
Attore/trice — Actor/actress
Musicista — Musician
Avvocato — Lawyer
Insegnante — Teacher
Architetto — Architect

Ingegnere   Engineer
Contadino/a   Farmer
Pompiere   Firefighter
Casalinga   Housewife
Bibliotecario/a   Librarian
Postino/a   Postman/woman
Traduttore/trice   Translator

Conclusion

> L' Italiana è lingua letteraria: fu scritta sempre, e non mai parlata; il che vuolsi ripetere perchè, o non fu detto, o ch'io mi sappia, non fu mai dimostrato: quindi originarono, e infellonirono le questioni e non cessano.

"The Italian is a literary language: it was always written, but never spoken. That this fact is going to repeat -or it was never told, or I didn't know – was never demonstrated: so this originated furious debates and they don't stop," once said Giovanni Boccaccio, an Italian writer, poet and important Renaissance humanist.

Learning the Italian language, as it has been reaffirmed a million times, is not easy. The effectiveness is given by the commitment. Enriching your knowledge with an additional language means, in any case, enriching another culture, another way of thinking.

Most Italians themselves do not believe in the effectiveness of the Italian language in the World. Even if not focused on economic attractiveness, the Italian language, uncommon for that purpose, is a practically unparalleled literary and cultural wealth.

With this volume, as well as having been dropped into the atmosphere of the Bel Paese, in the future you will have the possibility to extend your acquired knowledges to a wider atmosphere: an artistic, literary, cinematic, musical, religious and scientific history, full of coming and going.

If satisfying your curiosity about cultures and traditions means primarily learning a language, let's go this way! This has been a small step forward.

Part 2: Italian Short Stories

9 Simple and Captivating Stories for Effective Italian Learning for Beginners

Introduction

Since we are children, stories are a fundamental part of our formation. Whether they are told by our grandparents or parents or invented by ourselves, they can reflect our experience and also enrich it.

In this sense, from the beginning, the narration has been a modality of construction of human thought and knowledge: think of myths – stories built with the intent to explain natural phenomena and human life. These narratives – besides creating and passing on knowledge – allow education and understanding of certain cultural models. At the origins of Western culture, in ancient philosophy, narration and logical thinking were considered tools for building knowledge.

The many narratives that go through the life of each of us contribute to the construction of our formation. Telling, therefore, educates and allows the construction of an educational history, which in turn can be narrated, showing another aspect of the link between storytelling and education. Not only is it told to educate, but the same education can and must be told.

This book will present nine short stories developed to test your knowledge of Italian language. At the end of each narration are summaries and questions to test your understanding. Whether you read before going to sleep or lunchtime, these stories will help you go back in time, but with the current linguistic awareness!

Chapter 1: La storia del Signor Tempo – The Story of Mr. Time

"Mamma, quanto è lunga un'ora? Mamma, quante sono cento ore? Ma quando finisce il tempo?" chiedeva spesso Dino alla sua mamma. Ella, un giorno, decise di rispondergli raccontando la storia del Signor Tempo.

"Mom, how long is an hour? Mom, how many are a hundred hours? But when does the time end?" Dino often asked his mother.

One day, she decided to answer him by telling the story of Mr. Time.

C'era una volta, tanto tanto tempo fa, in un paese molto molto lontano, il Signor Tempo. Era un uomo buono ma girava per le vie sempre imbronciato e scontento perché, a suo dire, i giorni trascorrevano tutti uguali. Il suo sogno era quello di creare nelle giornate cambiamenti e varietà, per stupire gli uomini ma soprattutto i bambini.

Once upon a time, a long time ago, in a very far away country, there was Mr. Time. He was a good man, but he always went about the streets, always sulky and unhappy because, in his opinion, the days were all the same. His dream was to create changes and varieties in the days, to amaze men but especially children.

Decise allora di rivolgersi ai suoi quattro cari amici poiché lo aiutassero a realizzare questo suo grande desiderio. Così tutto sarebbe diventato più bello e vivace. Bastò chiamarli una volta per vederli arrivare immediatamente: il Vecchio Soffione, il Mago Nevoso, la Strega Terriccia e la Fata Ondina. Lo ascoltarono attentamente mentre esponeva il suo problema e ciascuno di loro trovò la soluzione.

He decided to turn to his four dear friends so they could help him realize his great desire. So everything would become more beautiful and lively. He only had to call them once to see them arrive immediately: the Old Showerhead, the Snowy Wizard, the Earthling Witch and the Wavy Fairy. They listened to him attentively while exposing his problem and each of them found the solution.

"Io sono il Vecchio Soffione e la cosa che so fare meglio, come dice il mio nome, è soffiare il vento. Il vento porterà le nuvole in cielo, farà cadere le foglie degli alberi e i ricci con le castagne. I bambini si divertiranno a raccoglierle! Così facendo porterò l'autunno, la stagione delle foglie rosse, gialle e arancioni, della ripresa della scuola e degli animali che vanno in letargo."

"I am the Old Showerhead and the thing that I do best, as my name says, is to blow the wind. The wind will bring clouds to the sky, drop the leaves of the trees and the burrs with their chestnuts. Children will have fun collecting them! In doing so, I will bring autumn, the season of red, yellow and orange leaves, and the recovery of school and hibernating animals."

"Io sono il Mago Nevoso e porterò con me il freddo e la neve. Arriverà l'inverno, la stagione in cui tutti dovranno coprirsi ben bene. I bambini potranno giocare a palle di neve aspettando l'arrivo di Babbo Natale!"

"I am the Snowy Wizard, and I will bring with me the cold and the snow. Winter will come, the season when everyone will have to cover up. Children can play snowballs waiting for Santa's arrival!"

"Eccomi qua, è arrivato il mio turno! Sono la Strega Terriccia, una strega buona s'intende. Io gironzolo qua e là sussurrando alla terra, ai fiori, agli alberi e alle tartarughe: "Sveglia…". Tutta la natura, ascoltando il mio richiamo, si risveglia con gioia perché è in arrivo la primavera. La stagione dove tutto rifiorisce, dove tutto si colora! Dove tutti i bambini possono finalmente tornare a giocare nei prati e nei parchi."

"Here I am, my turn has arrived! I am the Earthling Witch, a good witch of course. I wander around whispering to the earth, flowers, trees, and turtles: "Wake up..." All nature, listening to my call, awakens with joy because spring is coming. The season where everything flourishes, where everything is colored! Where all children can finally return to play in the meadows and parks."

"Ora tocca a me! Sono la Fata Ondina. Dopo la primavera io porterò l'estate, la stagione del sole, del mare e del gelato. È il tempo più spensierato e allegro, con i bambini che si godono la vacanza e il caldo."

"Now it's my turn! I'm the Wavy Fairy. After spring, I will bring the summer, the season of sun, sea and ice cream. It is the most carefree and cheerful time, with the children enjoying the holiday and the heat."

Il Signor Tempo accolse tutte queste idee e con aria soddisfatta disse: "Bene, bene. Faremo proprio come voi proponete. Arriverà l'autunno e poi l'inverno. Dopo sarà il tempo della primavera a cui seguirà l'estate. E così via, in un susseguirsi senza fine. Allora, amici miei, mettiamoci al lavoro! Uno per tutti e tutti per uno!".

Mr. Time accepted all these ideas and said with satisfaction: "Well, well. We will do just as you propose. Autumn will come and then winter. Then it will be the time of spring which will be followed by summer. And so on, in an endless succession. So, my friends, let's get to work! One for all, and all for one!"

1.1 – Summary

Il Signor Tempo è un uomo buono che gironzola in città. Egli, però, è triste perché i giorni sembrano tutti uguali. A tal proposito, si rivolge a quattro suoi amici: il Vecchio Soffione, portatore di vento e di autunno; il Mago Nevoso, il quale presenta l'inverno e il freddo; la Strega

Terriccia, simbolo di primavera, la quale grazie al suo canto sa far crescere di nuovo tutti gli elementi naturali; la Fata Ondina che porta il periodo più allegro e spensierato, cioè l'estate. Grazie a questi collaboratori, il Signor Tempo è motivato di nuovo.

      Mr. Time is a good man who wanders around the city. However, he is sad because the days seem all the same. In this regard, he turns to four of his friends: the Old Showerhead, bearer of wind and autumn; the Snowy Wizard, who presents winter and cold; the Earthling Witch, symbol of spring, which thanks to her song can make all the natural elements grow again; and the Wavy Fairy that brings the most cheerful and carefree period – the summer. Thanks to these collaborators, Mr. Time is motivated again.

1.2 – Vocabulary

Caldo = Hot

Castagna = Chestnut

Fata = Fairy

Freddo = Cold

Gelato = Ice cream

Giornata = Day

Idea = Idea

Lavoro = Work, job

Mago = Wizard

Quattro = Four

Soluzione = Solution

Strega = Witch

Tartaruga = Turtle

Tempo = Time

1.3 – Questions

1 – Perché il Signor Tempo è triste?

Why is Mr. Time sad?

2 – Collega i personaggi alle stagioni corrispondenti

a. Vecchio Soffione

b. Strega Terriccia

c. Fata Ondina

d. Mago Nevoso

1. Autunno

2. Inverno

3. Primavera

4. Estate

3 – La reazione del Signor Tempo al loro progetto è positiva o negativa?

The reaction of Mr. Time to their project is positive or negative?

4 – Perché la mamma racconta la storia del signor Tempo a Dino?

Why does the mom tell Dino the story of Mr. Time?

a. Perché il bambino piange – Because the child cries

b. Perché il bambino fa troppe domande – Because the child asks too many questions

c. Per far addormentare il bambino – To make the child fall asleep

5 – Qual è la tua stagione preferita? Perché?

What's your favourite season? Why?

1.4 – Answers

1 – Il Signor Tempo è triste perché le giornate sono tutte uguali.

Mr. Time is sad because days are all the same.

2 – A1, B3, C4, D2

3 – La reazione del Signor Tempo è positiva.

Mr. Tempo's reaction is positive.

4 – B

5 – La mia stagione preferità è… perché…

My favourite season is… because…

Chapter 2: Il singhiozzo della volpe – The Sob of the Fox

Le prime stelle stavano iniziando ad apparire nel cielo mentre Giacomo il giardiniere tornava alla sua casetta in fondo al parco. Aveva lavorato tutto il giorno ed era stanco ed affamato; non vedeva l'ora di cenare e riposarsi. Strada facendo, Giacomo vide la sua amica volpe risalire il sentiero verso di lui. Anche la volpe stava tornando a casa. "Buonanotte!" disse Giacomo, "Buonanotte... hic, Giacomo!" rispose la volpe. Aveva il singhiozzo.

The first stars were beginning to appear in the sky while Giacomo the gardener was returning to his cottage at the back of the park. He had worked all day and was tired and hungry; he could not wait to have dinner and rest. Along the way, Giacomo saw his friend, Fox, climb the path towards him. Even Fox was coming home.

"Goodnight!" Giacomo said.

"Goodnight ... hic, Giacomo!" the fox answered, with a sob.

Quella mattina la volpe stava bevendo una limonata, quando uno scoiattolo le raccontò una barzelletta a proposito di un pappagallo, un verme e una mazza da baseball e la volpe scoppiò a ridere. Fu allora che imparò che non è una buona idea ridere e bere allo stesso tempo. Aveva avuto il singhiozzo tutto il pomeriggio. "Mi domando se... hic... Giacomo conosce una cura per il singhiozzo".

On the morning of that day, Fox had been drinking lemonade when a squirrel told him a joke about a parrot, a worm, and a baseball bat. Fox had laughed. It was then that he'd learned that it is not a good idea to laugh and drink at the same time. He'd had the sob all afternoon.

"I wonder if ... hic ... Giacomo knows a cure for the sob."

Tornato a casa, Giacomo si ricordò che aveva ancora uno o due lavori da compiere. Per prima cosa bagnò le piante e poi ritirò il bucato. La volpe si affrettò a raggiungerlo. Non aveva paura del buio, ma dov'era Giacomo? Corse a cercarlo sul retro della casa, ma invece di trovare lui, trovò il suo bucato. Ruzzolò a terra in un gran fracasso, poi si ferì una zampa atterrando su dei vasi di fiori. "Che dolore...hic!" si lamentava la volpe. Giacomo, sorpreso dal baccano, andò a ispezionare da dove veniva, ma quando vide ciò che aveva provocato tanto rumore, si nascose velocemente. "Un fantasma!" urlò.

Back home, Giacomo remembered that he still had one or two jobs to do. First, he watered the plants and then he collected the laundry.

Fox hurried to join him. He was not afraid of the dark, but where was Giacomo? He ran to look for him at the back of the house, but instead of finding him, he found his laundry. He tumbled to the floor in a loud racket, then wounded a paw landing on flowerpots.

"What a pain ... hic!" complained Fox.

Giacomo, surprised by the din, went to inspect where it came from, but when he saw what had caused so much noise, he quickly hid.

"A ghost!" he screamed.

Era la prima volta che Giacomo vedeva un fantasma. Sapeva che doveva presentarsi, ma cosa avrebbe dovuto dire a un fantasma? Intanto restava immobile ad ascoltare. Si sentivano ancora i lamenti e i passi pesanti del fantasma quando, improvvisamente, ci fu un altro gran fracasso: "Hic!". Un sorriso apparve sul viso del giardiniere. Giacomo allungò di nuovo la testa dietro l'angolo della casa e questa volta vide qualcosa che lo fece scoppiare a ridere. "Ha bisogno di aiuto, signor Fantasma?" "Sì grazie" arrivò in risposta dall'interno di un barile, "potresti rimettermi dritto?".

It was the first time that Giacomo had seen a ghost. He knew he had to show himself, but what should he say to a ghost? Meanwhile, he remained still, to listen. He could still hear the lamentations and the heavy steps of the ghost when, suddenly, there was another great noise:

"Hic!"

A smile appeared on the gardener's face. Giacomo stretched his head back around the corner of the house, and this time he saw something that made him laugh.

"Do you need help, Mr. Ghost?"

"Yes, thank you," came a response from inside a barrel. "Could you put me back?"

Giacomo aiutò la volpe a rimettersi in piedi: "Mi hai fatto prendere uno spavento!" disse Giacomo. "Me ne sono preso uno anche io, ma indovina un po'? Mi è passato il singhiozzo!" rispose la volpe.

Giacomo helped Fox get back on his feet.

"You scared me!" Giacomo said.

"I got scared too, but guess what? The sob has passed!" replied Fox.

2.1 – Summary

Alla fine della sua giornata di lavoro, Giacomo il giardiniere torna a casa. Sul suo cammino incontra la sua amica volpe, la quale, a causa di una barzelletta, ora ha il singhiozzo e non sa come farlo passare. Giacomo fa il bucato ed innaffia le piante. La volpe vuole parlargli per chiedergli se c'è una cura al suo problema, ma, mentre lo cerca, si imbatte nel suo bucato. Non vede più nulla e va a sbattere a destra e a sinistra. Giacomo si spaventa perché crede sia un fantasma, ma non appena sente il singhiozzare sotto le lenzuola, subito capisce di chi si tratta. Il fantasma cade in un barile e Giacomo aiuta a rialzarsi. Lo spavento causato da questa caduta ha fatto passare il singhiozzo alla volpe.

At the end of his working day, Giacomo the gardener returns home. On his way, he meets his friend, Fox, who, because of a joke, now has a sob and does not know how to make it pass.

Giacomo does the laundry and waters the plants. Fox wants to talk to him to ask if there is a cure for his problem, but while he is looking for him, he gets covered with the laundry and start bumping into things.

Giacomo is frightened when he comes back to his house because he thinks he can hear a ghost, but as soon as he hears the sob from below the laundry, he immediately understands who it is. Fox accidentally falls into a barrel and Giacomo helps him get back out. The fright caused by Fox's fall into the barrel made the sob pass.

2.2 – Vocabulary

Bucato = Laundry

Fantasma = Ghost

Fracasso = Noise

Giardiniere = Gardner

Limonata = Lemonade

Pappagallo = Parrot

Parco = Park

Scoiattolo = Squirrel

Singhiozzo = Sob

Spavento = Fright

Vasi = Jars, vases

Verme = Worm

Volpe = Fox

2.3 – Questions

1 – Che lavoro svolge Giacomo?

What's Giacomo's job?

a. Allevatore - Farmer

b. Bibliotecario - Librarian

c. Giardiniere – Gardner

2 – Perché la volpe ha bisogno dell'aiuto di Giacomo?

Why does Fox need Giacomo's help?

a. Per cucinare – To cook

b. Per far crescere dei fiori – To make some flowers grow

c. Per far passare il singhiozzo – To make the sob pass

3 – Cosa incontra Giacomo mentre svolge i lavori domestici?

What scares Giacomo while he does housework?

a. Un fantasma – A ghost

b. Una volpe – A fox

c. Un ragno – A spider

4 – Per quale motivo alla volpe è venuto il singhiozzo?

Why does Fox have a sob?

5 – Come lo fa a cessare?

How does it stop?

2.4 – Answers

1 – C

2 – C

3 – A

4 – La volpe ha il singhiozzo perché, mentre rideva per una barzelletta, ha bevuto un sorso di limonata.

Fox has a sob because, while laughing at a joke, he took a sip of lemonade.

5 – Il singhiozzo finisce quando la volpe inciampa e cade in un barile, prendendo uno spavento.

The sob passes when Fox stumbles and falls into a barrel, taking a fright.

Chapter 3: Le zuppe magiche – The Magical Soups

Quando la strega Gaia si confrontò con una fotografia trovata su una rivista, si trovò bruttina. "Voglio trasformarmi" decise. "Con una delle mie zuppe magiche diventerò più affascinante di questa fotomodella". Andò a rileggersi tutti i suoi libri di cucina per scoprire la preparazione più adatta, ma non la trovò; decise allora di inventarsi una nuova ricetta. Fece l'inventario degli ingredienti presenti sui suoi scaffali: veleni, polvere di stelle, marmellate di lumaca, cacche di ogni genere. Si mise al lavoro; la luce della cucina restò accesa tutta la notte, mentre dal comignolo usciva una grossa nuvola di fumo nero.

When Gaia the Witch saw a photograph of a pretty model in a magazine, she felt ugly.

"I want to transform myself" she decided. "With one of my magical soups, I will become prettier than the model."

Gaia went to read all of her cookbooks to find the most suitable spell recipe, but she could not find it. So she decided to invent a new recipe. She made an inventory of the ingredients she had on her shelves: poisons, stardust, snail marmalades, and droppings of all kinds. She started working. The kitchen light remained lit all night, while a large cloud of black smoke came out of the chimney.

Nel grande calderone la strega buttò patate, carote, di tutto di più. Sul fornello a gas mise in una casseruola un po' di piselli e di fagiolini, una goccia di questo, un pizzico di questo. Nel forno a microonde sistemò su un piatto rotondo un po'dell'uno e un po'dell'altro. Infine aggiunse una cipolla. Schiacciando poi il bottone del microonde cantò: "Caro piccolo mio forno, fai girare tutto intorno, cuoci ben questa pappetta e domani sarò perfetta!".

In the big cauldron, the witch threw potatoes, carrots, and more of everything. On the gas stove, she put some peas and beans in a saucepan, a drop of this, and a pinch of that. In the microwave oven, she arranged on a round plate some of those ones and a little bit of these ones. Finally, she added an onion.

Then, pressing the microwave button, she sang: "Dear my little oven, turn everything around, cook this little mush and tomorrow I'll be perfect!"

Rifece l'operazione con altri ingredienti e quando tutto fu cotto e versato, si trovò davanti cinque piatti appetitosi. Prese un grande cucchiaio, lo affondò in un piatto, spalancò la bocca e… si fermò di colpo. "E se mi fossi sbagliata? E se mi stessi avvelenando?". Mise i piatti su un grande vassoio e girò per la casa chiamando i suoi animali. Ne diede uno al gatto che, zot, rimase fulminato ma sopravvisse. Ne diede uno al pipistrello, il quale perse subito l'equilibrio. Ne diede uno al rospo, che iniziò a fare delle bolle colorate. Ne diede uno anche al topo, il quale iniziò a credere di essere un divo del cinema. Uscita di casa ne diede uno persino al gufo, che si trasformò in un lampione acceso.

She made the spell recipe with all the ingredients, and when everything was cooked and dished out, five appetizing soup dishes sat before her. She took a large spoonful of food, opened her mouth and ... stopped suddenly.

"What if I am wrong? What if I am poisoning myself?"

She put the dishes on a large tray and walked around the house, calling for her animals. She gave one dish to the cat. *Zot*! It was electrocuted but survived. She gave one dish to the bat, which immediately lost its balance. She gave one dish to the toad, which began to blow colored bubbles. She gave one dish to the mouse, who believed that he was a movie star. After leaving the house, Gaia the Witch then gave one dish to the owl, which turned into a lit streetlamp.

Gaia pensò che tutto stava andando a meraviglia, promettendosi di mangiare le zuppe il giorno seguente. Se ne andò a dormire, sognando giorni meravigliosi che la aspettavano. Appena alzata, andò a recuperare i suoi animali: "Orrore!" gridò. Il gatto, il pipistrello, il rospo, il topo e il gufo si erano trasformati in copie di lei stessa, in formato ridotto. Cinque piccole Gaia guardavano Gaia.

Gaia thought that everything was going wonderfully, and promised herself she would eat the soups the following day. She went to sleep, dreaming of wonderful days ahead.

As soon as she got up, she went to retrieve her animals.

"Horror!" she cried. The cat, the bat, the toad, the mouse, and the owl had turned into small copies of herself. Five little Gaias looked at her.

"Vogliamo la zuppa!" chiesero in coro. Gaia si mise all'opera per nutrire la sua nuova famiglia. Addio fotomodella! Addio sogno di bellezza!

"We want the soup!" they chorused.

Gaia went to work to feed her new family.

"Goodbye, photo model! Goodbye dream of beauty!"

3.1 – Summary

Gaia la strega, guardando una foto su un giornale, si trova brutta, quindi decide di inventare un intruglio per diventare una fotomodella. Usando i vari ingredienti presenti nella sua cucina, crea cinque zuppe diverse. Prima di utilizzarle, però, per sicurezza le fa assaggiare ai suoi animali. Niente sembra andare storto, finché il giorno dopo, alzandosi, scopre che i suoi animali si sono trasformati in piccole copie di lei stessa! Essi chiedono ancora zuppa da mangiare, quindi Gaia decide di prendersi cura della sua nuova famiglia, abbandonando il sogno di diventare una fotomodella.

      Gaia the Witch feels ugly after looking at a photo in a magazine, so she decides to invent a magical soup to become a pretty model. Using the various ingredients she has in her kitchen, she creates five different soups. Before using them, however, for safety she makes her animals taste them. Nothing seems to go wrong, until the next day when she awakens and discovers that her animals have turned into small copies of herself! They ask for more soup to eat, so Gaia decides to take care of her new family, abandoning her dream of becoming a model.

3.2 – Vocabulary

Carote = Carrots

Cipolla = Onion

Cucchiaio = Spoon

Forno = Oven

Nero = Black

Nutrire = To feed

Patate = Potatoes

Pipistrelli = Bats

Polvere = Dust

Ricetta = Recipe

Rivista = Magazine

3.3 – Questions

1 - Che effetto ha la zuppa sul gufo?

What effect does the soup have on the owl?

a. Diventa un lampione acceso – It becomes a lit streetlamp

b. Perde l'equilibrio – It looses his balance

c. Si addormenta – It falls asleep

2 – Perché Gaia fa assaggiare le zuppe agli animali?

Why does Gaia make the animals taste the soups?

a. Perché potrebbero essere avvelenate – Because they could be poisonous

b. Perché hanno un cattivo odore – Because they have a bad smell

c. Perché si sono raffreddate – Because they became cold

3 – Perché la strega Gaia si sente brutta?

Why does Gaia feel ugly?

4 – Che cosa decide di fare a riguardo?

What does she decide to do about it?

5 – Come si conclude la vicenda?

How does the story end?

3.4 - Answers

1 – A

2 – A

3 – La strega Gaia si sente brutta perché non assomiglia alla modella nella foto sulla rivista.

Gaia feels ugly because she does not look like the pretty model in the magazine.

4 – Gaia decide di preparare delle zuppe magiche per diventare bella.

Gaia decides to prepare some magical soups to become beautiful.

5 – La storia finisce con la strega Gaia che prepara da mangiare per i suoi animali, i quali si sono trasformati in piccole copie di se stessa a causa delle zuppe magiche.

The story ends with Gaia the Witch preparing more soup for her animals, which have turned into small copies of her because of the magical soups.

Chapter 4: Triste e allegra – Sad and Happy

Roberto vive vicino al mare e gli piace tanto. Dalla finestra della camera da letto guarda la gente sulla spiaggia e le barche che passano sull'acqua. Quando è brutto tempo, Roberto sfida il vento e va a guardare le onde che si infrangono sugli scogli. Se c'è il sole, egli va in spiaggia con le sorelle, Marianna e Valentina. Le rincorre agitando le alghe bagnate. Quando si sentono stanchi, costruiscono castelli di sabbia e mangiano panini con la sabbia.

Roberto lives near the sea, and he really likes it. From the bedroom window, he looks at the people on the beach and at the boats passing over the water. When it is bad weather, Roberto defies the wind and goes to watch the waves crashing on the rocks. If it's sunny, he goes to the beach with his sisters, Marianna and Valentina. He runs after them, waving wet seaweed. When they feel tired, they build sandcastles and eat sand sandwiches.

A volte Roberto preferisce star solo con il mare. Gli piace restare lì quando la marea cala, lasciando sulla spiaggia alghe e sorprese di ogni genere. Roberto conserva le cose che il mare gli regala: possiede una stella marina, una chela di granchio e tante conchiglie dalle forme più disparate. Ha persino una noce di cocco.

Sometimes Roberto prefers to be alone with the sea. He likes to stay there when the tide's out, leaving seaweed and surprises of all kinds on the beach. Roberto preserves the things that the sea gives him: he has a starfish, a crab claw and many shells of different shapes. He even has a coconut.

Un giorno Roberto vede una coda di pesce in una pozza d'acqua tra gli scogli. Tuffa il suo retino e pesca una sirena. Le lacrime scorrono sul viso della sirena. "Perché sei triste?" domanda il ragazzo. "Perché il mare se n'è andato via e mi ha lasciata qui" singhiozza la sirena. "Non preoccuparti" dice Roberto "puoi venire a casa con me". Solleva delicatamente la sirena e la mette nella sua sacca, portandola a casa per farla vedere alla sua famiglia.

One day, Roberto sees a fishtail in a pool of water between the rocks. He dunks his net and catches a mermaid. Tears flow over the mermaid's face.

"Why are you sad?" asks Roberto.

"Because the sea has gone and left me here," the mermaid replies, sobbing.

"Do not worry," Roberto tells the mermaid. "You can come home with me."

He gently lifts the mermaid and puts her in his bag. He takes her home to show his family.

La mamma la trova bella e la abbraccia, mentre il papà consiglia di metterla nell'acqua per farla sentire a casa. La piscina in giardino viene riempita d'acqua e la sirena viene messa dentro. Lei muove la coda e nuota felicemente. Le sorelle di Roberto schizzano l'acqua dappertutto e giocano con lei. Roberto chiede alla sirena se è più felice e lei risponde: "A dire il vero sono triste e allegra allo stesso tempo. Mi piace la piscina, ma mi mancano i miei amici pesci, che nuotavano e cantavano con me". Roberto, così, le promette un pesce.

Roberto's mom finds the mermaid beautiful and hugs her, while Roberto's father advises putting the mermaid in water to make her feel at home. The pool in the back garden is filled with water, so they put the mermaid in it. She moves her tail and swims happily. Roberto's sisters splash water everywhere and play with the mermaid.

Roberto asks the mermaid if she is happier and she replies, "To be honest, I am sad and happy at the same time. I like the pool, but I miss my fish friends, who swam and sang with me."

So Roberto promises her a fish.

Roberto va al piccolo luna park sul lungomare, dove vince un pesce. Corre a casa con il pesciolino arancione chiuso in una busta, poi getta il pesce nella piscina. Il ragazzo si mette a sedere sull'erba con le sue sorelle e guarda il pesciolino arancione che nuota nella piscina. La sirena canta una canzone sul mare misterioso e cerca di giocare col pesce, che però continua a nuotare in tondo; non canta e non gioca.

Roberto goes to the small fairground on the seafront, where he wins a fish. He runs home with the orange fish enclosed in an envelope, then throws it into the pool. The boy sits on the grass with his sisters and watches the orange fish swimming in the pool. The mermaid sings a song on the mysterious sea and tries to play with the fish; however, it continues to swim in circles. It does not sing or play.

"Sei più felice ora?" le domanda Roberto. "Sono triste e allegra allo stesso tempo; questo pesce è simpatico, ma mi manca mio padre il mare. Il mare salato e pieno di onde, che mi sollevava e giocava con me" risponde la sirena. "Vedrai, la piscina diventerà come il mare" dice Roberto, e corre in bagno a prendere lo shampoo al profumo di alghe marine. Va in camera da letto e raduna sassi e conchiglie, poi scende in cucina a prendere una tazza di sale. Roberto torna di corsa alla piscina, ci getta dentro le conchiglie e i sassi, il sale e lo shampoo, poi mette le mani nell'acqua e la agita per far finta che ci siano le onde, come nel mare.

"Are you happier now?" Roberto asks.

"I am sad and happy at the same time. This fish is nice, but I miss my father, the sea. The salty sea full of waves, which used to lift me up and play with me," the mermaid replies.

"You'll see – the pool will become like the sea," Roberto says, and runs to the bathroom to get the shampoo with a seaweed scent.

He goes into the bedroom and collects pebbles and shells, then goes down to the kitchen to get a cup of salt. Roberto rushes back to the pool, throws in shells, stones, salt, and shampoo, then puts his hands in the water and shakes it to pretend that there are waves, as in the sea.

"Sei più felice ora?" chiede Roberto. "Sono ancora triste e allegra allo stesso tempo; mi piacciono le onde, ma mi manca mia madre il mare. Lei mi cullava e mi addormentava con le sue canzoni", risponde la sirena. "Posso farlo io" propone Roberto. Egli prende il braccio della sirena, la culla e canta una canzone, ma una lacrima scende dalla guancia della sirena. "Solo il mare può renderti felice, ti riporterò a casa" dice Roberto. La famiglia del ragazzo saluta la sirena prima che lei ritorni alla spiaggia.

"Are you happier now?" Roberto asks.

"I'm still sad and happy at the same time. I like the waves, but I miss my mother, the sea. She used to cradle me, and I used to fall asleep to her songs," the mermaid replies.

"I can do it for you," Roberto offers.

He takes the mermaid's arm, cradles it, and sings a song, but a teardrop falls from the mermaid's cheek.

"Only the sea can make you happy. I will take you home." Roberto tells the mermaid.

The boy's family says goodbye to the little mermaid before she returns to the beach.

"Addio! Spero che ora sarai più allegra" dice Roberto alla sirena. "Sono allegra e triste allo stesso tempo; allegra perché le onde salate del mare sono la mia casa, ma triste perché devo dirti addio. Perché non vieni a vivere con me in mezzo al mare, Roberto? Così non sarai più triste." Roberto pensa a come sarebbe bello fare amicizia con i pesci, ma poi pensa a sua madre,,a suo padre e alle sue sorelle. Non vuole lasciarli. Pensa alla sua casa e alla sua stanza e scuote la testa. La sirena agita la coda e si immerge nel mare. Va giù, sempre più in fondo, lontano da lui. Roberto è triste che la sirena se ne sia andata, ma anche allegro perché lei è di nuovo felice.

"Goodbye! I hope you will be happier now," Roberto calls out to the mermaid.

"I am happy and sad at the same time; happy because the salty waves of the sea are my home, and sad because I have to say goodbye. Why don't you come and live with me in the middle of the sea, Roberto? So you will not be sad again".

Roberto thinks about how nice it would be to make friends with the fish, but then he thinks about his mother, father, and sisters. He does not want to leave them. He thinks of his house and his room and shakes his head.

The mermaid flicks her tail and plunges into the sea. She swims down, deeper and deeper, away from Roberto.

Roberto is sad that the mermaid is gone,but is also cheerful because she is happy again.

Roberto torna a casa, dove lo aspettano Marianna e Valentina. Arriva il momento di andare a letto; quando Roberto è a letto, la mamma gli canta la canzone della sirena. Non appena se ne va, il ragazzo appoggia la conchiglia all'orecchio per sentire il rumore del mare e pensa alla sirena. Il suo sguardo va verso la finestra, verso il sentiero che conduce alla spiaggia e vede qualcosa. Una coda? Una mano che lo saluta? *Sono come la sirena* pensa, *sono triste e allegro allo stesso tempo. Lei sarà sempre mia amica: forse tornerà ancora a giocare con me.* Poi si addormenta.

Roberto returns home, where Marianna and Valentina wait for him. The time to go to bed arrives. When Roberto is in bed, his mom sings the mermaid's song. As soon as she leaves,

Roberto puts the shell to his ear to hear the sound of the sea and thinks about the mermaid. His gaze goes to the window, out to the path leading to the beach, and he sees something. A tail? A hand waving at him?

I'm like the mermaid, he thinks. *I'm sad and happy at the same time. She will always be my friend. Maybe she will come back to play with me again one day.*

Then he falls asleep.

4.1 – Summary

Roberto vive vicino al mare e ha due sorelle. Un giorno, mentre gioca al mare, egli pesca una sirena. Subito, ella diventa sua amica; la porta a casa sua per prendersene cura. Roberto mette la sirena in una piscina; lei, però, non si sente a casa. Egli fa di tutto per darle quella sensazione: le compra un amico pesce, posiziona conchiglie e sassi dentro la piscina, agita l'acqua per simulare le onde. Ciononostante la sirena si definisce sempre "triste e allegra allo stesso tempo" perché riconosce l'impegno di Roberto, ma le manca il mare. Il ragazzo capisce che lei appartiene al mare e la restituisce ad esso. Dopo essersi salutati, Roberto si sente triste e allegro allo stesso tempo; triste perché non potrà vedere spesso la sirena, allegro perché sa che ella adesso è felice e perché sa di avere un'amica che potrà andarlo a trovare ogni volta che vuole.

Roberto lives near the sea and has two sisters. One day, while playing by the sea, he catches a mermaid. Immediately, she becomes his friend. He takes her home to take care of her. Roberto puts the mermaid in a swimming pool; however, she does not feel at home. He does everything to give her that feeling: he buys her a fish, places shells and pebbles in the pool, shakes the water to simulate the waves. Nevertheless, the mermaid always tells him that she's sad and happy at the same time because she recognizes Roberto's efforts, but she misses the sea. Roberto finally realizes she belongs back in the sea and returns her to it. After saying goodbye, Roberto now feels sad and happy at the same time; sad because he won't be able to see the mermaid as often, but happy because the mermaid is now happy and he knows he has a friend who can visit him whenever she wants.

4.2 – Vocabulary

Acqua = Water

Amica = Friend (for a girl)

Barche = Boats

Canzone = Song

Coda = Tail

Conchiglie = Shells

Famiglia = Family

Granchio = Crab

Guancia = Cheek

Mare = Sea

Marea = Tide

Nuotare = To swim

Pesce = Fish

Piccolo = Tiny, little, small

Sale = Salt

Sentiero = Path, trail

Sirena = Mermaid

Spiaggia = Beach

Stella = Star

4.3 – Questions

1 – Dove vive Roberto?

Where does Roberto live?

a. Al lago – On a lake

b. Al mare – By the sea

c. In montagna – In the mountains

2 – Che cosa fa quando è bel tempo?

What does he do when the weather is good?

a. Va in spiaggia con le sorelle – He goes to the beach with his sisters

b. Va nei boschi con la mamma – He goes to the woods with his mom

c. Sta a casa – He stays at home

3 – Un giorno, che cosa pesca Roberto?

One day, what does Roberto catch?

a. Una stella marina – A starfish

b. Un granchio – A crab

c. Una sirena – A mermaid

4 – Che cosa fa Roberto per far sentire a casa la sua nuova amica?

What does Roberto do to make his new friend feel at home?

5 – Come si conclude la storia? Riesce Roberto nel suo intento?

How does the story end? Does Roberto manage in his purpose?

4.4 – Answers

1 – B

2 – A

3 – C

4 – Roberto mette la sua amica sirena nella piscina, riempiendola di sale, conchiglie, sassi e pesci, poi imita le onde del mare.

Roberto puts his mermaid friend in a pool, filling it with salt, shells, pebbles and fish, then imitates the waves of the sea.

5 – Roberto non riesce nel suo intento, ma capisce che è meglio per la sirena tornare nella sua vera casa, il mare.

Roberto fails in his purpose, but he understands that it is better for the mermaid to return to her true home, the sea.

Chapter 5: C'è una lucertola nel camino – There's a Lizard in the Chimney

Lucertola è uscita a prendere il sole, ma non si sente fortunata. Quasi subito, infatti, si scatena un temporale. Le nuvole nascondono il sole e inizia a piovere. Il vento è molto forte.

Lizard has gone out to sunbathe, but she does not feel lucky. Almost immediately, in fact, a storm begins. Clouds hide the sun, and it starts to rain. The wind is very strong.

Lucertola viene spinta verso un vecchio faggio, ma i rami si muovono in tutte le direzioni e rischiano di spezzarsi e caderle addosso. Lucertola irrigidisce la coda per non farsi del male e si guarda intorno, cercando un riparo adatto.

Lizard is pushed towards an old beech tree, but the branches move in all directions and are at risk of snapping and falling on her. Lizard stiffens her tail to avoid getting hurt and looks around, looking for suitable shelter.

All'improvviso vede una casa. Nel buio delle nuvole, una finestra brilla come se fosse appesa nel nulla. Una ragazzina bionda, svegliata dai tuoni, si è alzata a ritirare i panni stesi sul cornicione.

Suddenly, she sees a house. In the dim light, a window shines as if it were hanging in thin air. A blonde girl, awakened by thunder, had gotten up to collect the clothes hanging on the ledge to dry.

Lucertola fa un'ultima corsa sotto la pioggia e, salendo tramite le pareti colorate della casa, si infila nel comignolo. Si sente un colpo di vento e Lucertola perde l'equilibrio, scivolando giù per il camino.

Lizard makes a last run in the rain and climbs up and over the colored walls of the house. She slips down the chimney. A gust of wind sounds and Lizard loses her balance, sliding down the chimney chute.

Lucertola ha paura, anche se in casa c'è un bel tepore in confronto al vento freddo che soffia fuori. Sbatte un po' le zampette e la coda e cammina a dare un'occhiata in giro.

Lizard is afraid – even if at home there is warmth compared to the cold wind that blows outside. She slams her feet and tail a little and walks around the house.

All'ingresso si ferma e alza la testa. *Che strano*, pensa, *non c'è vento, né profumo di erba e alberi, terra o pioggia. La casa è ben chiusa, come una scatola di cartone.*

At the entrance to a room, she stops and raises her head.

How strange, she thinks. *There is no wind, nor the smell of grass, trees, earth or rain.*

The house is closed in, like a paper box.

Lucertola trova un animaletto in una gabbia: "Chi sei?" gli chiede. "Sono un criceto" risponde l'animale, attento a non avvicinarsi troppo a Lucertola. "Senti, il vento mi ha spinta giù per il camino di casa tua e ora non so come fare ad uscire. Sai dirmi come faccio a tornare libera?" gli chiede Lucertola.

Lizard finds a small animal in a cage.

"Who are you?" she asks.

"I'm a hamster" answers the animal, careful not to get too close to Lizard.

"Look, the wind pushed me down the chimney of your house, and now I do not know how to get out. Can you tell me how I can go free?" Lizard asks.

"Libera?" chiede stupito il criceto. "Non mi dire che vuoi tornare libera… immagino che vorrai essere al sicuro…" "Cosa vuol dire 'al sicuro'?" chiede Lucertola. "Io sono al sicuro in questa gabbia dove nessuno può farmi del male. Se non fossi dentro, magari mi avresti già morso", risponde il criceto. "Non è vero!" ribatte Lucertola sinceramente. Ella si allontana lasciando il criceto al sicuro dentro le sbarre della sua gabbia.

"Free?" asks the hamster in amazement. "Do not tell me you want to go free... I guess you want to be safe..."

"What does 'safe' mean?" Lizard asks.

"I am safe in this cage where no one can hurt me. If I weren't inside it, maybe you would have bitten me already," the hamster replies.

"That's not true!" Lizard says sincerely.

She walks away, leaving the hamster safe inside the bars of his cage.

In cucina un cane dorme placidamente nella cuccia. Lucertola è salita su una sedia e si schiarisce la gola. Il cane apre gli occhi: "Una lucertola! Che cosa ci fai tu qui?" chiede. "Il vento mi ha spinta giù per il camino" risponde Lucertola "e ora non so come andarmene. Come faccio a tornare libera?". Il cane sbadiglia. "Non vorresti invece che qualcuno si prendesse cura di te?", le chiede. "Cosa significa 'cura'?" domanda Lucertola. "Di me, per esempio, si prende cura la bambina: mi accarezza e poi mi porta a fare le passeggiate, dandomi dei biscotti" risponde il cane.

In the kitchen, a dog sleeps placidly in a kennel. Lizard climbs into a chair and clears her throat. The dog opens his eyes.

"A lizard! What are you doing here?" he asks.

"The wind pushed me down the chimney," Lizard answers, "and now I do not know how to leave. How can I be free?"

The dog yawns. "Wouldn't you rather someone take care of you?" he asks.

"What does 'care' mean?" Lizard asks.

"For example, the little girl takes care of me: she caresses me and then takes me for walks and gives me biscuits," the dog replies.

Lucertola assaggia un biscotto. è duro e ha uno strano gusto di pesce. Non è buono come gli insetti, ma non è male. "Posso mangiarne un altro?" chiede Lucertola, dato che ha molta fame. "Puoi prenderne quanti ne vuoi", risponde il cane. Quando la ciotola è vuota, Lucertola si pulisce la bocca con l'aiuto delle zampe. "Grazie mille!" dice al cane. "Non ringraziare me!" dice il cane "i biscotti che hai mangiato sono della gatta!".

Lizard tastes a biscuit. It is hard and has a strange taste of fish. It's not as good as insects, but it's not bad.

"Can I eat another?" Lizard asks – since she is very hungry.

"You can have as many as you want," the dog replies.

When the bowl is empty, Lizard cleans her mouth with the help of her legs.

"Thank you very much!" she says to the dog.

"Do not thank me. The biscuits you just ate were the cat's!" the dog says.

Al piano di sopra la bambina è sveglia, seduta sul letto. Il temporale si è calmato, ma lei non riesce più a dormire. Allora prende la torcia che di solito usa per leggere sotto le coperte. Quando Lucertola entra in camera sua, la bambina accende la torcia. Nel fascio di luce, le zampette di Lucertola brillano come un tessuto prezioso. "Ti prego, aiutami" chiede Lucertola. "Il vento mi ha fatta cadere giù per il camino e ora non so più come uscire. Come faccio a tornare libera?" "Libera? Forse vuoi essere amata!" "Cosa vuol dire essere 'amata'?". La bambina accarezza Lucertola dolcemente: "Io ti amerò! Ti terrò al sicuro come il mio criceto e mi prenderò cura di te come faccio con il cane e la gatta".

Upstairs, the girl is awake, sitting on her bed. The storm has calmed down, but she cannot sleep anymore. Then she takes the flashlight she usually uses to read under the covers.

When Lizard enters the room, the little girl turns on the flashlight. In the beam of light, the lizard's legs shine like a precious fabric.

"Please, help me. The wind made me fall down the chimney, and now I do not know how to get out. How can I be free?" Lizard asks the girl.

"Free? Maybe you want to be loved!"

"What does 'loved' mean?"

The girl gently caresses Lizard. "I will love you! I will keep you safe, as I do with my hamster, and I will take care of you, as I do with my dog and cat. "

Lucertola è felice. Si rilassa e sembra quasi che dorma. Ella sta quasi per promettere di restare per sempre, ma poi sente un rumore che viene dal piano di sotto. *Forse è una porta che sbatte?* pensa. Un soffio di vento arriva a sfiorare la sua coda e Lucertola riconosce l'odore del legno, dell'erba e delle foglie. Senza voltarsi indietro, corre via dalla stanza e segue la scia lasciata dal vento. In cucina, il cane dorme ancora nella sua cuccia. Lì vicino una gatta lecca il latte da un piatto. La sua pelliccia ha l'odore della terra bagnata, l'odore della libertà.

Lizard is happy. She relaxes, and it almost seems as if she is sleeping. She is about to promise to stay forever, but then she hears a noise coming from downstairs.

Maybe it's a door slamming? Lizard thinks.

A breath of wind touches her tail and Lizard recognizes the smell of wood, grass, and leaves. Without looking back, she runs away from the room and follows the trail left by the wind.

In the kitchen, the dog still sleeps in his kennel. Nearby, a cat licks milk from a plate. The cat's fur has the smell of wet earth. The smell of freedom.

La gatta lecca l'ultima goccia di latte e guarda Lucertola. "Sei tu che hai mangiato i miei biscotti?" chiede la gatta. "È stato il cane a dirmi che potevo, mi ha detto che erano tuoi solo quando li avevo ormai mangiati tutti" risponde Lucertola. "Fa sempre così, non ti preoccupare! Per fortuna mentre ero fuori ho mangiato un topolino!" dice la gatta. "Fuori? Allora sai dirmi come andare fuori?" domanda Lucertola. La gatta fa cenno di seguirla e si avvicina alla porta-finestra. Lucertola vede che c'è una porticina sulla parte bassa della porta, proprio sopra il pavimento. "È il mio ingresso privato. Te lo farò usare, ma solo per questa volta!" dice la gatta a Lucertola.

The cat licks the last drop of milk and looks at Lizard.

"Are you the one who ate my cookies?" the cat asks.

"It was the dog who told me I could. He only told me they were yours when I had eaten them all," Lizard replies.

"He always does that. Do not worry. Luckily, while I was out, I ate a mouse!" the cat says.

"Out? So can you tell me how to be free?" Lizard asks.

The cat gestures to follow her and goes in front of the French door. Lizard sees that there is a small door at the bottom of the door, just above the floor.

"It's my private entrance. I'll let you out, but only this time!" the cat tells Lizard.

Lucertola guarda attraverso la porticina: il temporale è finito e l'aria è di nuovo calma. In cielo è tornato a splendere il sole, mentre le nuvole si sono allontanate. Lucertola sa che adesso tutto andrà bene. "Per favore, saluta da parte mia il criceto, il cane e la bambina" dice Lucertola alla gatta. Ma la gatta non l'ascolta nemmeno perché è troppo impegnata a mangiare i biscotti del cane che ha trovato sotto il tavolo.

Lizard looks through the little door. The storm is over, and the air is calm again. The sun is back in the sky, and the clouds are gone. Lizard knows that now everything will be fine.

"Please say hello to the hamster, the dog, and the girl for me," Lizard says to the cat.

But the cat does not even listen because she's too busy eating some dog cookies she found under the table.

5.1 – Summary

Lucertola vuole andare a prendere il sole, quando all'improvviso comincia un forte temporale. Per ripararsi, scala il muro di una casa e si rifugia sotto il tetto del camino. Una folata di vento la fa cadere all'interno della casa, dove fa di tutto per tornare libera. Durante la sua ricerca, incontra vari animali che vivono lì, tra cui un criceto e un cane, che la lascia mangiare i biscotti della gatta. Tutti gli animali le insegnano una lezione, spiegandole che cosa vuol dire per loro essere liberi. Durante il suo cammino incontra anche la bambina di casa, la quale si propone di prendersi cura di lei, ma non appena Lucertola sente di nuovo l'odore della natura, desidera tornare fuori ed essere libera. In questo modo incontra la gatta, la quale le mostra la via per uscire dalla casa e, quando Lucertola le chiede di ringraziare tutti coloro che l'hanno aiutata, la gatta è impegnata a mangiare i biscotti del cane!

Lizard wants to go sunbathing when suddenly a storm begins. So she climbs the wall of a house and takes refuge in a chimney. A gust of wind makes her fall inside the house, and she does everything to try and get out. During her search, she meets various animals which live in the house, including a hamster and a dog that lets her eat the cat's biscuits. All the animals teach her a lesson, explaining what it means for them to be free. During her walk, she also meets the little girl who lives in the house, who intends to take care of Lizard. However, as soon as Lizard smells the scent of nature again, she wants to be back outside, free. She then meets the cat, who shows her the way out of the house, and when Lizard asks the cat to thank all those who helped Lizard, the cat eats the dog's biscuits instead!

5.2 – Vocabulary

Biscotto = Biscuit, cookie

Coda = Tail

Criceto = Hamster

Erba = Grass

Gabbia = Cage

Latte = Milk

Lucertola = Lizard

Nuvole = Clouds

Paura = Fear

Pesce = Fish

Porta = Door

Sole = Sun

Tavolo = Table

Temporale = Thunderstorm, storm

Uscire = To get out, to go out

5.3 – Questions

1 – Che cosa vuole fare Lucertola all'aria aperta?

What does Lizard want to do in the open air?

a. Andare a caccia – To go hunting

b. Fare scorte di cibo – Take stocks of food

c. Prendere il sole – To sunbathe

2 – Perché la lucertola vuole ripararsi?

What does Lizard need shelter from?

a. Per il temporale – The thunderstorm

b. Per il sole cocente – The scorching sun

c. Per degli animali predatori – Some predators

3 – Cercando riparo, dove si ritrova?

Looking for shelter, where does she find herself?

a. In una fattoria – In a farm

b. In una casa- In a house

c. In un supermercato – In a supermarket

4 – Dove si trova il criceto?

Where is the hamster?

a. In una gabbia – In a shelter

b. Sul divano – On the couch

c. Nel frigorifero – In a cage

5 – Di cosa sanno i biscotti che il cane offre a Lucertola?

What do the cookies the dog offers Lizard taste like?

a. Di pesce – Fish

b. Di carne – Beef

c. Di mela – Apple

6 – Che cosa significa per il cane "prendersi cura di qualcuno"?

What does the dog mean by 'care'?"

7 – Che cosa propone la ragazzina a Lucertola?

What does the little girl propose to Lizard?

8 – Che mezzo utilizza la gatta per far uscire la lucertola?

What means does the cat use to get Lizard out of the house?

9 – Qual è il clima quando Lucertola riesce ad uscire?

What is the climate when Lizard manages to get back outside?

10 – Come finisce la storia?

How does the story end?

5.4 – Answers

1 – C

2 – A

3 – B

4 – A

5 – A

6 – Prendersi cura di qualcuno significa accarezzare, fare passeggiate e dare i biscotti.

Taking care of someone means to caress, take walks and give biscuits.

7 – La ragazzina propone alla lucertola di amarla e di prendersi cura di lei.

The little girl proposes that she will love and take care of Lizard.

8 – Per uscire dalla casa la gatta suggerisce una porticina.

To get out, the cat suggests the cat flap.

9 – Quando Lucertola esce, il temporale è passato e il cielo è senza nuvole.

When Lizard gets out, the thunderstorm is gone and the sky is cloudless.

10 – La storia finisce con la gatta che si vendica, mangiando i biscotti del cane.

The story ends with the cat taking revenge on the dog by eating the dog biscuits.

Chapter 6: Bolle di sapone – Soap Bubbles

Finalmente Pasqua! Marcello uscì da scuola, salutando il maestro e augurando a tutti buone vacanze. Corse a casa, dove era sicuro che avrebbe trovato tante uova di cioccolato. Quando arrivò a casa, zia Laura, vedendolo così eccitato, cercò di calmarlo, ma Marcello corse subito in cucina. Lì trovò solamente un uovo e divenne triste; quando però si accorse che la zia aveva preparato il pacchetto dell'uovo con tanto amore, le fece un sorriso. Lo aprì felice, chiedendosi che cosa avrebbe potuto contenere.

Finally, Easter! As Marcello left the school, he said goodbye to his teacher and wished everyone happy holidays. He ran home, where he was sure he would find many chocolate eggs. When he got home, Aunt Laura, seeing him so excited, tried to calm him down, but Marcello immediately ran into the kitchen. He only found one egg and became sad; when, however, he realized that his aunt had decorated the egg with so much love, he gave her a smile. He opened it happily, wondering what it could contain.

Dentro trovò un piccolo tubetto azzurro con un po' di acqua opaca per fare le bolle di sapone. Per amore della zia, Marcello finse di essere contento, ringraziandola e andando subito a letto sperando di sognare tutte le sorprese che non aveva ricevuto. Prima di addormentarsi egli aprì il tubetto e fece molte bolle di sapone, riempiendo tutta la camera da letto. *Che gioco inutile e noioso!* pensò il bambino, riempiendo così tanto la stanza che non si riuscivano a vedere gli altri giocattoli. "Farò l'ultima bolla e andrò a dormire" disse.

Inside, he found a small blue tube with some opaque water to make soap bubbles. For his aunt's sake, Marcello pretended to be happy, thanking her and going straight to bed, hoping to dream of all the surprises he had not yet received. Before falling asleep, however, he opened the tube and made lots of soap bubbles, which filled the whole bedroom.

What a useless and boring game! thought Marcello, the bubbles filling the room so much that he could not see the other toys.

"I'll make one last bubble and go to sleep," he said.

Marcello ne fece una talmente grande che ci si ritrovò intrappolato. Con meraviglia, uscì dalla finestra, volando sempre più in alto verso la luna. Il bambino vedeva il mondo dall'alto; spinto da un leggero vento, sorvolò le campagne e il mare, passando tra le nuvole che sembravano fatte di panna montata. Marcello si sentiva leggero e felice. La bolla di sapone scese sulla spiaggia, posandosi accanto ad un uomo con la barba che riposava all'ombra di una palma. La bolla si dissolse e Marcello si ritrovò in spiaggia in pigiama. "Buonasera, signore" disse esitando, "cosa ci fa qui solo?" "Sono Babbo Natale in vacanza! Mi sto riposando sulla mia isoletta, dopo le fatiche del Natale. Portare i doni è un lavoro molto duro!" rispose l'uomo barbuto

Marcello made the last bubble so big that he became trapped in it. With wonder, he bobbed out of the window, flying higher and higher, towards the moon. He saw the world from above as he was pushed by a light wind, soaring over the countryside and the sea, and passing through the clouds that looked as if they were made of whipped cream. Marcello felt light and happy.

The soap bubble finally landed on a beach, settling next to a bearded man resting in the shade of a palm tree. The bubble dissolved and Marcello found himself on the beach in his pajamas.

"Good evening, sir," Marcello said hesitantly. "What are you doing here alone?"

"I'm Santa Claus on vacation! I'm resting on my little island after the efforts of Christmas. Bringing gifts is a very hard job!" the bearded man replied.

"Sono contento che tu sia arrivato! Anche mio figlio Luigi ne sarà felice, lui è sempre così solo! Te lo faccio conoscere" disse Babbo Natale accompagnando Marcello dentro una casa vicino alla spiaggia. Entrarono in una stanza piena di meravigliosi giocattoli; qui il figlio di Babbo Natale stava guardando annoiato la televisione. I due bambini si guardarono negli occhi e capirono che sarebbero diventati amici. Luigi tornò a sorridere, spegnendo il televisore e proponendo a Marcello tanti giochi da fare. Scesero in spiaggia a giocare tra le onde e costruirono una zattera per fare il giro delle isole adiacenti, ma Babbo Natale, vedendoli segare, spiegò loro che le piante erano rare e non potevano essere tagliate.

"I'm glad you arrived! Even my son, Luigi, will be happy, he is always so alone! I'll let you meet him," Santa Claus added, and accompanied Marcello inside a house near the beach.

They entered a room full of wonderful toys; here, the son of Santa Claus, Luigi, was watching the television. He looked bored. The two children looked into each other's eyes and realized that they would become friends. Luigi smiled, turned off the television and proposed to Marcello that they should play lots of games together. They went down to the beach and played in the waves. They also built a raft to circle the adjacent islands, but Santa Claus, seeing them sawing, explained that the plants were rare and could not be cut.

I due bambini fecero solamente il giro dell'isola su cui erano già. Trovarono tante palme e tante simpatiche scimmie. Insieme si divertirono a raccogliere le noci di cocco in grandi canestri e giocarono fino al tramonto. Quando tornarono a casa, Luigi propose a Marcello di guardare la televisione, ma quest'ultimo non era entusiasmato dalle proposte dell'altro bambino. "Sai, Luigi, ho nostalgia di zia Laura. Chissà come sarà in pena se non mi trova a casa! Penso che domani dovrò lasciarti" sussurrò Marcello con un'espressione triste.

The two children only wandered around the island they were already on. They found so many palm trees and lots of nice monkeys. Together, they enjoyed gathering coconuts into large baskets and played until sunset. When they returned home, Luigi suggested he and Marcello watch television, but the latter was not impressed by the other child's proposal.

"You know, Luigi, I miss Aunt Laura. She will be upset if she does not find me at home! I think I'll have to leave you tomorrow," whispered Marcello with a sad expression.

La mattina dopo si trovarono tutti e tre sulla spiaggia e Marcello cominciò a fare bolle di sapone. Luigi lo guardava stupito: non aveva mai sentito di un gioco fatto solo di acqua e sapone e guardò incantato la danza leggera di quelle sfere trasparenti. Finalmente Marcello riuscì a fare una bolla abbastanza grande per entrarci e salire in cielo. "Ciao Luigi! Ciao Babbo Natale! Vi prometto che tornerò nelle prossime vacanze!" gridò il bambino agitando le mani.

The next morning, Marcello, Luigi, and Santa Claus went back to the beach, and Marcello began to make soap bubbles. Luigi looked at him in amazement: he had never heard of a game made only of soap and water and looked at the light dance of transparent spheres. Finally, Marcello managed to make a bubble large enough to enter, and he floated up into the sky.

"Bye, Luigi! Bye, Santa! I promise I'll come back next holidays!" shouted Marcello, waving his hands.

Quando Marcello tornò alla sua casetta, entrò zitto zitto in camera sua. C'era un grande silenzio perché la zia dormiva ancora. Stanco della sua avventura, si infilò a letto e piombò in un profondo sonno. Al risveglio corse in cucina, dove la zia aveva apparecchiato il tavolo con la colazione. "Zia! Come è bella la sorpresa che mi hai fatto! Di tutte le uova al cioccolato del mondo hai scelto la più fantastica!" disse il bambino. Zia Laura sorrise e abbracciò il nipotino, poi fecero colazione mentre Marcello raccontava la sua avventura.

When Marcello returned to his house, he quietly entered his room. There was a great silence because Aunt Laura was sleeping. Tired from his adventure, he slipped into bed and fell into a deep sleep.

When he woke up, he ran into the kitchen, where his aunt had set the table for breakfast.

"Aunt Laura! How beautiful is the surprise you made me! Of all the chocolate eggs in the world, you chose the most fantastic!" Marcello said.

Aunt Laura smiled and hugged her nephew. Then they ate breakfast while Marcello told her all about his adventure.

Con un po' di fantasia, anche le semplici bolle di sapone sono un gioco fantastico. Senza fantasia i giochi più ricchi diventano noiosi. Zia Laura non seppe dire se il viaggio all'isola di Babbo Natale fosse stato solo un sogno o un fatto reale, ma da quell'anno iniziò a mettere tanti tubetti blu tra i regali che portava a tutti i bambini del mondo.

With a little imagination, even the simple soap bubbles are a fantastic game. Without imagination, the the most expensive game become boring. Aunt Laura could not tell if the trip to the island and Santa Claus were just a dream or a fact for Marcello, but from that year onward, she put many blue tubes among the gifts that she brought to all the children of the world.

6.1 – Summary

Arrivano le vacanze di Pasqua e Marcello, tornando a casa, spera di trovare tante uova di cioccolato ad aspettarlo. La zia gliene ha regalata solamente una e il bambino finge di esserne felice: dentro trova un tubetto blu pieno di acqua e sapone per fare le bolle. Prima di andare a dormire ci gioca un po': l'ultima bolla è la più grande di tutte e riesce a trasportare Marcello su una piccola isola. Lì Babbo Natale che si sta riposando dopo il suo lavoro di Natale. Egli è felice di incontrare Marcello, tant'è che lo presenta a suo figlio Luigi, il quale è sempre annoiato e guarda la televisione. Insieme i due bambini fanno tanti giochi fino a sera. A Marcello manca molto sua zia Laura, quindi grazie al tubetto blu fa un'altra bolla grande per tornare a casa. Quando rivede la zia, è felice e la ringrazia per la sua grande sorpresa di Pasqua. Da quel giorno, ogni Pasqua zia Laura prepara tanti tubetti blu da regalare a tutti i bambini del mondo.

Easter holidays arrive, and Marcello hopes to find lots of chocolate eggs waiting for him at home after school. His Aunt Laura only gives him one, and the child pretends to be happy. Inside the egg, he finds a little blue tube full of water and soap to make bubbles. Before going to sleep, he plays with it: the last bubble is the biggest of all and manages to transport Marcello to a small island. There, he finds Santa Claus, who is resting after his Christmas work. He is happy to meet Marcello and introduces him to his son, Luigi, who is always bored and watches television. Together, the two children play lots of games until the evening. Marcello misses Aunt Laura, so uses the blue tube to make another big bubble to return home. When he sees Aunt Laura again, he is happy and thanks her for his great Easter surprise. Every Easter afterward, Aunt Laura prepares many little blue tubes to give to all the children of the world.

6.2 – Vocabulary

Adiacente = Adjacent

Avventura = Adventure

Azzurro = Light blue

Colazione = Breakfast

Cucina = Kitchen

Danza = Dance

Dormire = To sleep

Figlio = Son

Giocattoli = Toys

Gioco = Game, toy

Natale = Christmas

Noioso = Boring

Nostalgia = Homesickness

Onde = Waves

Pigiama = Pajamas

Sapone = Soap

Silenzio = Silence

Sogno = Dream

Sorriso = Smile

Tramonto = Sunset

Vacanze = Holidays

6.3 – Questions

1 – In quale periodo dell'anno è ambientata la storia?

In which period of the year is the story set?

a. Natale – Christmas

b. Pasqua – Easter

c. Capodanno – New Year's Day

2 – Che cosa spera di trovare Marcello?

What does Marcello hope to find?

a. Tante uova di cioccolata – Lots of chocolate eggs

b. Tanti pacchetti – Lots of toys

c. Un amico – A friend

3 – Che regalo gli fa la zia?

What does Aunt Laura give him as a present?

a. Solo un uovo con un tubetto di bolle – An egg with a blue tube of bubbles

b. Tante uova con tante sorprese diverse – Lots of eggs with lots of surprises

c. La zia non gli fa nessun regalo – Nothing

4 – Marcello è contento della sua sorpresa?

Is Marcello happy about his surprise?

a. No, ma fa finta di esserlo – No, but he pretends to be

b. Sì, molto – Yes

c. No, non lo è – No

5 – Chi incontra il bambino sull'isola?

Who does Marcello meet on the island?

a. Sua zia Laura – Aunt Laura

b. L'uomo ragno - Spiderman

c. Babbo Natale – Santa Claus

6 – Perché Babbo Natale è felice di far incontrare Marcello con suo figlio Luigi?

Why is Santa happy for Marcello to meet Luigi?

7 – Perché Luigi è colpito dalle bolle di sapone di Marcello?

Why is Luigi impressed by Marcello's soap bubbles?

8 – Perché Marcello vuole tornare a casa?

Why does Marcello want to return home?

9 – Riesce a ritornare a casa? Come?

Does Marcello manage to return home? How?

10 – Cosa fa la zia dopo che Marcello le ha raccontato la sua avventura?

What does Aunt Laura do after Marcello tells her about his adventure?

6.4 – Answers

1 – B

2 – A

3 – A

4 – A

5 – C

6 – Babbo Natale è felice di far incontrare suo figlio a Marcello perché il figlio è sempre annoiato e triste.

Santa Claus is happy to let his son meet with Marcello because his son is always bored and sad.

7 – A Luigi piacciono le bolle di Marcello perché sono semplici, ma allo stesso tempo sono un bellissimo gioco.

Luigi likes Marcello's bubbles because they are simple, but at the same time, it's a beautiful game.

8 – Marcello vuole tornare a casa perché ha paura che la zia si preoccupi per lui.

Marcello wants to go home because he's afraid his aunt is worried about him

9 – Sì, Marcello riesce a tornare a casa soffiando un'altra bolla grandissima che lo porta in giro.

Yes, Marcello manages to return home by blowing another huge bubble that carries him into the sky and back to his house.

10 – Dopo che Marcello ha raccontato la sua avventura, ora la zia ogni anno regala a Pasqua tubetti di bolle di sapone a tutti i bambini del mondo.

After Marcello talked about his adventure, every year at Easter, Aunt Laura gives soap tubes to all the children of the world.

Chapter 7: Il pacchetto verde – The Green Package

Nevica e il vento è gelido. La nonna è andata a prendere Patrizia alla stazione e la tiene stretta per mano perché è un po' faticoso camminare nella neve fresca. Patrizia è comunque contenta di essere di nuovo con lei e di rivedere la sua bella casa. È bellissimo trascorrere le vacanze di Natale dalla nonna. Ella sa raccontare tante stupende favole e inventare i giochi più divertenti. Ogni volta che viene a trovarla, Patrizia trova un bel regalo: un nuovo libro o un album per disegnare.

It's snowing, and the wind is cold. Grandma went to pick up Patrizia at the station and holds her by the hand because it's a bit tiring to walk in the fresh snow. However, Patrizia is happy to be with Grandma again and to see her beautiful house. Spending the Christmas holidays at Grandma's is wonderful. She can tell so many wonderful stories and invents fun games. Every time Patrizia visits her, she finds a nice present: a new book or a drawing album.

Patrizia e la nonna si recano insieme in paese. Lì Patrizia potrebbe giocare con gli altri bambini mentre la nonna fa la spesa dal panettiere e dal lattaio, ma i bambini hanno le facce annoiate e non ne hanno alcuna voglia. La nonna finisce presto di fare la spesa perché nei negozi non c'è nessuno di buon umore che si ferma a scambiare due chiacchiere, proprio nessuno che ha tempo per qualche parola gentile. Sulla strada del ritorno, la nonna sta in silenzio. Patrizia capisce che la nonna sta riflettendo.

Patrizia and her grandmother go to the village together. There, Patrizia could play with the other children while her grandmother is shopping at the bakery and the milkman, but the children have bored faces and do not want to play. Grandma ends up finishing her shopping soon because there's no one in the shops in a good mood who stops to chat. No one has time for a few kind words. Grandma is silent on the way back home. Patrizia understands that her grandmother is reflecting.

"Il pacchetto è pronto, Patrizia!" Dice la nonna quella stessa sera. La bambina alza gli occhi dall'album da disegno. Vorrebbe chiederle subito per chi è e che cosa contiene, ma la nonna fa capire che il pacchetto verde è un segreto.

"The package is ready, Patrizia!" Grandma says that evening.

Patrizia looks up from the drawing book. She would like to ask Grandma right away who it is for and what it contains, but her grandmother makes it clear that the green package is a secret.

Il giorno seguente Patrizia e la nonna escono presto di casa con il pacchetto verde. Lungo la strada coperta dalla neve incontrano il boscaiolo. Vive da poco tempo nel villaggio e tutti sanno che è solo. La nonna gli si avvicina e gli porge il pacchetto verde. "Che cosa devo farne?" chiede il boscaiolo sorpreso. "È per te" dice Patrizia, "ma non lo aprire, altrimenti ciò che è dentro si perderà". Il boscaiolo è pieno di stupore e chiede che cosa contiene. La nonna risponde "Fortuna e felicità" e gli stringe la mano.

The following day, Patrizia and her grandmother leave the house early with the green package. Along the snow-covered road, they meet the lumberjack. He recently came to live in the village, and everyone knows he is alone. Grandma approaches him and hands him the green package.

"What should I do with it?" asks the surprised lumberjack.

"It's for you," replies Patrizia, "but do not open it; otherwise, what is inside is going to get lost."

The lumberjack is full of amazement and asks what it contains.

Grandma answers, "Fortune and happiness," and shakes his hand.

Patrizia si stupisce della felicità del boscaiolo. Chiede alla nonna se è possibile preparare altri pacchetti uguali. "No, Patrizia, uno solo è abbastanza" risponde la nonna. Nel bosco il boscaiolo pensa che finalmente anche lui ha degli amici e prende di ottimo umore il suo cammino. Quando lo spazzacamino lo vede arrivare, cerca di nascondersi. È timido perché i bambini lo prendono in giro. Il boscaiolo gli porge il pacchetto verde: "Tieni, questo è per te! Questa volta sono io che porto fortuna!" "Oh grazie!" dice lo spazzacamino arrossendo in faccia.

Patrizia is amazed at the happiness of the lumberjack. She asks her grandmother if she can prepare other identical packages.

"No, Patrizia, only one is enough," Grandma replies.

In the woods, the lumberjack thinks that, finally, he has friends too and is in a good mood. When the chimney sweeper sees him walking down the path, he tries to hide. He is shy because children make fun of him.

The lumberjack hands him the green package: "Here, this is for you! This time it's me that brings luck!"

"Oh, thank you!" says the chimney sweeper, blushing.

Lo spazzacamino è felice: non si nasconde più, sorride alla gente e tutti lo salutano gentili. Mentre lavora sui tetti, vede attraverso la finestra la piccola Anna: "Non sei a giocare? Sei ammalata?" chiede ad Anna. È così: Anna è malata e ha l'influenza. Lo spazzacamino le porta allora il pacchetto verde, rassicurandola che con quello guarirà presto. Anna nasconde il pacchetto. "Chi lo trova lo può tenere, ma non va aperto!" dice agli amici che vanno a farle visita. I bambini frugano dappertutto. Finalmente Monia scopre il pacchetto sopra l'armadio e lo porta a casa sua.

The chimney sweeper is happy; he does not hide anymore, he smiles at the people, and they all say hello to him. While working on the roofs, he sees through a window little Anna.

"Are not you playing? Are you sick?" he asks Anna.

Yes, Anna is sick. She has the flu. The chimney sweep gives her the green package, reassuring Anna that she will soon recover. Anna hides the package.

"Those who find it can keep it, but it should not be opened!" she says to some friends who visit her.

The children rummage everywhere. Finally, Monia discovers the package in the wardrobe and takes it to her house.

Nascosti in cantina, i bambini vorrebbero aprire il pacchetto verde. Andrea lo gira tra le mani e lo scuote, mentre Monia non resiste e tira un po' il nastro. Improvvisamente, però, davanti alla finestra si sente qualcuno che grida in modo disperato. "È mio padre! Sentite odore di fumo? Poveretto, sta bruciando il pane!" urla Martina. Anna si precipita dal panettiere, il papa di Martina, e gli dà il pacchetto verde, dicendogli che porta fortuna.

Hidden in the cellar, the children would like to open the green package. Andrea turns it over in his hands and shakes it, while Monia does not resist and pulls the tape a little. Suddenly, however, in front of the window, they hear someone shouting desperately.

"My papa! Do you smell smoke? Poor Papa, he's burning the bread!" shouts Martina.

Anna rushes to the bakery and gives the baker, Martina's father, the green package, telling him that it brings good luck.

Ma il panettiere non lo tiene a lungo. Lo passa con la pala alla moglie del falegname che teme di rimanere senza pane. "Domani ci sarà di nuovo pane fresco" la tranquillizza sorridendo. Durante la notte la moglie del falegname sente piangere nella casa dei vicini. Essi sono preoccupati perché i loro figli sono lontani, non riuscendo così a dormire. "Ecco il pacchetto, ma non apritelo: porta fortuna e felicità!" dice la moglie del falegname ai suoi vicini

However, the baker does not hold the green package for long. He passes it with the shovel to the wife of the carpenter who fears running out of bread.

"Tomorrow there will be fresh bread again," the baker reassures the carpenter's wife.

During the night, the carpenter's wife hears crying inside the neighbors' house. They are worried because their children are far away and so they are unable to sleep.

"Here is a package, but do not open it: it brings luck and happiness!" the carpenter's wife tells her neighbors.

Tempo dopo, Patrizia e la nonna si recano nuovamente in paese. Ora si sentono allegre chiacchiere venire dai negozi e i bambini hanno tanta voglia di correre e giocare. Patrizia va sulla slitta con Andrea, mentre gli altri costruiscono insieme pupazzi di neve e ridono tirandosi palle di neve. Un uomo viene a sedersi vicino alla nonna e le racconta che cosa è successo qua e là e di come la gente da qualche tempo è più felice grazie ad un misterioso pacchetto verde. Non si sa da chi né da dove provenga. "Sai" dice la nonna, "non lo si deve aprire, ma porta fortuna a tutti coloro che lo ricevono in regalo!".

Sometime later, Patrizia and her grandmother go back to the village. Now they hear cheerful talk coming from the shops, and the children want to run and play. Patrizia goes on the sled with Andrea, while the others build snowmen together and laugh throwing snowballs. A man comes to sit next to Grandma and tells her what happened here and how people have been happier thanks to a mysterious green package. They do not know who or where it came from.

"You know," Grandma says, "you should not open it, but it brings good luck to all those who receive it as a gift!"

Le vacanze purtroppo terminano e Patrizia deve ripartire. Vacanze così emozionanti non le aveva passate prima e già pensa a quando ritornerà. La nonna invece è un po' triste: senza la nipote si sentirà un po' sola. Intanto alla stazione arrivano gli amici di Patrizia per salutarla. Subito i bambini si accorgono che la nonna è triste, chiedendole se vorrebbe ricevere il pacchetto verde. Patrizia ride e batte le mani: "È di nuovo qua, nonna, è ritornato! Avevi ragione, uno solo bastava, e tu ora non sarai più triste!".

Unfortunately, the holidays end and Patrizia has to leave again. She had not had such an exciting vacation before, and she already thinks about when she will return. Grandma, on the other hand, is a little sad: without her granddaughter, she will feel lonely.

Meanwhile, Patrizia's friends arrive at the station to say goodbye. Immediately, the children realize that Grandma is sad and ask her if she would like the green package.

Patrizia laughs and claps her hands. "It's here again, Grandma. It's back! You were right, only one was enough, and you will not be sad anymore!"

7.1 – Summary

Durante le vacanze di Natale Patrizia va dalla nonna. Facendo spese in paese, le due si accorgono che le persone sono tristi e che i bambini non vogliono giocare, quindi ritornano a casa. La nonna progetta un pacchetto verde dal contenuto segreto, ma che porta fortuna a chi lo riceve. Esso passa tra le mani di varie persone, tra cui il boscaiolo e lo spazzacamino, i quali vengono spesso messi in disparte dagli altri abitanti. Grazie a questo pacchetto, essi diventano più felici e vengono accettati dalle altre persone. Quando passa tra le mani dei bambini, essi sono curiosi del loro contenuto, ma non esitano ad aiutare chi ha più bisogno, tra cui il panettiere. Quest'ultimo lo passa alla moglie del falegname, la quale a sua volta lo dona ai vicini di casa preoccupati per i loro figli. Grazie al pacchetto, tutto il paese è di nuovo felice. Purtroppo le vacanze finiscono e Patrizia deve tornare a casa, rattristendo così la nonna che si sentirà sola senza di lei. I bambini si accorgono subito della sua tristezza e le regalano il pacchetto verde. Il pacchetto può anche essere uno solo, ma è sufficiente a portare felicità a tutti.

During the Christmas holidays, Patrizia goes to her grandmother's house. Shopping in the village, the two realize that people are sad and that children do not want to play, so they go home. Grandma designs a green package with secret contents, but which brings good luck to those who receive it. It passes into the hands of various people, including the lumberjack and the chimney sweep, who are often put aside by the other inhabitants. Thanks to this package, they become happier and are accepted by other people. When it passes into the hands of children, they are curious about the package's contents but do not hesitate to help those in need, including the baker. The baker passes it to the carpenter's wife, who in turn gives it to her neighbors who are worried about their children. Thanks to the package, the whole village is happy again. Unfortunately, the holidays end and Patrizia must return home, thus saddening her grandmother who will feel lonely without her. The children are immediately aware of Grandma's sadness and give her the green package. The package might just be one, but it brings happiness to everyone.

7.2 – Vocabulary

Armadio = Wardrobe

Boscaiolo = Lumberjack

Falegname = Carpenter

Favole = Tales

Felicità = Happiness

Fortuna = Luck

Giocare = To play

Influenza = Flu

Lattaio = Milkman

Moglie = Wife

Nastro = Tape

Neve = Snow

Pacchetto = Packet

Paese = Village

Pane = Bread

Panettiere = Baker

Spazzacamino = Chimney sweep

Stazione = Station

Triste = Sad

Vacanze = Holidays

7.3 – Questions

1 – Di che colore è il pacchetto preparato dalla nonna?

What color is the package prepared by Grandma?

a. Rosso – Red

b. Verde – Green

c. Oro – Gold

2 – Che cosa porta alle persone il pacchetto?

What does the package bring to people?

a. Fortuna e felicità – Luck and happiness

b. Soldi e fortuna – Money

c. Pane e formaggio – Bread and cheese

3 – Chi è il primo a riceverlo?

Who is the first to receive the package?

a. Il boscaiolo – The lumberjack

b. Lo spazzacamino – The chimney sweep

c. Gli amici di Anna – Anna's friends

4 – Perché Anna riceve il pacchetto verde?

Why does Anna receive the green package?

a. Perché deve studiare – Because she has to study

b. Perché si sente sola – Because she feels lonely

c. Perché è malata – Because she's sick

5 – Dove si nascondono i bambini a studiare il pacchetto?

Where do the children hide to study the package?

a. In giardino – In the garden

b. In cantina – In the cellar

c. Nella stanza di Anna – In Anna's room

6 – Perché la nonna decide di creare il pacchetto verde?

Why does Drandma decide to make the green package?

7 – A chi è destinato il pacchetto?

Whom is the package intended for?

8 – Perché il pacchetto va al panettiere?

Why the package go to the baker?

9 – Come è il paese dopo che tutti lo hanno ricevuto?

How's the village after everyone receives the package?

10 – Come mai la nonna finisce col ricevere il pacchetto?

Why does Grandma finish with the package?

7.4 – Answers

1 – B

2 – A

3 – A

4 – C

5 – B

6 – Perché nota che tutti in paese sono tristi e vuole migliorare la situazione.

Because she notices that everyone in the village is sad and she wants to improve the situation.

7 – Il pacchetto è destinato a coloro in difficoltà.

The package is intended for those in need.

8 – Il pacchetto verde va al panettiere perché il pane si sta bruciando.

The green package goes to the baker because his bread is burning.

9 – Dopo che il pacchetto è stato ricevuto, il paese è di nuovo vitale e felice.

After the package has been received, the village is again vital and happy.

10 – La nonna finisce col riceverlo perché è triste per la partenza della nipote Patrizia.

Grandma ends up receiving it because she is sad because of the departure of her granddaughter, Patrizia.

Chapter 8 - Il pettirosso di carta – The Paper Robin

Era una notte di luna piena. Nel suo studio in cima alla torre, una pittrice stava ancora lavorando. Il giorno dopo era il compleanno di sua figlia e, in gran segreto, le stava preparando un regalo. Solo il suo gatto aveva il permesso di guardare. "Dipingerò un pettirosso talmente bello e vivo che saprà persino volare!" disse l'artista.

It was a full moon night. In her study, at the top of the tower, a painter was still working. The next day was her daughter's birthday, and secretly, she was preparing a present for her. Only the cat was allowed to watch.

"I will paint a robin so beautiful and alive that it will even fly!" said the artist.

Quando ebbe finito, la pittrice andò a riposare. Il gatto entrò nella stanza e, dopo un lungo sbadiglio, si addormentò in un angolo. Si era addormentato da poco quando una voce gridò: "Ma io non volo! Non sono capace di volare!". Il gatto si svegliò all'improvviso, si sfregò gli occhi e si grattò le orecchie per essere certo di non sognare: a parlare era stato il pettirosso dipinto! "È ovvio che non puoi volare: sei solo un pettirosso di carta!" brontolò, "quindi tieni chiuso il becco e lasciami dormire!". "Ma io devo saper volare!" protestò il pettirosso, "lo ha detto la pittrice. Dimmi, come si fa a volare?".

When she had finished, the painter went to rest. The cat entered the room, and after a long yawn, fell asleep in a corner.

It had just fallen asleep when a voice shouted, "But I do not fly! I cannot fly!"

The cat woke up, rubbed its eyes and scratched its ears to make sure it wasn't dreaming. It was the painted robin talking!

"It's obvious you cannot fly; you're just a paper robin!" the cat said with a grumble. "So keep your beak closed and let me sleep!"

"But I must know how to fly!" the robin protested. "The painter said so. Tell me how to fly."

A quel punto il gatto si arrabbiò. Egli non sopportava di essere disturbato durante il sonno, così prese il pettirosso di carta, lo gettò dalla finestra e tornò nel suo angolo a dormire. Il foglio volò nell'aria e andò a posarsi sui rami di un albero. Lì stavano pernottando tre grossi corvi.

At that point, the cat got angry. It could not bear to be disturbed during sleep, so it took the painted robin, threw it out of the window, and went back to its corner to sleep. The sheet flew into the air and landed on the branches of a tree. Three large crows were spending the night there.

"So volare!" gridò il pettirosso di carta. "Cosa c'è di tanto straordinario?" chiese uno dei corvi, svegliato da quelle grida: "Tutti gli uccelli sanno volare!". "Chi fa tutto questo baccano?" chiese il secondo corvo. "Scusate, sono emozionato perché sto imparando a volare" rispose il pettirosso, "so già volare dall'alto verso il basso. Ora voglio imparare a volare dal basso verso l'alto: potreste aiutarmi?"

"I can fly!" shouted the paper robin.

"What's so extraordinary?" asked one of the crows, woken by the robin's cries. "All birds can fly!"

"Who's making all this noise?" asked the second crow.

"Sorry, I'm excited because I'm learning to fly," the robin replied. "I already know how to fly from top to bottom. Now I want to learn to fly from the bottom to the top. Could you help me?"

"Ma quell'uccello è di carta!" esclamò il terzo corvo. "È di carta e sa parlare!" dissero i primi due, sbalorditi. I tre corvi borbottarono qualcosa tra di loro, poi si voltarono verso il pettirosso. "Signor uccello", gli dissero, "noi non siamo che dei poveri corvi ignoranti e non capiamo le cose complicate. Però possiamo accompagnarti dalla civetta. Lei ha letto molti libri, conosce ogni segreto e siamo certi che ti saprà aiutare". Il pettirosso di carta accettò la proposta con entusiasmo. I tre corvi lo afferrarono con il loro becco e lo portarono dalla civetta.

"But that bird is made of paper!" exclaimed the third crow.

"It's made of paper and can speak!" said the first two crows, stunned.

The three crows muttered something between them, then turned to the robin.

"Mr. Bird," they said, "we are but poor ignorant crows, and we do not understand complicated things. But we can accompany you to the owl. She has read many books, knows every secret, and we're sure she can help you."

The paper robin accepted their proposal with enthusiasm. The three crows grabbed the paper robin with their beak and took him to the owl.

La civetta abitava sulle mura di un castello. Non appena la videro, i corvi aprirono il becco e lasciarono cadere il pettirosso di carta. "Eccola! Mostrale che cosa sai fare" gli dissero. "Signora civetta, io ho un grosso problema: voglio imparare a volare. Come vedi, so già farlo verso il basso. Ma come si fa a volare verso l'alto?" chiese l'uccello, cercando di non cadere a terra. La civetta lo osservò con molta attenzione, pensò a lungo, poi disse: "Vedo che tu non sei un vero uccello. Sei soltanto un disegno, ma sai parlare e questo è un fatto raro! Sei forse un pettirosso magico?" "Non lo so" fece l'uccello di carta "ma dicono che tu sia saggia, mi potresti aiutare?". La civetta disse di sì, dicendogli che lo avrebbe accompagnato dagli storni non appena fosse arrivato il giorno.

The owl lived on the walls of a castle. As soon as the crows saw her, they opened their beak and let the paper robin fall.

"Here she is! Show her what you can do," the crows told the robin.

"Lady Owl, I have a big problem: I want to learn how to fly. As you can see, I already know how to do it downwards. But how do I fly upwards?" the robin asked, trying not to fall to the ground.

The owl looked at him very carefully, thinking for a long time, then she replied, "I see you're not a real bird. You are only a drawing, but you can speak, and this is a rare fact! Are you a magical robin?"

"I do not know," replied the paper robin. "But the crows said you were wise. Could you help me?"

"Yes," the owl said and told the robin that she would accompany it to the starlings as soon as dawn rose.

La famiglia degli storni si trovava sul tetto di una torre in riva al mare, posto adatto per le lezioni di volo. Il pettirosso di carta chiese se potevano insegnare anche a lui. "Ben volentieri!" risposero gli storni, "cominciamo subito!". Lo portarono sulla cima del tetto e lo spinsero nel vuoto. L'uccello di carta volteggiò qua e là nella brezza del mare, senza fare nessun movimento verso l'alto. Dopo un po' infatti cadde sugli scogli. "Non sono capace a far niente!" pianse, "non imparerò mai a volare come voi!". Gli storni lo consolarono: "Tu sei forse un uccello di città. Là abitano dei nostri parenti: forse loro saranno capaci di insegnarti meglio di noi. Ti porteremo da loro!".

The starlings were on the roof of a tower by the sea, which was suitable for flying lessons.

The paper robin asked the starlings if they could teach him to fly.

"Very willingly!" replied the starlings. "Let's start now!"

They took him to the top of the roof and pushed him into the void. The paper robin circled here and there in the sea breeze, making no movement upward. After a while, he fell on the rocks.

"I'm not able to do anything!" he cried. "I'll never learn how to fly like you!"

The starlings consoled him. "You are perhaps a city bird. There live some of our relatives. Perhaps they will be able to teach you better than us. We will bring you to them."

La città era popolata da molti uccelli. "Cugini carissimi! Qui abbiamo un caso speciale. Questo pettirosso vorrebbe volare ma non riesce. Potete fare qualcosa? Come vedete, lui è diverso da noi" dissero gli storni. Le rondini risposero che non era un vero uccello e i passeri affermarono di non aver mai visto un pettirosso così strano. "È un capolavoro d'arte! Noi ce ne intendiamo!" dissero i piccioni. "Gli uomini quando fanno un dipinto così lo appendono ad una parete, in casa o in un museo. Poi vengono gli altri ad ammirarlo. Sembra vivo ma non lo è, è soltanto un dipinto. Ecco perché il vostro pettirosso non potrà mai volare". Gli storni furono costernati. L'uccello di carta cadde dal loro becco ed iniziò a volteggiare.

The city was populated by many birds.

"Dearest cousins, here we have a special case. This robin would like to fly but he can't. Can you do something? As you see, he is different from us," the starlings said.

The swallows replied that the robin was not a real bird and the sparrows claimed they had never seen such a strange robin.

"He is a masterpiece of art! We understand it!" the pigeons said. "After men do a painting, they hang it on a wall, at home or in a museum. Then others come to admire it. It looks alive, but it is not; it is only a painting. That's why your robin will never fly."

The starlings were dismayed. The paper robin fell from one of their beaks and began to twirl in the air.

"Quindi io sono un uccello importante? Vorrei soltanto sapere a cosa serve. Tutti gli altri possono volare come vogliono, mentre io sono solo un disegno, prigioniero su un foglio di carta!" disse il pettirosso con delusione. Mentre scendeva sotto i tetti della città, il pettirosso ebbe un attimo di paura. Tre gatti erano lì ad aspettarlo e, si sa, i gatti non sono sempre amici degli uccellini. Per fortuna uno di loro era il gatto della pittrice e lo riconobbe. Lo afferrò e lo riportò sano e salvo nello studio sulla torre.

"So I'm an important bird? I just want to know what it's for. Everyone else can fly as they want, while I'm just a drawing, a prisoner on a piece of paper!" the robin said, disappointed.

As he descended beneath the rooftops of the city, the robin had a moment of fear. Three cats were there waiting for him, and cats are seldom friends with birds. Fortunately, one of them was the painter's cat and recognized him. He grabbed the bird and brought him back to the safety of the study in the tower.

"Scusa pettirosso, non credevo tu fossi un capolavoro!" disse il gatto. "Ho sbagliato a gettarti dalla finestra, mi dispiace molto". L'uccello di carta lo perdonò: "Grazie a te ho fatto un bellissimo viaggio e ho conosciuto molti amici. Me ne ricorderò sempre quando sarò appeso ad una parete!". In quel momento nella stanza entrò la pittrice, fischiettando in modo allegro. Prese il pettirosso di carta e ne costruì un bellissimo aquilone. Poi mostrò il regalo a sua figlia e insieme si recarono sulla collina. Lassù c'era molto vento e il pettirosso si alzò altissimo nel cielo.

"Sorry, Robin, I did not think you were a masterpiece!" said the cat. "I was wrong to throw you out the window. I'm very sorry."

The paper robin forgave the cat. "Thanks to you I had a wonderful trip, and I met many friends. I will always remember it when I'm hanging on a wall!" the robin said.

At that moment, the painter entered the room, whistling cheerfully. She took the paper robin and built a beautiful kite out of it. Then she showed the gift to her daughter, and together, they went to a hill. There was a lot of wind up there, and the robin rose very high in the sky.

Da lontano lo videro i suoi amici e gli fecero i complimenti. "Avete visto? Il vento mi ha insegnato a volare verso l'alto!" urlò il pettirosso, "il mio sogno si è avverato!".

From a distance, his friends saw the robin and congratulated him for finally being able to fly.

"Did you see? The wind taught me how to fly upwards!" the robin shouted to them. "My dream came true!"

8.1 – Summary

Una pittrice dipinge un pettirosso per il regalo di compleanno di sua figlia. Di notte, questo pettirosso prende vita e disturba il gatto, il quale lo butta giù dalla finestra. Finito il suo volo, incontra tre corvi a cui chiede come volare, senza però avere un riscontro positivo. Essi lo portano dalla civetta, considerata saggia e in grado di poter aiutare l'uccello di carta. Lei riconosce una rarità nel pettirosso, ma non sa aiutarlo, indirizzandolo agli storni, grandi maestri di volo. Questi ultimi però non sono in grado di insegnargli a volare e lo mandano dai loro parenti cittadini. In città solo i piccioni sanno ricordargli che è un dipinto e quindi molto più importante di un uccello volante. Il pettirosso vola via scoraggiato, finché non incontra il gatto della pittrice, il quale si scusa per averlo buttato dalla finestra. La pittrice costruisce un aquilone con l'uccello di carta: finalmente il pettirosso può volare, esaudendo il suo sogno.

A painter paints a robin for her daughter's birthday present. At night, the robin comes to life and disturbs the cat, who throws it out the window. After its flight, the robin meets three crows, asking them how to fly, but without having a positive response. They bring him to the owl, considered wise enough to help the paper bird. She recognizes a rarity in the robin, but cannot help him, directing him to the starlings, great masters of flight. The starlings, however, are not able to teach him to fly and send him to their relatives in the city. In the city, only pigeons can remind the robin that he is a painting and therefore he's much more important than a flying bird. The robin flies away discouraged until he meets the painter's cat, who apologizes for throwing the robin out of the window. The painter builds a kite out of the robin. Finally, the robin can fly, fulfilling his dream.

8.2 – Vocabulary

Angolo = Corner

Aquilone = Kite

Becco = Beak

Capolavoro = Masterpiece

Carta = Paper

Casa = Home, house

Cielo = Sky

Città = City

Civetta = Owl

Collina = Hill

Compleanno = Birthday

Corvi = Crows

Dipinto = Painting

Gatto = Cat

Gentilezza = Kindness

Imparare = To learn

Importante = Important

Mare = Sea

Mura = Walls

Museo = Museum

Parlare = To speak

Passeri = Sparrows

Paura = Fear

Pettirosso = Robin

Piccioni = Pigeons

Pittrice = Painter (woman)

Prigioniero = Prisoner

Problema = Problem

Rondini = Swallows

Sognare = To dream

Sogno = Dream

Storni = Starlings

Torre = Tower

Uccelli = Birds

Vento = Wind

Viaggio = Trip, journey

Volare = To fly

8.3 – Questions

1 – Inizialmente per cosa nasce il pettirosso?

Initially, what is the robin made for?

a. Per un'esposizione d'arte – An art exhibition

b. Per un regalo di compleanno – A birthday present

c. Per passatempo – A pastime

2 – Quale animale domestico possiede la pittrice?

Which pet does the painter own?

a. Un cavallo – A horse

b. Un cane – A dog

c. Un gatto – A cat

3 – Quali sono i primi animali che incontra il pettirosso?

What are the first animals the robin meets?

a. Dei corvi – Some crows

b. Dei cervi – Some deer

c. Delle lumache – Some snails

4 – Cosa vorrebbe imparare l'uccello di carta?

What does the robin want to learn?

a. A disegnare – To draw

b. A cantare – To sing

c. A volare – To fly

5 – Quale animale è saggio e potrebbe aiutare il pettirosso?

Which animal is wise and could help the robin?

a. La civetta – The owl

b. Il piccione – The pigeon

c. La rondine – The swallow

6 – In quale direzione il pettirosso è già capace di volare?

In which direction is the robin already able to fly?

7 – E in quale direzione gli piacerebbe imparare ad andare?

And in which direction would he like to learn to go?

8 – Il pettirosso è felice di essere un capolavoro? Perché?

Is the robin happy to be a masterpiece? Why?

9 – Riesce ad imparare a volare? Come?

Does he manage to learn to fly? How?

10 – Il pettirosso riesce ad avverare il suo sogno di volare?

Does the robin succeed in fulfilling his dream of flying?

8.4 – Answers

1 – B

2 – C

3 – A

4 – C

5 – A

6 – Il pettirosso sa volare dall'alto in basso.

The robin can fly from top to bottom.

7 – Il pettirosso vorrebbe saper volare dal basso verso l'alto.

The robin would like to know how to fly from bottom to top.

8 – No, egli non è felice di essere un capolavoro perché vorrebbe volare come tutti gli altri uccelli.

No, he is not happy to be a masterpiece because he would like to fly like any other bird.

9 – Sì, il pettirosso riesce ad imparare a volare grazie all'aiuto di un aquilone.

Yes, the robin can learn to fly thanks to the help of a kite.

10 – Sì, egli riesce ad avverare il suo sogno.

Yes, he succeeds in fulfilling his dream.

Chapter 9: Un roseto sotto terra – A Rose Garden Under the Ground

Arriva la notte e la gente si affretta ad arrivare a casa. Il signor Giovanni guarda tutto dal suo balcone. Dopo aver portato in casa un germoglio che prendeva il sole, egli chiude con cura la finestra. Il signor Giovanni si prepara ad andare a lavorare. Si allaccia le scarpe ed esce di casa. Cammina lungo la strada che scende in città, fino al viale in cui c'è la fermata della metropolitana.

Night is coming, and people are quick to get home. Mr. Giovanni looks at everything from his balcony. After bringing into the house a sprout that absorbed the sun, he carefully closes the window. Mr. Giovanni is getting ready to go to work. He fastens his shoes and leaves the house. He walks along the road that goes down into the city until the avenue, where there is the subway stop.

Il signor Giovanni lavora di notte. Egli fa lo spazzino in metropolitana. Un tempo, quando la stazione era nuova, gli abitanti erano felici di scendere e salire le scale splendenti. Col passare degli anni, però, l'intera stazione si è rovinata. Ciononostante, il signor Giovanni ogni sera spazza via lo sporco dai gradini. Grazie a lui la fermata luccica e ritrova il bell'aspetto che aveva un tempo.

Mr. Giovanni works at night. He is a street sweeper at the subway. Once, when the station was new, the inhabitants were happy to come down and climb the shining stairs. Over the years, however, the whole station has been ruined. Nevertheless, every night, Mr. Giovanni sweeps the dirt from the steps. Thanks to him the station glitters and finds the good looks it once had.

Quella notte, mentre il signor Giovanni pulisce l'ingresso, sente per caso la conversazione tra due viaggiatori della sera. "Non senti questo odore?" "Che schifo! Ed è anche peggio quando il treno si avvicina". Poi il treno arriva e copre il rumore delle loro voci.

That night, while Mr. Giovanni is cleaning the entrance, he overhears a conversation between two evening travelers.

"Do you smell that?"

"How disgusting! And it's even worse when the train approaches."

Then the train arrives and drowns out the noise of the voices.

Il signor Giovanni entra nella galleria e guarda l'ultimo vagone allontanarsi. La galleria torna buia e silenziosa. Quell'odore c'è veramente! È un cattivo odore, veramente disgustoso! Il signor Giovanni è disperato. Tutto questo lavoro per niente! E tutto questo pulire per niente!

Mr. Giovanni enters the gallery and looks at the last carriage leaving. The gallery is dark and silent. The smell really exists! It's a bad smell, really disgusting! Mr. Giovanni is desperate. All this work for nothing! And all this clean up for nothing!

Come al solito, il signor Giovanni torna a casa all'alba, poco prima che passi il primo treno. Siccome egli lavora di sera, è più comodo dormire di giorno. Il ricordo dell'odore in metropolitana e le parole dei viaggiatori gli impediscono di addormentarsi. La stessa sera va a lavorare prima del solito, pulendo la stazione con maggiore cura, poi torna in galleria. Asciuga pozzanghere e pavimenti, lava la sporcizia e la muffa sulle pareti. Strofina e lucida con acqua e sapone. Ad un certo punto, dietro le bolle di sapone, compare il colore blu delle piastrelle che era scomparso tempo fa. Strofinando con più foga, scopre una presa d'aria; toglie i rifiuti che ostruiscono il passaggio dei raggi di luna e degli spifferi d'aria. Riesce a sentire il rumore delle automobili e della strada. Tutto ad un tratto gli viene un'idea.

As usual, Mr. Giovanni returns home at dawn, just before the first train passes. Since he works in the evening, it is more comfortable to sleep during the day. The memory of the smell in the subway and the words of the travelers prevent him from falling asleep.

The same evening, he goes to work earlier than usual, cleaning the station with greater care, then returns to the gallery. He dries puddles on the floor, washes the dirt and mold on the walls, and rubs and polishes with soap and water. At one point, behind the soap bubbles, the blue color of the tiles that disappeared long ago reappears. While rubbing, Giovanni finds an air vent that was covered by waste. This prevented the air and the moonlight to get inside the station. After removing the waste, he starts to hear the city noises and suddenly, he gets an idea.

Lì dove c'era la sporcizia, il signor Giovanni depone un po' di terra e pianta il germoglio che ha portato da casa. Per non farlo sentire solo, ne compra degli altri simili. Ora, in questa galleria scura, lo spazzino ha un piccolo roseto colorato tutto suo. Da allora il signor Giovanni continua a pulire la metropolitana, senza dimenticarsi però di innaffiare le sue rose. Ora nessun passeggero si lamenta del cattivo odore, anzi, la corrente d'aria porta spesso un profumo fresco. I volti della gente che aspetta il treno si illuminano.

Where the dirt was, Mr. Giovanni puts some plants and the sprout from his home. So the sprout doesn't get lonely, he buys more sprouts to keep it company. Now, in this dark gallery, the street sweeper has a small colorful rose garden all of his own. Since then, Mr. Giovanni continues to clean the subway, without forgetting to water his roses. Now no passenger complains of the bad smell; in fact, the current of air often brings a fresh scent. The faces of the people waiting for the train light up.

I raggi del sole e le gocce di pioggia attraversano la presa d'aria e raggiungono i germogli di rose, facendoli crescere. Una mattina di primavera, un arbusto del roseto compare in alto sul marciapiede. Un bambino grida: "Mamma! Mamma!", ma nessuno ci fa caso. Intanto le rose continuano a crescere e dopo molto tempo la gente nota quelle strane rose che spuntano da un tombino.

The rays of the sun and raindrops pass through the air (vent?) and reach the buds of roses, making them grow.

One spring morning, a rosebush shrub appears on the sidewalk.

A child cries, "Mom! Mom!" but nobody notices.

Meanwhile, the roses continue to grow, and after a long time, people finally start to notice the strange roses sprouting from a manhole.

La voce delle rose sbocciate gira per tutta la città. Lo stesso giorno, un quotidiano pubblica una fotografia e la radio va a fare l'intervista agli impiegati della metropolitana. Ogni giorno la folla si accalca per osservare questo roseto che cresce sotto la città. Ma l'agitazione non dura a lungo e la gente si stufa velocemente delle rose, rendendo le visite più rare. Il luogo diventa di nuovo tranquillo; solo le rose continuano a crescere.

News of the bloomed roses spreads throughout the city. The same day, a newspaper publishes a photograph of the roses, and a radio host goes to interview the subway employees. Every day a crowd gathers to observe the roses growing under the city. But the spectacle does not last long, and people start to get over the roses, making their visits rarer. The place becomes quiet again; only the roses continue to grow.

La primavera seguente fioriscono altre rose . Così accade ogni anno, facendo profumare il quartiere. Poco a poco, gli abitanti tornano a sorridere. Gli uccelli vengono a cantare e la gente si sente a suo agio a riposare in questo luogo profumato. Sotto terra il piccolo roseto diffonde i suoi freschi profumi. I passi lenti del signor Giovanni si avvicinano. Anche oggi egli pulirà la fermata della metropolitana prima di andare a trovare il suo caro roseto sotto terra. E un sorriso inarca sul suo viso.

The following spring, other roses bloom. This happens every year, making the neighborhood smell amazing. Little by little, the inhabitants return to smile. Birds come to sing, and people feel comfortable resting in such a fragrant place. Under the ground, the small rose garden spreads its fresh scents. Mr. Giovanni's slow steps approach them. Even today he is going to clean the subway stop before going to find his dear rose garden under the ground. A smile arches on his face.

9.1 – Summary

Il signor Giovanni è da sempre uno spazzino alla fermata della metropolitana. Un giorno, nonostante il suo incessante impegno, sente dei passeggeri lamentarsi del cattivo odore. Egli quindi decide di mettere tutto a lucido trovando una presa d'aria. Lì decide di piantare delle rose, che portano un buon profumo alla fermata e provocano meraviglia in tutti i passanti che le vedono. Lo stupore alla fine si placa, ma il signor Giovanni non smette di prendersi cura del suo roseto e così ogni primavera l'atmosfera è più serena e profumata, portando allo spazzino una piccola ma grande soddisfazione.

Mr. Giovanni has always been a street sweeper at the subway station. One day, despite his unremitting efforts, he hears passengers complaining of the bad smell. He then decides to polish everything and finds an air vent. There he decides to plant some roses, which bring a pleasant scent to the subway stop and people marvel at the rose garden. The amazement eventually dies down, but Mr. Giovanni does not stop taking care of his rose garden. And so every spring the atmosphere is more serene and fragrant, bringing the street sweeper a small, yet great satisfaction.

9.2 – Vocabulary

Ciononostante = Neverthless

Crescere = To grow

Fermata = Stop (of a public transport)

Germoglio = Sprout

Inarcare = To arch

Odore = Smell

Profumo = Scent

Roseto = Rose garden

Sorriso = Smile

Spazzino = Sweeper, scavenger

Vagone = Wagon

Viale = Avenue, Boulevard

9.3 – Questions

1 - Che lavoro fa il signor Giovanni?

What's Mr. Giovanni's work?

a. Spazzino – A street sweeper

b. Meccanico – A mechanic

c. Giardiniere – A gardener

2 – Quando lavora?

When does he work?

a. Nel pomeriggio – In the afternoon

b. Al mattino – In the morning

c. Di notte – At night

3 – Quando dorme di solito il signor Giovanni?

When does Mr. Giovanni usually sleep?

a. Nel pomeriggio – In the afternoon

b. Di giorno – During the day

c. Di notte – At night

4 – Che cosa possiede con cura?

What does he own and care for?

a. Un animale – A pet

b. Un germoglio – A sprout

c. Un libro antico – An old book

5 – Chi si accorge del cattivo odore?

Who notices the bad smell?

a. Un bambino – A kid

b. Dei passeggeri – Some passengers

c. Una signora anziana – An old woman

6 – Come si sente il signor Giovanni quando scopre il cattivo odore? Perché?

How does Mr. Giovanni feels when he discovers the bad smell? Why?

7 – Che cosa decide di fare?

What does he decide to do?

8 – Che tipo di fiori pianta?

What type of flowers does he plant?

9 – Come viene presa la nuova situazione?

How is the new situation taken?

10 – Il finale è positivo o negativo? Perché?

Is the end positive or negative? Why?

9.4 – Answers

1 – A

2 – C

3 – B

4 – B

5 – B

6 – Il signor Giovanni si sente scoraggiato perché lavora sempre duramente.

Mr. Giovanni feels discouraged because he always works hard.

7 – Decide di profumare la stazione piantando dei germogli.

He decides to perfume the station by planting some sprouts.

8 – Il signor Giovanni pianta delle rose.

Mr. Giovanni plants some roses.

9 – La nuova situazione è presa con troppo entusiasmo ed interesse.

The new situation is taken with too much enthusiasm and interest.

10 – Il finale è positivo perché il signor Giovanni continua a curare le sue rose e a profumare la stazione della metropolitana.

The ending is positive because Mr. Giovanni continues to cure his roses and to perfume the subway station.

Conclusion

The story is a simple way that is useful, among many other purposes, to check if you can understand the contents. Usually, we start from the simplest plots, then test ourselves with the most complicated and intrinsic ones. Even stories that seem more mundane and accessible can be useful: how did it go with this book? What difficulties did you have during the journey? How did you manage to solve them? Did you learn new terms and abilities?

Do not stop at these stories of kindness, witches and soap bubbles; now it's your turn. An idea could be to invent new short stories, using terms and expressions that you have learned, but also hazarding new formulas and phrases. How about a talking horse in the middle of the desert? Or an Egyptian child on holiday in the Maldives? Everything is possible, and everything can be useful in the sphere of education.

"Where there has been devastation, the story reconstructs a form, removes the threads, re-establishes broken links. The story is a raft in the middle of the shipwreck, Noah's ark after the flood, tenderness instead of horror, voice instead of silence, justice against violence, order in chaos, bank to oblivion. Life continues in the time of the story." (Benedetta Tobagi)

If you enjoyed this book, can you please leave a review for it?

Thanks for your support!

Part 3: Italian Phrase Book

The Ultimate Italian Phrase Book for Travel in Italy Including Over 1000 Phrases for Accommodations, Eating, Traveling, Shopping, and More

Introduction

Italian is a Romance language spoken by not only Italian people: in this category there are also inhabitants of Switzerland, San Marino and Vatican City. The first Italian language as we know it first appeared in 10th Century, written for a poetry and a lawsuit use.

In the literary field, there are a lot of Italian writers who are very famous not only in their homecountry: I bet you already know about Dante Alighieri - who made a religious journey in Paradise - or Petrarch and Boccaccio, two authors really loved also abroad.

Flying over the "ancient" aspect of the Italian language, even now there are many characters of Italian nationality and roots that can be noteworthy both inside and outside the Bel Paese. If food and music can be considered characters, too, then the list gets even bigger!

As you may already be aware of, knowing and studying the grammar of a foreign language means being halfway to mastering it. In order to obtain every shade of the new idiom you are learning, you'd need to advance in native people's everyday life. Experimenting with common ways of saying, typical behaviors and new ways of thinking should be on the agenda when you want to improve or learn a new language different from yours.

Unfortunately, teleportation hasn't been created, yet, and travelling – even if always easier – isn't always doable. How to start interacting, then? How to begin to know all the elements of a new culture if you are not physically present inside its cradle?

Every language owns expressions and words in combinations which are very considerable. In Italian Country – in North, Center and South – there exists a common terminology, too. The dialects, unfortunately, will not be contemplated, since they are practically innumerable; they would make this guide an infinite book of different words and nuances which make the same concept! Let us offer the Italian language in its objective form.

In this guide I'm going to take care of offering useful phrases and vocabulary, ways of saying and practical uses of Italian language. I'm going to provide pronunciation and translation under every element I'll write. Don't hesitate to read this book aloud and to experiment with the phrases that I will present!

Chapter 1 – Basis

The first thing to say about Italian pronunciation is that every letter in a word must be pronounced. There are no silent letters - except for the letter "h" – but sometimes there may be diphthongs, thripthongs and hiatuses, which come from the combination of vowels and consonants.

1.1 Single letters pronunciation

A [Ah]//
B [Bee]//
C [Chee]//
D [Dee]//
E [Ay]//
F [Effay]//
G [Gee]//
H [Ahkka]//
I [Ee]//
L [Ellay]//
M [Emmay]//
N [Ennay]//
O [Oh]//
P [Pee]//
Q [Koo]//
R [Erray]//
S [Essay]//
T [Tee]//
U [Oo]//
V [Vee]//
W [Dohpeeahvoo]//
X [Eeks]//
Y [Eepseelohn]//
Z [Zayta]

1.2 Combinations pronunciation

CH [K]

GH ["G" like in word "goal"]

GN [Ny]

GLI ["lli" like in word "million"]

GU [Ghoo]

QU [Koo]

SC [Sk]

SCH [Sk]

SCI [Shee]

SCE [Sha]

1.3 Numbers

1.3.1 Cardinal numbers

0 [Dze-ro]

1 [Oono]

2 [Doo-ay]

3 [Tray]

4 [Kwa-tro]

5 [Cheen-kway]

6 [Say]

7 [Set-tay]

8 [Ot-to]

9 [No-vay]

10 [Dee-ay-chee]

11 [Oon-dee-chee]

12 [Do-dee-chee]

13 [Tray-dee-chee]

14 [Kwat-tor-dee-chee]

15 [Qwen-dee-chee]

16 [Say-dee-chee]

17 [Deechas-set-tay]

18 [Dee-chot-to]

19 [Dee-chan-novay]

20 [Ven-tee]

21 [Ven-too-no]

22 [Ven-tee-doo-ay]

23 [Ven-tee-tray]

24 [Ven-tee-kwat-tro]

25 [Ven-tee-cheen-kway]

26 [Ven-tee-say]

27 [Ven-tee-set-tay]

28 [Vent-otto]

29 [Vent-tee-no-vay]

30 [Trayn-ta]

40 [Kwaran-ta]

50 [Cheen-kwanta]

60 [Ses-santa]

70 [Set-tanta]

80 [Ot-tanta]

90 [No-vanta]

100 [Chen-to]

110 [Chen-to dee-ay-chee]

1000 [Meel-lay]

2000 [Dooay-meela]

1.000.000 [Oon meel-yo-nay]

1.000.000.000 [Oon meel-yardo]

1.3.2 Ordinal numbers

1° [Pree-mo]

2° [Say-kon-do]

3° [Tayr-tzo]

4° [Qwar-to]

5° [Qween-to]

6° [Say-sto]

7° [Sayt-tee-mo]

8° [Ot-tavo]

9° [No-no]

10° [Dee-chee-mo]

11° [Oon-dee-chay-see-mo]

12° [Do-dee-chay-see-mo]

13° [Tray-dee-chay-see-mo]

14° [Qwat-tordee-chay-see-mo]

15° [Qween-dee-chay-see-mo]

16° [Say-dee-chay-see-mo]

17° [Dee-cha-sayt-tay-see-mo]

18° [Dee-chyot-tay-see-mo]

19° [Dee-chyan-novay-see-mo]

20° [Vayn-tay-see-mo]

21° [Ven-too-nay-see-mo]

22° [Ven-tee-doo-ay-see-mo]

23° [Ven-tee-tray-ay-see-mo]

24° [Ven-tee-kwat-tray-see-mo]

25° [Ven-tee-cheen-kway-see-mo]

26° [Ven-tee-say-ay-see-mo]

27° [Ven-tee-set-tay-see-mo]

28° [Vent-ot-tay-see-mo]

29° [Vent-tee-no-vay-see-mo]

30° [Trayn-tay-see-mo]

40° [Kwaran-tay-see-mo]

50° [Cheen-kwan-tay-see-mo]

60° [Ses-santay-see-mo]

70° [Set-tantay-see-mo]

80° [Ot-tantay-see-mo]

90° [No-vantay-see-mo]

100° [Chen-tay-see-mo]

110° [Chen-to dee-chee-mo]

1000° [Meel-lay-see-mo]

2000° [Dooay-mee-lay-see-mo]

1.000.000° [Oon meel-yo-nay-see-mo]

1.000.000.000° [Oon meel-yar-day-see-mo]

1.4 Time

Scusi, che ore sono?
[Skoo-say kay oray sono?]
Excuse me, what time is it?

Sono le…
[Sono lay…]
It's…

È… [with midday, midnight, one o'clock]
[Ay…]
It's…

In Italy the full 24-hour clock is mostly used. After mezzogiorno [medzo-dgeeorno], midday, Italian people use the corresponding hour number. For example there is le tredici [13:00], le sedici [16:00], le venti [20:00].

È l'una.
[Ay loo-na]
It's 1 o'clock.

È mezzogiorno.
[Ay may-tso-dgeeorno]
It's midday.

È mezzanotte.
[Ay medza-nottay]
It's midnight.

Sono le due.
[Sono lay doo-ay]
It's two o'clock.

Sono le due e dieci.
[Sono lay doo-ay ay dee-achee]
It's ten past two.

Sono le due e un quarto.
[Sono lay doo-ay ay oon kwar-to]
It's a quarter past two.

Sono le due e venti.
[Sono lay doo-ay ay vayn-tee]
It's twenty past two.

Sono le due e mezza.
[Sono lay doo-ay ay me-dza]
It's half past two.

Sono le due e trentacinque.
[Sono lay doo-ay ay trayn-ta-cheen-qway]
It's two thirty-five.

Manca un quarto alle tre.
[Ma-nca oon kwar-to allay tray]
It's a quarter to three.

Sono le tre meno un quarto.
[Sono lay tray may-no oon kwar-to]
It's a quarter to three.

Sono le tre meno cinque.
[Sono lay tray may-no cheen-qway]
It's five to three.

A che ora…?
[A kay ora?]
At what time?

A che ora apre la biblioteca?
[A kay ora apray la bee-blyo-tay-ka?]
What time does the library open?

A che ora chiude il negozio?
[A kay ora apray eel nay-go-tzyo?]
What time does the shop close?

A che ora comincia la partita?
[A kay ora komeen-cheea la par-tee-ta?]
What time does the match start?

A che ora finisce il pranzo?
[A kay ora phee-nee-chee eel pran-tzo?]
What time does the lunch end?

Prima delle due.
[Pree-ma day-lay doo-ay]
Before two o'clock.

Dopo le due.
[Dopo lay doo-ay]
After two o'clock.

1.4.1 Useful words about time

Oggi [Odg-ee]
Today

Domani [Doma-nee]
Tomorrow

Ieri [Ye-ree]
Yesterday

Stasera [Stasay-ra]
This evening

Stanotte [Sta-nottay]
This night

Stamattina [Stama-teena]
This morning

Mattina [Mat-teena]
Morning

Pomeriggio [Pomay-ree-gyo]
Afternoon

Sera [Say-ra]
Evening

Notte [Not-tay]
Night

1.5 Date

Che data è oggi?
[Kay data ay od-gee?]
What date is it today?

Che giorno è oggi?
[Kay dgeeor-no ay od-gee?]
What day is it today?

In che mese siamo?
[Een kay may-say sya-mo?]
What month is it?

Oggi è…
[Odg-ee ay…]
Today it's…

In the Italian language, in order to indicate the date, the ordinal numbers are not used, but the cardinal numbers are. The only case in which the rule does not apply is for the first day of each month.

È il primo maggio.
[Ay eel pree-mo madg-yo]
It's the first of May.

È il cinque marzo.
[Ay eel cheen-kway mar-tzo]
It's March the fifth.

È il venti di aprile.
[Ay eel vay-ntee dee apree-lay]
It's April the twentieth.

Oggi è lunedì.
[Od-jee ay loo-nay-dee]
Today it's Monday.

Domani è martedì.
[Doma-nee ay mar-tay-dee]
Tomorrow it's Tuesday.

1.5.1 Useful words about date

1.5.1.1 Days of the week

Lunedì [loo-nay-dee]
Monday

Martedì [Mar-tay-dee]
Tuesday

Mercoledì [Mer-ko-lay-dee]
Wednesday

Giovedì [Jovay-dee]
Thursday

Venerdì [Vay-nay-rdee]
Friday

Sabato [Sa-bato]
Saturday

Domenica [Do-may-nee-ka]
Sunday

1.5.1.2 Months

Gennaio [Dg-ay-nayo]
January

Febbraio [Pheb-ray-o]
February

Marzo [Mar-tzo]
March

Aprile [Apree-lay]
April

Maggio [Mad-jo]
May

Giugno [Dgoo-nyo]
June

Luglio [Lool-yo]
July

Agosto [A-gosto]
August

Settembre [Say-taymb-ray]
September

Ottobre [Otto-bray]
October

Novembre [Novay-mbray]
November

Dicembre [Dee-chaym-bray]
December

1.5.1.3 Seasons

Inverno [Een-vayr-no]
Winter

Primavera [Preema-vay-ra]
Spring

Estate [Ay-sta-tay]
Summer

Autunno [Aoo-too-no]
Autumn

1.6 Colors

Arancione [Aran-chyo]
Orange

Argento [Ar-dgyayn-to]
Silver

Avorio [Avo-ryo]
Ivory

Azzurro [Adzoor-ro]
Light blue

Bianco [Bee-an-ko]
White

Blu [Bloo]
Blue

Bordeaux [Bor-do]
Burgundy

Giallo [Dgyal-lo]
Yellow

Grigio [Gree-dgyo]
Gray

Lilla [Leel-la]
Lilac

Marrone [Mar-ro-nay]
Brown

Nero [Nay-ro]
Black

Ocra [Ok-ra]
Ochre

Oro [O-ro]
Gold

Rosa [Ro-sa]
Pink

Rosso [Ros-so]
Red

Verde [Vayr-day]
Green

Viola [Vee-ola]
Purple

Chapter 2 - Travelling in Italy

2.1 At the airport

Vorrei un biglietto solo andata per l'Italia.
[Vor-ray oon beel-aytto sola andata payr lee-taleea]
I want a one-way ticket to Italy.

Vorrei un biglietto andata e ritorno per l'Italia.
[Vor-ray oon beel-aytto andata ay ree-torno payr lee-taleea]
I want a return ticket to Italy.

Vorrei un biglietto andata e ritorno per l'aeroporto di…
[Vor-ray oon beel-aytto andata ay ree-torno payr lay-roporto dee…]
I want a return ticket to the airport of…

Vorrei un biglietto ridotto per…
[Vor-ray oon beel-aytto ree-dotto payr…]
I want a reduced ticket to…

Quanto costa il biglietto?
[Qwan-to kos-ta eel beel-aytto?]
How much does the ticket cost?

C'è qualche posto last minute?
[Chay qwal-kay posto last minute?]
Is there a last-minute seat?

A che ora è il volo per l'aeroporto di…?
[Ah kay ora ay eel volo payr lay-roporto dee…?]
What time is the flight to the airport of…?

Quanto dura il volo per…?
[Qwan-to doo-ra eel vo-lo payr…?]
How long does the flight to… last?

A che ora arriviamo a…?
[Ah kay orah ar-ree-veeamo a…?]
What hour do we arrive to…?

C'è lo scalo all'aeroporto?
[Chay lo ska-lo al-layro-porto?]
Is there a stop at the airport?

Quanto dura lo scalo?
[Qwan-to doo-ra lo ska-lo?]
How much does the stop last?

Scusi, come arrivo all'aeroporto?
[Skoo-see, koh-may ahr-reevo allay-roporto?]
Sorry, how do I get to the airport?

Esiste un autobus per l'aeroporto?
[Ay-see-stay oon autobus payr lay-roporto?]
Is there a bus for the airport?

Posso arrivare all'aeroporto a piedi?
[Pos-so ar-ree-va-ray al-layro-porto a pyay-dee?]
May I arrive at the airport by feet?

Stiamo andando a…
[Stee-amo andando a…]
We're travelling to…

Qual è il mio gate?
[Qwal-ay eel myo gayt?]
What's my gate?

Il mio gate è il numero 2.
[Eel mee-oh gate ay eel noo-may-ro doo-ay]
My gate is number 2.

Il gate è aperto.
[Eel gate ay apayr-to]
The gate is open.

Il gate è ancora chiuso.
[Eel gate ay ankoh-ra kee-ouso]
The gate is still closed.

L'imbarco è all'uscita numero…
[Leen-bahr-ko ay aloo-sheeta noo-mayro…]
Boarding is at the exit number…

Buon viaggio!
[Bwon vee-ageeo]
Have a nice trip!

Dove prendo il mio bagaglio?
[Do-vay prayn-do eel meeo bagal-yo?]
Where do I take my luggage?

Dove sono i bagagli del volo da…?
[Do-vay sono ee ba-galy dayl volo da…?]
Where are the luggages of the flight from…?

Il suo bagaglio è al rullo numero…
[Eel soo-o ba-gal-yo ay ahl roul-loh noo-may-roh…]
Your luggage is on the roller number…

Ha il passaporto, per favore?
[Ah eel passa-por-to, per fa-vou-ray?]
Do You have the passport, please?

Io uso la carta d'identità.
[Eeo uso la kar-ta dee-dayn-teeta]
I use the identity card.

Io uso il passaporto.
[Eeo uso eel passa-por-to]
I use the passport.

Il mio bagaglio non è arrivato.
[Eel mee-yo bagal-yo non ay ar-reeva-to]
My luggage hasn't arrived.

Scusi, non trovo il mio bagaglio.
[Skoo-see, non trovo eel myo baga-lyo]
Excuse me, I can't find my luggage.

Penso che il mio bagaglio sia andato perso.
[Payn-so kay eel myo baga-lyo sya andato payr-so]
I think my luggage went lost.

La mia valigia è arrivata danneggiata.
[La mee-ya va-leeja ay ar-reeva-ta dan-nedja-ta]
My luggage arrived damaged.

Scusi, dove posso cambiare i soldi?
[Scoo-see, dou-vay poss-o kam-bee-arey e sol-dee?]
Excuse me, where may I change money?

Posso cambiare i soldi qui in aeroporto?
[Pos-so kam-bya-ray ee sol-dee qwee een a-ayro-porto?]
May I change my money here at the airport?

Come posso arrivare in città?
[Ko-may poss-o arr-ee-varay een cee-ttah?]
How may I get to the city?

Quanto costa il taxi per questa via?
[Qwan-to kos-ta eel taxi payr qwes-ta vee-a?]
How much is the taxi for this street?

Posso usare il treno/autobus per arrivare all'alloggio?
[Pos-so usa-ray eel tray-no/au-to-boos payr arree-va-ray al allo-dgyo?]
May I use the train/bus to arrive to the accomodation?

Come posso arrivare all'hotel, per favore?
[Kom-ay posso arreeva-ray allo-tayl, payr favo-ray?]
How may I get to the hotel, please?

Posso acquistare qui il biglietto per il bus?
[Pos-so aqwee-sta-ray qwee eel bee-lyayt-to payr eel bus?]
May I buy here the ticket for the bus?

2.2 At the accommodation

If you are going to stay in a *albergo* [al-bayr-go], hotel, keep in mind these formulas that will come in handy according to your needs: *mezza pensione* [may-tza payn-syo-nay] is when you just need accommodation, breakfast and sometimes another meal to your choice. *Pensione completa* [payn-syo-nay kom-play-ta] includes accommodation, breakfast, lunch and dinner. All inclusive is common mostly in luxury hotels.

Abbiamo bisogno di un posto in cui stare.
[Ab-bee-amo bee-so-nyo dee oon posto een koo-ee sta-ray]
We need a place to stay.

Sto cercando un alloggio.
[Sto chayr-kando oon al-lo-dgyo]
I'm looking for an accomodation.

Sto cercando un hotel.
[Sto chayr-kando oon ho-tayl]
I'm looking for a hotel.

Avete un alloggio da consigliarmi per pochi giorni?
[Avay-tay oon al-lo-dgyo da kon-see-lyar-mee payr po-kee gyor-nee?]
Do you have an accommodation to suggest for a few days?

Avete una camera disponibile?
[A-vay-tay oona ka-may-ra dees-ponee-bee-lay?]
Do you have an available room?

Quante stelle ha questo hotel?
[Qwan-tay stayl-lay a qway-sto otayl?]
How many stars does this hotel have?

Posso vedere prima la camera?
[Posso vay-day-ray pree-ma la ka-may-ra?]
May I see the room first?

Ho prenotato tramite Internet.
[O pray-notato tra-mee-tay Een-tayr-nayt]
I booked through the Internet.

Ho prenotato con il nome di…
[O pray-notato kon eel no-may dee…]
I booked with the name of…

Ho prenotato una camera singola.
[O pray-notato oona ka-mayra see-ngola]
I booked a single room.

Ho prenotato una camera doppia.
[O pray-notato oona ka-mayra doppya]
I booked a double room.

Ho prenotato uno spazio campeggio.
[O pray-notato oono spa-tzyo kam-pay-dgyo]
I booked a camping square.

Ho prenotato un bungalow.
[O pray-notato oon banga-lo]
I booked a bungalow.

Vorrei prenotare una camera singola.
[Vor-ray pray-nota-ray oona ka-mera seen-gola]
I want to book a single room.

Vorrei prenotare una camera doppia.
[Vor-ray pray-nota-ray oona ka-mera dopp-ya]
I want to book a double room.

Vorrei usufruire della mezza pensione.
[Vor-ray oo-soo-phroo-eeray dayl-la may-tza payn-syo-nay]
I'd like to have a half-board staying.

Vorrei usufruire della pensione completa.
[Vor-ray oo-soo-phroo-eeray dayl-la payn-syo-nay kom-play-ta]
I'd like a staying with a full board.

Potrei avere un soggiorno tutto incluso?
[Po-tray avay-ray oon sod-jor-no ol een-kloo-seev?]
Could I have an all-inclusive staying?

Vorrei prenotare per 3 notti.
[Vor-ray pray-nota-ray payr tray not-tee]
I want to book for 3 nights.

Quanto costa per… giorni?
[Qwan-to ko-sta payr… jor-nee?]
How much does it cost for… days?Quanto costa la stanza per 4 giorni?
[Qwan-to costa la stan-dza payr qwa-tro dgior-nee?]
How much is the room for 4 days?

Quanto costa a persona?
[Qwan-to costa payr payr-sona?]
How much does it cost per person?

Vorrei una camera con bagno privato.
[Vor-ray oona ka-mayra kon ba-nyo pree-vato]
I want a room with a private toilet.

Vorrei una camera doppia con letti separati.
[Vor-ray oona ka-mayra dop-pya kon let-tee say-para-tee]
I want a double room with separate beds.

Vorrei una camera per non fumatori.
[Vor-ray oona ka-mayra payr non phoo-mato-ree]
I'd like to have a room for non-smokers.

Vorrei una camera dove è possibile fumare.
[Vor-ray oona ka-may-ra do-vay ay pos-see-bee-lay phoo-ma-ray]
I want a room where it is possible to smoke.

Vorrei uno spazio per il camper.
[Vor-ray oono spa-tzyo payr eel kam-payr]
I want a square for the camper.

Avete una camera più economica?
[A-vay-tay oona ka-may-ra pee-o ay-ko-nomee-ka?]
Do you have a cheaper room?

Avete una camera più silenziosa?
[A-vay-tay oona ka-may-ra pee-oo see-layn-tzyo-sa?]
Do you have a quieter room?

Avete una camera più spaziosa?
[A-vay-tay oona ka-may-ra pee-o spa-tzyo-sa?]
Do you have a larger room?

C'è uno spazio camper più spazioso?
[Chay oono spa-tzyo kam-payr pyoo spa-tzyoso?]
Is there a larger camping square?

La colazione è inclusa nel prezzo?
[La kola-zionay ay een-clusa nayl prayz-zo?]
Is breakfast included in the price?

La cena e il pranzo sono inclusi nel prezzo?
[La chay-na ay eel pran-tzo sono een-kloo-see nayl pray-tzo?]
Are dinner and lunch included in the price?

Quanto costa la tassa di soggiorno?
[Qwan-to ko-sta la tassa dee sodgyo-rno?]
How much is the tourist tax?

Fino a che ora è aperta la reception?
[Fee-no a kay oray ay apayr-ta la ray-shayptyon?]
Until what time is the reception open?

Avete il deposito bagagli?
[A-vay-tay eel day-po-see-to ba-ga-lee?]
Do you have luggage storage?

C'è il servizio in camera?
[Ch-ay eel sayr-vee-tseeo een camay-ra?]
Is there room service?

Il servizio in camera è incluso nel prezzo?
[Eel sayr-vee-tseeo een kam-ayra ay een-kluso nayl pray-tso?]
Is room service included in the price?

Disponete di un ascensore per gli ospiti?
[Dee-spo-nay-tay dee oon a-shayn-so-ray payr lee ospee-tee?]
Do you have a lift for the guests?

A che ora è il check-out?
[A kay ora ay eel check-out?]
What time is the room check-out?

Avete una cartina della città?
[Avay-tay oona kar-tee-na dayl-la cheet-tah?]
Do you have a map of the city?

Il vostro parcheggio è a pagamento?
[Eel vostro par-kay-dgyo ay a paga-mayn-to?]
Is your parking for a fee?

Il riscaldamento/condizionatore è a pagamento?
[Eel reeskalda-maynto/kon-dee-tsyona-toray ay a paga-maynto?]
Is the heating/air conditioning to pay?

C'è un ristorante nel campeggio?
[Che oon ree-storantay nayl kam-pay-geeo?]
Is there a restaurant in the campsite?

Possiamo usufruire del ristorante dell'hotel?
[Pos-see-amo oosoo-froo-eeray dayl ree-sto-rantay dayl lo-tayl?]
Can we use the hotel restaurant?

L'elettricità è compresa nel prezzo?
[Elet-treechee-ta ay komp-raysa nayl pray-tso?]
Is electricity included in the price?

L'acqua calda è compresa nel prezzo?
[Lak-wa kal-da ay komp-raysa nayl pray-tso?]
Is hot water included in the price?

Le pulizie sono comprese nel prezzo?
[Kay poo-lee-zyay sono kom-pray-say nayl pray-tzo?]
Is cleaning included in the price?

La mia stanza è sporca.
[La mya stan-tza ay spor-ka]
My room is dirty.

La mia stanza non è stata pulita.
[La mya stan-tza non ay sta-ta poo-lee-ta]
My room hasn't been cleaned.

L'aria condizionata non funziona.
[La-ree-a kon-dee-tzyo-nata non phoon-zyo-na]
The air conditioning does not work.

La mia chiave non funziona.
[La mee-a kya-vay non phoon-zyo-na]
My key does not work.

Mi sono chiuso/chiusa fuori dalla stanza.
[Mee sono kyoo-so/kyoo-sa phoo-oree dal-la stan-tza]
I got locked out of the room.

Manca l'acqua calda.
[Man-ka laqwa kal-da]
Hot water is missing.

Il mio vicino di stanza fa troppo rumore.
[Eel myo vee-chee-no dee stan-tza fa trop-po roo-mo-ray]
My room neighbour is too loud.

Il mio vicino di bungalow è troppo rumoroso.
[Eel myo vee-chee-no dee banga-lo ay trop-po roo-moroso]
My bungalow neighbour is too loud.

Siamo al completo, mi dispiace.
[See-amo al komplay-to, mee dees-peeacay]
We are full, I'm sorry.

Come preferisce pagare?
[Ko-may pray-phay-ree-shay pa-ga-ray?]
How would you like to pay for that?

Vuole pagare subito o alla partenza?
[Woo-lay paga-ray soo-bee-to o al-la par-tayn-za?]
Do you want to pay now or when you're departing?

Vorrei pagare subito.
[Vor-ray paga-ray soo-bee-to]
I'd like to pay immediately.

Vorrei pagare alla fine, se è possibile.
[Vor-ray paga-ray al-la phee-nay, say ay pos-see-bee-lay]
I'd like to pay at the end, if it is possible.

2.3 Money

Accettate i pagamenti in dollari?
[Ac-chayt-ta-tay ee paga-mayn-tee en dol-la-ree?]
Do you accept payments in dollars?

Accettate i pagamenti in sterline?
[Ac-chayt-ta-tay ee paga-mayn-tee een stayr-lee-nay ?]
Do you accept payments in pounds?

Accettate la carta di credito?
[Ac-chayt-ta-tay la kar-ta dee kray-dee-to?]
Do you accept credit cards?

Potrebbe cambiarmi i soldi, per favore?
[Po-trayb-bay kam-bee-armee ee sol-dee, payr favo-ray?]
Can you change money for me, please?

Dove posso cambiare i miei soldi?
[Do-vay posso kam-bee-arey ee myay sol-dee?]
Where can I get money changed?

Quanto costano le commissioni di cambio?
[Qwan-to kos-tano lay kom-mees-syo-nee dee kam-byo?]
How much are exchange fees?

C'è un bancomat nelle vicinanze?
[Chay oon ban-ko-mat nayl-lay vee-chee-nan-tzay?]
Is there an ATM nearby?

C'è una banca nelle vicinanze?
[Chay oona ban-ka nayl-lay vee-chee-nan-tzay?]
Is there a bank nearby?

Potrebbe prestarmi dei soldi, per favore?
[Po-trayb-bay pray-star-mee day sol-dee, payr favo-ray?]
Could you lend me some money, please?

Dove posso fare un prestito?
[Do-vay posso pha-ray oon pray-stee-to?]
Where may I make a loan?

2.3.1 At the bank

Vorrei ritirare 100 euro, per favore.
[Vor-ray ree-tee-ra-ray chayn-to ay-ro, payr favo-ray]
I'd like to withdraw 100 euros, please.

Vorrei fare un prelievo.
[Vor-ray pha-ray oon pray-lyay-vo]
I want to make a withdrawal.

Vorrei prelevare…
[Vor-ray pray-lay-va-ray…]
I'd like to withdraw…

Potrebbe cambiarmi i soldi, per favore?
[Po-trayb-bay kam-bee-armee ee sol-dee, payr favo-ray?]
Could you give me some smaller notes?

Vorrei pagare in contanti.
[Vo-lyo paga-ray een kon-tan-tee]
I'd like to pay in notes, please.

Vorrei fare un bonifico bancario, per favore.
[Vor-ray pha-ray oon bo-nee-phee-ko banka-ryo, payr favo-ray]
I would like to make a bank transfer, please.

Vorrei trasferire del denaro su questo conto.
[Vor-ray tras-phay-ree-ray dayl day-naro soo qway-sto kon-to]
I'd like to transfer some money to this account.

Vorrei trasferire denaro all'estero.
[Vor-ray tras-phay-ree-ray dayna-ro al-lay-stero]
I want to transfer some money abroad.

Vorrei aprire un conto bancario.
[Vo-lyo a-pree-ray oon kon-to ban-ka-ryo]
I'd like to open a bank account.

Potrebbe comunicarmi il mio saldo attuale?
[Potrayb-bay ko-moo-nee-karmee eel myo saldo at-too-alay?]
Could you tell me my current balance?

Potrei avere un estratto conto, per favore?
[Po-tray a-vay-ray oon ay-strat-to kon-to, payr favo-ray?]
Could I have a statement, please?

Vorrei cambiare i miei soldi.
[Vor-ray kam-bya-ray ee myay sol-dee]
I'd like to change my money.

Vorrei cambiare i miei soldi in…
[Vor-ray kam-bee-are ee myay sol-dee een…]
I'd like to change my money in…

Corone [Koro-nay] Crowns

Dollari [Dol-la-ree] Dollars

Euro [Ay-oo-ro] Euros

Franchi [Fran-kee] Francs

Rubli [Roo-blee] Rubles

Sterline [Stay-rlee-nay] Pounds

Vorrei ordinare delle valute straniere.
[Vor-ray or-dee-naray dayl-lay va-loo-te stra-nyay-ray]
I'd like to order some foreign currency.

Qual è il tasso di cambio dell'euro?
[Qwan-to kos-ta eel kam-byo een ay-oo-ro?]
What's the exchange rate for euros?

Ho perso la mia carta di credito.
[O payr-so la mya kar-ta dee kray-dee-to]
I've lost my credit card.

Vorrei fare una carta di credito con voi.
[Vor-ray pha-ray oona kar-ta dee kray-dee-to kon vo-ee]
I'd like to have a credit card with you.

Ho dimenticato il mio codice PIN.
[O dee-mayn-tee-kato eel myo ko-dee-chay PIN]
I've forgotten my PIN code.

Chapter 3 - Everyday life

3.1 Greetings, thanking, saying yes or no

Buongiorno!
[Bwon-dgorno!]
Good morning!

Buon pomeriggio.
[Bwon po-may-reed-gyo]
Good afternoon.

Buonasera.
[Bwona-say-ra]
Good evening.

Salve.
[Sal-vay]
Good morning.

Ciao!
[Chow]
Hello – Bye bye!

Arrivederci.
[Arree-vay-daye-rcee]
Goodbye.

Buonanotte.
[Bwona-nottay]
Good night.

Piacere di conoscerla.
[Pyay-chay-ray dee kono-shayr-la]
Nice to meet you.

A più tardi!
[A py-oo tar-dee!]
See you later!

Ci vediamo domani!
[Cee vay-dee-amo do-manee]
See you tomorrow!

Ci vediamo domenica!
[Cee vay-dee-amo do-may-neeka]
See you on Sunday!

Ci rivediamo a settembre!
[Cee vay-dee-amo a set-taymb-ray!]
See you again in September!

Come stai?
[Ko-may sta-ee?]
How are you?

Che cosa mi racconti?
[Kay ko-sa mee rak-kon-tee?]
What's up?

Come sta, signore/signora?
[Ko-may sta, see-nyo-ray/see-nyo-ra?]
How are you, Sir/Madam?]

Come va?
[Ko-may va?]
How are you?
In a most friendly way.

Sto bene.
[Sto bay-nay]
I'm fine.

Non sto molto bene.
[Non sto molto bay-nay]
I'm not fine at all.

Sto abbastanza bene.
[Sto abbastan-tza bay-nay]
I'm fine enough.

Sto male.
[Sto ma-lay]
I'm not fine.

Grazie!
[Gra-tzy-ay!]
Thank you!

Grazie mille!
[Gra-tzy-ay meel-lay!]
Thank you very much!

La ringrazio.
[La reen-gra-tzyo]
I thank you.

Prego.
[Pray-go]
You are welcome.

Non c'è di che!
[Non chay dee kay!]
You're welcome!

Per favore/per piacere.
[Payr pha-voray/payr pya-chay-ray]
Please.

Per cortesia.
[Payr kor-tay-sya]
Please.

Mi dispiace.
[Mee dees-pya-chay]
I'm sorry.

Scusa/scusi.
[Skoo-sa/skoo-see]
Sorry.

Mi scusi…
[Mee skoo-see]
Excuse me…

Sì.
[See]
Yes.

No.
[No]
No.

Davvero?
[Dav-vay-ro?]
Really?

Così così.
[Ko-see ko-see]
So and so.

Forse.
[Phor-say]
Maybe.

Magari.
[Maga-ree]
Perhaps.

Certo!
[Chayr-to!]
Sure!

Ovvio.
[Ov-vee-o]
Obvious.

Certo che no!
[Chayr-to kay no!]
Of course not!

Certo che sì!
[Chayr-to kay see!]
Of course yes!

Direi di sì.
[Dee-ray dee see]
I guess so.

Direi di no.
[Dee-ray dee no]
I don't guess so.

3.2 Talking about the weather

Che tempo fa oggi?
[Kay tempo ph-a od-gee?]
What's the weather today?

Che tempo farà domani?
[Kay tempo pha-ra doma-nee?]
What will be the weather tomorrow?

Che cosa dicono le previsioni meteo?
[Kay ko-sa dee-kono lay pray-vee-seeyo-nee dayl may-tayo?]
What do the weather forecasts say?

Quali sono le previsioni per…?
[Qwa-lee sono lay pray-vee-syo-nay payr…?]
What are the forecasts for...?

Oggi è una bellissima giornata!
[Od-gee ay oona bayl-lees-seema jor-nata!]
Today it's a beautiful day!

Oggi non è una bella giornata.
[Od-gee non ay oona bayl-la jorn-ata]
Today is not a good day.

Domani farà caldo.
[Doma-nee pha-ra kal-do]
Tomorrow it's going to be hot.

Oggi fa freddo.
[Od-gee fa frayd-do]
Today it's cold.

La giornata è umida.
[La jor-nata ay oo-mee-da]
The day is very humid.

Piove!
[Pee-ovay!]
It's raining!

Nevica!
[Nay-vee-ka!]
It's snowing!

È nuvoloso.
[Ch-ay noo-voloso]
It's cloudy.

C'è molto vento.
[Ch-ay molto vayn-to]
It's very windy.

C'è un temporale.
[Ch-ay oon taym-pora-lay]
There's a thunderstorm.

Quanti gradi ci sono?
[Qwan-tee gra-dee ch-ee sono?]
What is the temperature?

Quanti gradi ci sono qui dentro?
[Qwan-tee gra-dee ch-ee sono qw-ee dayn-tro?]
How many degrees are there in here?

Oggi ci sono 20 gradi.
[Od-gee ch-ee sono vayn-tee gra-dee]
Today there are 20 degrees.

Pensi che domani pioverà/nevicherà?
[Payn-see kay doma-nee pee-ovay-ra/nay-vee-kay-ra?]
Do you think that it will rain/snow tomorrow?

Pensi che domani ci sarà nebbia/vento/un temporale?
[Payn-see kay doma-nee chee sara nayb-beea/vayn-to/oon taym-poralee?]
Do you think there will be fog/wind/a storm tomorrow?

La mia stagione preferita è…
[La mya sta-jyo-nay pray-phay-ree-ta ay…]
My favourite season is…

3.3 Going around

Vorrei arrivare in centro.
[Vor-ray arree-va-ray een chayn-tro]
I would like to arrive to the centre.

Dove mi consiglia di andare?
[Do-vay mee kon-see-lya dee anda-ray?]
Where do you suggest me to go?

C'è qualche attrazione nei dintorni?
[Chay qwal-kay attra-tzyo-nay nay deen-tor-nee?]
Are there some attractions nearby?

Scusi, come posso andare/arrivare…?
[Skoo-see, ko-may pos-so anda-ray/ar-ree-varay…?]
Sorry, how may I get to…?

Scusi, come posso andare alla stazione?
[Skoo-say, ko-may posso anda-ray alla sta-tsyo-nay?]
Excuse me, how may I get to the station?

Scusi, come posso arrivare in centro?
[Skoo-say, ko-may posso ar-ree-va-ray een chayn-tro?]
Excuse me, how may I get to the centre?

È lontano il centro da qui?
[Ay lontano eel chain-tro?]
Is the centre far from here?

Quanto dista…?
[Qwan-to dees-ta…?]
How far is…?

Quanto dista la stazione?
[Qwan-to dee-sta la sta-tsyo-nay?]
How far is the station?

Dov'è…?
[Dov-ay…?]
Where is…?

Dov'è il museo?
[Do-vay eel moo-say-o?]
Where is the museum?

Come posso arrivarci?
[Ko-may pos-so ar-ree-var-chee?]
How can I get there?

Può aiutarmi ad arrivarci?
[Pwo ayoo-tar-mee a ar-ree-var-chee?]
Can you help me to get there?

Dove posso trovare/comprare una cartina della città?
[Do-vay posso trova-ray/kompra-ray oona kar-tee-na dayl-la chee-ttà?]
Where can I find/buy a map of the city?

Potrebbe indicare la strada sulla cartina?
[Pot-rayb-bay een-dee-karay sool-la kar-tee-na la strada?]
Could you indicate the road on the map?

Può disegnare la strada sulla cartina, per cortesia?
[Pwo dee-say-nya-ray la strada sool-la kar-tee-na, payr korte-sya?]
Can you draw the way on the map, please?

Qual è l'autobus per arrivare in centro?
[Qwal-ay la-ooto-boos payr arree-va-ray een chain-tro?]
What is the bus to get to the center?

Quando passa il prossimo autobus?
[Qwan-do passa eel pros-see-mo aoo-to-boos?]
When is the next bus?

C'è un tram per arrivare qui?
[Chay oon tram payr ar-ree-vay-ray qwee?]
Is there a tram to get here?

Scusi, mi può dire quando è la mia fermata?
[Skoo-see, mee pwo dee-ray qwan-do ay la meea fayr-mata?]
Excuse me, can you tell me when we arrive to my stop?

Sto cercando la fermata della metropolitana.
[Sto cher-kando la fayr-mata dayl-la may-tropo-lee-tana]
I'm looking for the subway stop.

Che linea della metropolitana devo prendere?
[Kay lee-nay-a dayl-la may-tropo-lee-tana day-vo prayn-day-ray?]
What subway line do I have to take?

Vorrei comprare un biglietto per…
[Vor-ray kompra-ray oon bee-lyayt-to payr…]
I would like to buy a ticket for…

Vorrei comprare un biglietto per l'autobus.
[Vor-ray kompra-ray oon beel-aytto payr l-aoo-to-boos?]
I would like to buy a bus ticket.

Quanto costa un biglietto per la metropolitana?
[Qwan-to ko-sta oon beel-aytto payr la may-tropo-lee-tana?]
How much does a subway ticket cost?

Dov'è il supermercato più vicino?
[Dov-ay eel soo-payr-mayr-kato peeo vee-cee-no?]
Where is the nearest supermarket?

Dove posso trovare una banca?
[Dov-ay posso trova-ray oona ban-ka?]
Where may I find a bank?

La stazione è lontana 2 metri/chilometri.
[La sta-tsyo-nay ay lontana doo-ay may-tree/kee-lomay-tree]
The station is 2 meters/kilometers far.

Sto andando in centro.
[Sto andando een chayn-tro]
I'm going downtown.

Dove posso trovare un taxi?
[Do-vay posso trova-ray oon taxi?]
Where may I find a taxi?

Quanto costa il taxi per il centro?
[Qwan-to ko-sta eel taxi payr eel chayn-tro?]
How much is the taxi to the center?

Devo prendere il treno/la metropolitana/il tram.
[Day-vo prayn-day-ray eel tray-no/la maytro-polee-tana/eel tram]
I have to take the train/the subway/the tram.

Quali sono gli orari del tram?
[Qwa-lee sono lee ora-ree payr eel tram?]
What are the tram timetables?

Vorrei noleggiare una macchina.
[Vor-ray no-lay-dgeea-ray oona mak-kee-na]
I'd like to hire a car.

Dov'è il noleggio più vicino?
[Do-vay eel no-lay-dgeeo pee-oo vee-chee-no?]
Where is the nearest rental?

Dov'è il parcheggio più vicino?
[Do-vay eel park-kay-dgee-o pee-oo vee-chee-no?]
Where is the nearest parking?

Quali strade posso percorrere?
[Qwa-lee stra-day posso payr-kor-ray-ray?]
Which roads can I travel?

C'è una zona a traffico limitato?
[Chay oona tzo-na a traph-pheeko lee-mee-tato?]
Is there a limited traffic area?

Posso parcheggiare qui?
[Posso par-kay-dgee-are qwee?]
May I park here?

C'è un bagno pubblico nei dintorni?
[Chay oon ba-nyo poob-blee-ko nay deen-tor-nee?]
Is there a public toilet nearby?

3.3.1 Useful vocabulary to go around

Accanto a [Ak-kan-to a]
Next to

All'angolo [Al-langolo]
At the corner

Davanti a [Davan-tee a]
Opposite to

Destra [day-stra]
Right

Dietro a [Dee-ay-tro a]
Behind

Sinistra [See-nee-stra]
Left

Vicino a [Vee-chee-no a]
Near to

Entrata [Ayn-trata]
Entry

Uscita [Oo-shee-ta]
Exit

Arrivi [Arree-vee]
Arrivals

Battello [Bat-tayl-lo]
Boat

Bicicletta [Bee-chee-klayt-ta]
Bicycle

Biglietteria [Beel-yet-tay-reea]
Ticket office

Biglietto giornaliero [Beel-yet-to jor-na-lyay-ro]
Dialy ticket

Binario [Bee-na-ryo]
Platform

Centro [Chayn-tro]
City centre

Cinema [Chee-nay-ma]
Cinema

Città [Chee-ttah]
Town

Imbarco [Eem-bar-ko]
Boarding gate

Macchina [Mak-kee-na]
Car

Metropolitana [May-tropo-lee-tana]
Subway

Motocicletta [Moto-chee-klayt-ta]
Motorbike

Ospedale [Os-pay-da-lay]
Hospital

Parcheggio [Par-kay-dgyo]
Parking

Partenze [Par-tayn-tzay]
Departures

Pronto soccorso [Pron-to sok-kor-so]
Emergency room

Stadio [Sta-dyo]
Stadium

Stazione [Sta-tzyo-nay]
Station

Treno [Tray-no]
Train

Veterinario [Vay-tay-ree-na-ryo]
Vet

3.4 (Doing the) shopping

Dov'è il supermercato?
[Do-vay eel soo-payr-mayr-kato?]
Where is the supermarket?

In che giorni c'è il mercato locale?
[Een kay dgyor-nee chay eel mer-kato loka-lay?]
What days is the local market open?

Dove posso comprare del cibo?
[Do-vay posso kom-pra-ray dayl chee-bo?]
Where may I buy some food?

Sto cercando un souvenir.
[Sto chayr-kan-do oon soo-vay-neer]
I'm looking for a souvenir.

Sto solo dando un'occhiata.
[Sto solo dando oon ok-kee-ata]
I'm just watching.

Mi potrebbe aiutare, per favore?
[Mee po-trayb-bay ayoo-ta-ray, payr favo-ray?]
Can you help me, please?

Dove posso trovare…?
[Do-vay posso tro-va-ray…?]
Where may I find…?

Potrebbe darmi…?
[Po-trayb-bay dar-mee…?]
Could you give me…?

Per favore, potrei avere…?
[Payr favo-ray, po-tray a-vay-ray…?]
Please, may I have…?

Avete del sale?
[A-vay-tay eel sa-lay?]
Do you have salt?

Vorrei comprare due mele.
[Vor-ray kom-pra-ray doo-ay may-lay]
I want to buy two apples.

Vorrei questo.
[Vor-ray qw-ay-sto]
I'd like to have this.

Quanto costa?
[Qwan-to kos-ta?]
How much does is cost?

Quanto costa al chilo?
[Qwan-to kos-ta al kee-lo?]
What's the price per kilo?

Posso pagare con la carta di credito?
[Posso paga-ray kon la kar-ta dee kre-dee-to?]
Can I pay with credit card?

È troppo caro.
[Ay troppo ka-ro]
It's too expensive.

Non me lo posso permettere.
[Non may lo posso payr-mayt-tay-ray]
I can't afford it.

Avete qualcosa di più economico?
[A-vay-tay qwal-kosa dee pee-oo ay-kono-meeko?]
Do you have something cheaper?

Potrebbe farmi uno sconto?
[Po-trayb-bay far-mee oono skon-to?]
Could you give me a discount?

In Italy there are sales. Sales refer to end-of-season sales with discounted prices of clothing and accessories. Usually they occur in two periods of the year: at the beginning of January after Christmas holidays for winter clothing and early July for the summer.

Posso assaggiarlo?
[Po-tray as-sa-dgee-aray?]
May I taste it?

Posso provarlo?
[Pos-so provar-lo?]
May I try it?

Posso provare questa gonna?
[Posso prova-ray qwes-ta gonna?]
May I try on this skirt?

Porto la taglia 40.
[Porto la ta-lee-a qwa-ranta]
I wear size 40.

Porto il numero 38.
[Porto eel noo-may-ro trayn-totto]
I wear shoe size number 38.

A quale taglia corrisponde?
[A qwa-lay ta-lya kor-rees-pon-day?]
What size does it correspond to?

Pay attention to Italian sizes! They have differences compared to those of other countries. Check the conversion table before asking for a specific size, or let the shop assistants help you out!

È troppo grande.
[Ay trop-po gran-day]
It's too big.

È troppo piccolo.
[Ay trop-po peek-kolo/peek-kola]
It's too small.

Vorrei una taglia più grande.
[Vor-ray oona ta-lee-a pee-oo gran-day]
I'd like to have a bigger size.

Vorrei una taglia più piccola.
[Vor-ray oona ta-lee-a pee-oo peek-kola]
I'd like to have a smaller size.

Quanti giorni ho per il cambio?
[Qwan-tee jor-nee o payr eel kam-byo?]
How many days do I have for a change?

C'è la garanzia? Di quanto tempo è?
[Chay la garan-tzya? Dee qwan-to taym-po ay?]
Is there a guarantee? How much time is it?

Ne vorrei di più.
[Nay vor-ray dee pee-oo]
I want more.

Ne vorrei di meno.
[Nay vor-ray dee may-no]
I want less.

Lo prendo!
[Lo prayn-do!]
I'll take it!

Non lo prendo, mi dispiace.
[Non lo prayn-do, mee dees-pya-chay]
I won't take it, I'm sorry.

Avrebbe un sacchetto, per cortesia?
[A-vrayb-bay oona bor-see-na, payr kor-tay-sya?]
Do you have a carrier bag, please?

Avete una carta fedeltà?
[A-vay-tay oona kar-ta phay-dayl-tah?]
Do you have a fidelity card?

Posso usare la carta di credito per pagare?
[Pos-so oosa-ray la kar-ta dee kray-dee-to payr paga-ray?]
May I use the credit card to pay?

Posso pagare in contanti?
[Pos-so paga-ray een kon-tantee?]
May I pay with cash?

Ecco il suo resto.
[Ek-ko eel soo-o rays-to]
Here's your change.

Ecco il suo scontrino.
[Ayk-ko eel soo-o skon-tree-no]
Here's your receipt.

Tenga lo scontrino per la garanzia.
[Tayn-ga lo skon-tree-no payr la garan-tzya]
Keep the receipt for the guarantee.

Potrei avere una fattura, per cortesia?
[Po-tray avay-ray oona phat-too-ra, payr kor-tay-sya?]
May I have an invoice, please?

3.4.1 Shops names

Agenzia [A-jayn-tzya]
Agency

Bottega [Bot-tay-ga]
Parlour

Cappelleria [Kap-payl-lay-rya]
Headgear shop

Centro commerciale [Chayn-tro kom-mayr-cheea-lay]
Shopping center

Concessionaria [Kon-chays-syo-narya]
Car dealership

Discount [Dees-ka-oont]
Discount supermarket

Edicola [Ay-dee-kola]
Newsstand

Emporio [Aym-poryo]
Emporium

Farmacia [Pharma-cheea]
Pharmacy

Ferramenta [Phayr-ra-mayn-ta]
Ironmongery

Fiorista [Phyo-reesta]
Florist

Fruttivendolo [Froot-tee-vayn-dolo]
Grocery shop

Gelateria [Jay-latay-rya]
Ice-cream shop

Libreria [Lee-bray-reea]
Bookshop

Macelleria [Ma-chayl-lay-reea]
Butchery shop

Merceria [May-rchay-rya]
Haberdashery

Panificio [Pa-nee-phee-chyo]
Bakery shop

Parrucchiere [Par-rook-kyay-ray]
Hairdresser

Pescheria [Pay-skay-rya]
Fish shop

Supermercato [Soo-payr-mayr-kato]
Supermarket

Tabaccheria [Tabak-kay-reea]
Tabacconist's

Vineria [Vee-nay-rya]
Winery shop

Vivaio [Vee-vayo]
Vivarium

3.4.2 Food vocabulary

Arancia [Aran-chee-a]
Orange

Burro [Boor-ro]
Butter

Caffè [Kaf-fay]
Coffee

Carota [Ka-rota]
Carrot

Cipolla [Chee-pol-la]
Onion

Formaggio [Phor-madgyo]
Cheese

Fragola [Phra-gola]
Strawberry

Insalata [Een-salata]
Salad

Latte [Lat-tay]
Milk

Limone [Lee-mo-nay]
Lemon

Mela [May-la]
Apple

Olio [O-lee-o]
Oil

Pane [Pa-nay]
Bread

Patata [Pata-ta]
Potato

Pepe [Pay-pay]
Pepper

Pera [Pay-ra]
Pear

Pesce [Pay-shay]
Fish

Pomodoro [Pomo-doro]
Tomato

Sale [Sa-lay]
Salt

Uova [Wo-va]
Eggs

Zucchero [Tsoo-kay-ro]
Sugar

3.4.3 Other articles

Antidolorifico [An-tee-dolo-ree-fee-ko]
Painkiller

Assorbente [Assor-bayn-tay]
Sanitary napkin

Calze [Kal-tzay]
Socks

Camicia [Ka-mee-chee-a]
Shirt

Cartolina [Kar-to-lee-na]
Postcard

Francobollo [Phran-kobol-lo]
Stamp

Giacca [Dgee-ak-ka]
Jacket

Gonna [Gon-na]
Skirt

Guida turistica [Goo-eeda too-rees-tee-ka]
Tourist guide

Maglietta [Ma-lyayt-ta]
T-shirt

Mappa [Map-pa]
Map

Mutande [Moo-tan-day]
Underwear

Pannolino [Pan-no-lee-no]
Diaper

Pantaloni [Panta-lonee]
Trousers

Preservativo [Pray-sayr-vatee-vo]
Condom

Reggiseno [Ray-dgee-say-no]
Bra

Sigarette [See-ga-rayt-tay]
Cigarettes

3.5 At the hair saloon

Vorrei tagliare i capelli, per favore.
[Vor-ray ta-lyare ee ka-payl-lee, payr favo-ray]
I'd like a haircut, please.

Devo prendere l'appuntamento?
[Day-vo a-vay-ray lap-poon-tamayn-to?]
Do I need to book?

Potrei prendere un appuntamento?
[Po-tray prayn-day-ray oon ap-poon-ta-mayn-to?]
May I make a reservation?

Che cosa consiglia per i miei capelli?
[Kay ko-sa kon-see-lya payr ee myay ka-payl-lee?]
What do you recommend for my hair?

Ho tanta forfora, può aiutarmi?
[O tanta phor-phora, pwo a-yoo-tar-mee?]
I have a lot of dandruff, could you help me?

Vorrei i capelli più corti.
[Vor-ray ee ka-payl-lee py-oo kor-tee]
I'd like shorter hair.

Può applicarmi le extension?
[Pwo ap-plee-kar-mee lay ay-stayn-syon?]
Could you apply me the extensions?

Vorrei fare una piega liscia.
[Vor-ray pha-ray oona pyay-ga lee-shya]
I'd like a straight blow-dry.

Vorrei avere i capelli mossi.
[Vor-ray a-vay-ray ee ka-payl-lee mos-see]
I'd like to have wavy hair.

Vorrei fare la permanente liscia/riccia.
[Vor-ray pha-ray la payrma-nayn-tay lee-shya/reech-chya]
I'd like to do the straight/curly permanent.

Mi farebbe la frangia, per favore?
[Mee pha-rayb-bay la phran-gya, payr favo-ray?]
Would you give me the fringe, please?

Vorrei questo taglio di capelli.
[Vor-ray qwes-to tal-yo dee ka-payl-lee]
I want this haircut.

Può farmi i capelli così?
[Pwo pahr-mee ee ka-payl-lee ko-see?]
Could you make my hair like this?

Potrebbe tagliarmi la barba?
[Potrayb-bay ta-lyar-mee la barba?]
Could you cut my beard?

Potrebbe regolarmi la barba?
[Potrayb-bay ray-golar-mee la barba?]
Could you regulate my beard?

Può tingermi la barba?
[Pwo teen-jayr-mee lay barba?]
Can you dye my beard?

Può farmi i baffi?
[Pwo phar-mee ee baph-phee?]
Can you do a mustache for me?

Solo una spuntata, grazie.
[Solo oona spoon-tata, gra-tzy-ay]
Just a trim, please.

Li vorrei corti fino a qui.
[Lee vor-ray kor-tee phee-no a qwee]
I would like them to be up to here.

Voglio tingere i miei capelli color…
[Vo-lyo teen-dgyay-ray ee myay ka-payl-lee ko-lor…]
I want to dye my hair in … color.

Vorrei un colore di capelli più chiaro/scuro.
[Vor-ray oon kolo-ray dee ka-payl-lee pee-oo kya-ro/skoo-ro]
I'd like a lighter/darker hair colour.

Vorrei colorare le punte.
[Vor-ray kolo-ra-ray lay poon-tay]
I'd like to dye my hair ends.

Posso fare un trattamento?
[Pos-so pha-ray oon trat-ta-mayn-to?]
May I make a hair treatment?

Ha dei prodotti per capelli?
[A day prodot-tee payr ka-payl-lee?]
Do you have some hair products?

3.6 Eating out

In Italy there are many types of restaurants.

The classical *ristorante* [ree-storan-tay], restaurant, is one of the best places to eat. Usually inside it you can find an experienced chef and a very prepared staff. The food must be of high quality and probably the bill will be slightly high! But if you want to find quality and fine dining, this is the right place.

The *trattoria* [trat-to-rya] is a casual place to go eating where you can find a fixed menu at a low price. Usually trattorias focus on typical dishes, perhaps with a hint of modernity.

The *osteria* [o-stay-rya], then, is a place to eat very similar to the trattoria. The osteria, however, can have more rooted origins and a more regional menu, if not even local.

Maybe you already know what a *pizzeria* [pitz-say-rya] is. If you want to eat one of the most famous Italian dishes, here's the perfect place for you! As well as pizza margherita, a pizzeria has many variations that delight: from pizza with ham to pizza with vegetables. Hawaiian pizza is not covered, of course!

The *enoteca* [ay-no-tay-ka] focuses mainly on the tasting and on the degustation of wines. The culinary choice is limited, but if the wine is to your liking, this is the right place to make your taste buds dance. Besides, Italy has a very wide variety of wines: from the north to the south there are more than 400 types! The real challenge would be to taste them all, perhaps accompanied with typical snacks!

If you go in a *taverna* [ta-vayr-na] it seems to be in an English pub. The difference between the two lies in the products sold: in a taverna you prefer wine to beer or any other modern alcoholic drink!

Dove mi consiglia mangiare?
[Do-vay mee kon-see-lya dee man-dgya-ray?]
Where do you recommend eating?

Mi potrebbe consigliare un buon ristorante?
[Mee po-trayb-bay kon-see-lee-aray oon bwon ree-storan-tay?]
Could you recommend a good restaurant?

Dove vorresti andare a mangiare?
[Do-vay vor-ray-stee anda-ray a man-dgya-ray?]
Where would you like to go to eat?

Dov'è il ristorante?
[Do-vay eel ree-storan-tay?]
Where is the restaurant?

Dove posso fare colazione?
[Do-vay posso fa-ray kola-tzeeo-nay?]
Where may I have breakfast?

Dove posso pranzare?
[Do-vay posso pran-tza-ray?]
Where may I have lunch?

Dov'è un buon posto per cenare?
[Do-vay oon bwon posto do-vay chay-na-ray?]
Where's a good place where I may have dinner?

Ho prenotato un tavolo per due.
[O pray-notato oon ta-volo payr doo-ay]
I booked a table for two.

Vorrei prenotare un tavolo per 5 persone.
[Vor-ray pray-no-taray oon ta-volo payr cheen-qway payr-so-nay]
I would like to reserve a table for 5 people.

Ho molta fame.
[O molta pha-may]
I'm very hungry.

Potrei vedere il menù, per favore?
[Po-tray vay-day-ray eel may-noo, payr favo-ray?]
May I see the menu, please?

Avete il menù per turisti?
[A-vay-tay eel may-noo payr too-ree-stee?]
Do you have the menu for tourists?

Avete il menù brunch?
[Avay-tay eel may-noo branch?]
Do you have the brunch menu?

Qual è il piatto del giorno?
[Qwal ay eel peeat-to dayl dgeeor-no?]
What is the dish of the day?

Che cosa mi consiglia?
[Kay ko-sa mee kon-see-lya?]
What do you suggest?

Quali sono gli ingredienti di questo piatto?
[Qwa-lee sono lee een-gray-dee-ayntee dee qwes-to peeat-to?]
What are the ingredients of this dish?

Avete dei piatti vegetariani?
[A-vay-tay day pyat-tee vay-dgayta-reea-nee?]
Do you have any vegetarian dishes?

Avete dei piatti vegani?
[A-vay-tay day pyat-tee vay-ga-nee?]
Do you have any vegan dishes?

Avete la lista dei vini?
[A-vay-tay la lees-ta day vee-nee?]
Do you have the wine list?

Che cosa mi consiglia da bere?
[Kay ko-sa mee kon-see-lya da bay-ray?]
What do you recommend me to drink?

Qual è il vino locale?
[Qwal ay eel vee-no lo-ka-lay?]
What's the local wine?

Quali dolci avete?
[Qwa-lee dol-chee a-vay-tay?]
Which desserts do you have?

Che piatti di pesce avete?
[Kay peeat-tee dee pay-shay a-vay-tay?]
Which fish dishes do you have?

Servite alcolici?
[Sayr-vee-tay al-ko-lee-chee?]
Do you serve alchool?

Sono allergico/allergica a…
[Sono al-layr-dgee-ko/al-layr-dgee-ka a…]
I'm allergic to…

Prendo questo piatto.
[Prayn-do qwes-to peeat-to]
I'll have this dish.

Vorrei…
[Vor-ray…]
I'd like…

Vorrei questo.
[Vor-ray qway-sto]
I want this one.

Vorrei un piatto di pasta al pomodoro.
[Vor-ray oon pee-atto dee pasta al pomo-doro]
I would like a plate of pasta with tomato sauce.

Vorrei una pizza margherita.
[Vor-ray oona pee-tza mar-gay-ree-ta]
I would like a pizza margherita.

Warning! Traditional pizza is cooked with mozzarella cheese and tomato. If you have any allergy to one of the two ingredients, do not hesitate to ask:

Una pizza… bianca, per favore!
[Oona pee-tza… bee-anka, payr favo-ray!]
A white… pizza, please!
When you want a pizza without tomato.

Una pizza… rossa, per favore!
[Oona pee-tza… ros-sa, payr favo-ray!]
A red… pizza, please!
When you want a pizza without mozzarella.

Vorrei bere dell'acqua naturale.
[Vor-ray bay-ray dayl-la-qwa na-too-ralay]
I'd like to drink some still water.

Prendo una bottiglia di vino rosso.
[Prayn-do oona bot-tee-lya dee vee-no ros-so]
I'll take a bottle of red wine.

Bevo un bicchiere di bollicine, grazie.
[Bay-voo on beek-kyay-ray dee bol-lee-chee-nay, grat-zye]
I'll have a glass of sparkly wine, please.

Una birra, per favore!
[Oona beer-ra, payr favo-ray!]
A beer, please!

Senza ghiaccio, grazie!
[Sayn-tza ghee-at-chyo, gra-tzye!]
No ice, please!

Vorrei un caffè, per favore.
[Vor-ray oon kaf-fay, payr favo-ray]
I'd like a coffee, please.

In Italy, if you really want to say it all, coffee has become a kind of cult lately: just think of the famous espresso coffee! The types of coffee – or its variations – are many. Coffee in Italy can be *liscio* [lee-shee-o], plain, when there is no addition. The *macchiato* [mak-kee-ato], dappled, coffee contains milk. Do you want hot or cold milk? The macchiato may be *macchiato caldo* [mak-kya-to kal-do] if the milk is hot or *macchiato freddo* [mak-kya-to frayd-do] if the milk is at the room temperature. Ask for a *corretto* [kor-rayt-to] if you want alcohol inside your coffee. You may ask to put your favourite alcholic drink in it, but the most used addition is *grappa*, an distillated drink made out processing wine.

Avete un digestivo per me?
[A-vay-tay oon deejay-stee-vo payr may?]
Do you have a digestive for me?

Scusi, dove si trova il bagno, per favore?
[Skoo-see, do-vay see trova eel ba-nyo, payr favo-ray?]
Excuse me, where is the toilet, please?

Sono sazio/sazia.
[Sono sa-tzyo/sa-tzya]
I'm full.

Vorrei dell'altro, per favore.
[Vor-ray dayl-laltro, payr favo-ray]
I'd like to have more, please.

Potrebbe portare il conto, per favore?
[Po-trayb-bay porta-ray eel kon-to, payr favo-ray?]
Could you bring the bill, please?

Il servizio è incluso?
[Eel sayr-vee-tzeeo ay een-kloo-so?]
Is service included?

Il conto, per favore!
[Eel kon-to, payr favo-ray!]
The bill, please!

Possiamo fare conti separati?
[Pos-see-amo pha-ray kon-tee say-para-tee?]
Can we have separate bills?

Posso pagare con la carta?
[Posso pa-ga-ray kon la kar-ta?]
May I pay with a card?

Accettate i buoni pasto?
[A-chayt-tatay ee bwo-nee pasto?]
Do you accept meal vouchers?

Tipping in Italy is considered optional. If you really want to do it, but do not know how much to give, evaluate! The meters of comparison are above all the quality of the service and the total sum of the final bill. One of the methods also used by many Italians is to use the change of your bill as a tip. In that case you could say: "Tenga pure il resto!" [Tayn-ga poo-ray eel rays-to!], "Keep the change!".

3.6.1 What's on the menu?

Acqua frizzante [A-qwa ph-ree-dzan-tay]
Sparkling water

Acqua naturale [A-qwa na-too-ra-lay]
Still water

Analcolico [Anal-ko-lee-ko]
Non-alcoholic

Antipasti [An-tee-pas-tee]
Starters

Aperitivi [A-pay-ree-tee-vee]
Appetizers

Bibite [Bee-bee-ta]
(Soft) drinks

Cappuccino [Kap-poo-tchee-no]
An Italian coffee with double espresso and milk foam

Contorni [Kon-tor-nee]
Side dishes

Coperto [Ko-payr-to]
Cover charge

Dolci [Dol-chee]
Desserts

Liquore [Lee-qwo-ray]
Liquor

Primi piatti [Pree-mee pee-at-tee]
First course

Secondi piatti [Say-kon-dee pee-at-tee]
Main course

3.7 (On the) phone

C'è qualche offerta telefonica per turisti?
[Chay qwal-kay oph-phayr-ta tay-lay-pho-nee-ka payr too-ree-stee?]
Is there any telephone offer for tourists?

Potrei avere una scheda SIM italiana, per favore?
[Po-tray a-vay-ray oona seem eeta-lee-ana, payr favo-ray?]
May I have an Italian SIM card, please?

Qual è il tuo numero?
[Qwal-ay eel too-o noo-may-ro?]
What's your number?

Il mio numero è…
[Eel myo noo-may-ro ay…]
My telephone number is…

Vorrei fare una telefonata, per favore.
[Vor-ray fa-ray oona tay-lay-fonata, payr favo-ray]
I'd like to make a phone call, please.

Potrei fare una chiamata, per favore?
[Pot-ray pha-ray oona kya-mata, payr favo-ray?]
May I make a call, please?

Voglio chiamare all'estero.
[Vo-lyo kee-ama-ray al-lay-stay-ro]
I want to call abroad.

Quali sono le tariffe per chiamare all'estero?
[Qwa-lee sono lay taree-phay payr kya-maray al-lay-stay-ro?]
What are the rates for calling abroad?

Chiamare costa … al minuto.
[Kya-ma-ray kos-ta… al mee-noo-to]
Calling costs … per minute.

Chiamare all'estero costa… al minuto.
[Kya-ma-ray al-lay-stay-ro kos-ta… al mee-noo-to]
Calling abroad costs… per minute.

Potrebbe prestarmi il telefono, per cortesia?
[Potrayb-bay pray-star-mee eel tay-lay-fono, payr kor-tay-sya?]
Could you lend me the phone, please?

C'è una cabina telefonica nelle vicinanze?
[Chay oona ka-bee-na tay-lay-pho-nee-ka nayl-lay vee-chee-nan-tzay?]
Is there a telephone box nearby?

Qual è il numero per chiamare…?
[Qwal-ay eel noo-mayro payr kya-ma-ray…?]
What's the phone number to call…?

Pronto!
[Pron-to!]
Hello!

Chi parla?
[Kee parla?]
Who is it?

Sono Luca.
[Sono Loo-ka]
It's Luca speaking.

Posso parlare con qualcuno che parla inglese?
[Posso parla-ray kon qwal-koo-no kay parla een-glay-say?]
Can I talk to someone who speaks English?

Parla…?
[Parla…?]
Do you speak…?

Inglese [Een-glay-say] English

Francese [Phran-chay-say] French

Tedesco [Tay-day-sko] German

Spagnolo [Spa-nyo-lo] Spanish

Italiano [Eeta-lya-no] Italian

Olandese [Olanday-say] Dutch

Cinese [Chee-nay-say] Chinese

Giapponese [Jyap-po-nay-say] Japanese

Pronto, vorrei parlare con Maria.
[Pronto, vor-ray parla-ray kon Ma-rya]
Hello, I'd like to talk to Maria.

Può mettermi in contatto con…?
[Pwo mayt-tayr-mee een kon-tat-to kon…?]
Can you get me in touch with…?

Scusi, posso parlare con il direttore?
[Skoo-say, posso parla-ray kon eel dee-rayt-toray?]
Excuse me, may I talk to the manager?

Posso lasciare un messaggio a Giuseppe?
[Posso la-sheea-ray oon mays-sadgyo a Dgyoo-sayp-pay?]
May I leave a message to Giuseppe?

Può dire che ho chiamato?
[Pwo dee-ray kay o keea-mato?]
Can you say I called?

Mi scusi, ho sbagliato numero.
[Mee skoo-say, o sba-lee-ato noo-may-ro]
Sorry, wrong number.

È caduta la linea.
[Ay ka-doo-ta la lee-nay-a]
I've been cut off.

Resta in linea!
[Ray-sta een lee-nay-a!]
Hold the line!

Non ti sento, la linea è disturbata.
[Non tee sayn-to, la lee-nay-a ay dees-toor-bata]
I can't hear you, the line is disturbed.

Richiamerò più tardi.
[Ree-kya-may-ro pyoo tar-dee]
I'll call again later.

Richiamo domani.
[Ree-kya-mo doma-nee]
I'll call back tomorrow.

Ti richiamo più tardi.
[Tee ree-kyamo pyoo tar-dee]
I'll call you later.

Scriverò un messaggio.
[Skree-vay-ro oon mays-sad-jyo]
I'll write a message.

Ti contatterò per e-mail.
[Tee kon-tat-tay-ro payr mayl]
I'll contact you via e-mail.

Qual è il tuo indirizzo e-mail?
[Qwal-ay eel too-o een-dee-ree-tzo mail?]
What's your e-mail address?

Come posso contattarti?
[Ko-may pos-so kontat-tar-tee?]
How may I contact you?

3.8 Making plans

Che cosa fai stasera?
[Kay ko-sa fa-ee sta-say-ra?]
What are you doing tonight?

Che cosa facciamo oggi?
[Kay ko-sa fa-chya-mo od-gee?]
What do we do today?

Che cosa vuoi fare?
[Kay ko-sa voo-oee fa-ray?]
What do you want to do?

Che cosa potremmo fare?
[Kay kosa potraym-mo pha-ray?]
What could we do?

Vorresti andare al cinema?
[Vor-ray-stee anda-ray al chee-nay-ma?]
Would you like to go to the cinema?

Andiamo al parco.
[An-dee-amo al par-ko?]
Let's go the the park.

Visitiamo la città?
[Vee-see-tya-mo la cheet-tah?]
Do we visit the city?

Andiamo a…!
[An-dee-amo a…!]
Let's go to…!

Andiamo a mangiare fuori stasera!
[An-dee-amo a man-djay-ray foo-oree sta-say-ra!]
Let's go out for dinner tonight!

Vorresti uscire?
[Vor-ray-stee oo-schee-ray?]
Do you want to go out?

Vorrei…
[Vor-ray…]
I'd like to…

Potremmo…
[Po-traym-mo…]
We could…

Che ne dici di…?
[Kay nay dee-chee dee…?]
What about…?

Che ne dici di guardare un film?
[Kay nay dee-chee dee gwar-da-ray oon feelm?]
What about watching a movie?

Ti piacerebbe vederci per un caffè?
[Tee pia-chay-rayb-bay vay-dayr-chee payr oon kaf-fay?]
Do you fancy meeting for a coffee?

Beviamo qualcosa insieme?
[Bay-vee-amo qwal-kosa een-syay-may?]
Do we drink something together?

A che ora ci incontriamo?
[A kay ora chee een-kon-trya-mo?]
What time shall we meet?

A che ora è l'incontro?
[A kay ora ay leen-kontro?]
What time is the meeting?

Incontriamoci alle…
[Een-kon-tryamo-chee al-lay…]
Let's meet at…

Potremmo incontrarci alle sette.
[Po-traym-mo een-kon-trar-chee al-lay sayt-tay]
We could meet at seven o'clock.

Ci vediamo alle otto!
[Chee vay-dee-amo al-lay otto!]
See you at eight o'clock!

Non posso.
[Non pos-so]
I can't.

Sono impegnato/impegnata.
[Sono eem-pay-nyato/eem-pay-nyata]
I'm busy.

Devo lavorare.
[Day-vo lavora-ray]
I have to work.

Possiamo fare un'altra volta, se vuoi.
[Pos-sya-mo pha-ray oon altra volta, say woo-oee]
We can meet another time, if you want.

Facciamo la prossima volta!
[Fach-chyamo la pros-see-ma volta!]
Let's meet the next time!

3.8.1 Some ideas

Andare a ballare [Anda-ray a bal-la-ray]
Go to the disco

Andare a bere qualcosa [Anda-ray a bay-ray qwal-kosa]
Go out for a drink

Fare una passeggiata [Pha-ray oona pas-say-dgya-ta]
To go out for a walk

Guardare un film [Gwar-da-ray oon feelm]
Watching a movie

Lavorare [Lavora-ray]
To work

Mangiare fuori [Man-dgya-ray phoo-oree]
Eating

Guardare la televisione [Gwar-da-ray la tay-lay-vee-syo-nay]
To watch television

Leggere [Lay-dgyay-ray]
To read

Andare ad un concerto [Anda-ray ad oon kon-chayr-to]
To go to a concert

Visitare la città [Vee-see-ta-ray la cheet-ta]
To visit the city

Riposare [Ree-posa-ray]
To rest

3.9 Spare time

3.9.1 At the museum

Quanto costa l'entrata?
[Qwan-to kos-ta layn-trata?]
How much is it to get in?

Avete lo sconto studenti?
[A-vay-tay lo skon-to stoo-dayn-tee?]
Do you have a student discount?

Il museo è accessibile ai disabili?
[Eel moo-say-o ay ach-chays-see-bee-lay da-ee dee-sa-bee-lee?]
Is the museum accessible by the disabled?

Posso portare un accompagnatore?
[Pos-so porta-ray oon ak-kompa-nyato-ray?]
May I bring a conductor?

A che ora chiudete?
[A kay ora kyoo-day-tay?]
What time do you close?

In quali giorni è aperto il museo?
[Een qwa-lee jor-nee ay apayr-to eel moo-say-o?]
On which days is the museum open?

In quali giorni è chiuso?
[Een qwa-lee jor-nee ay kyoo-so?]
On which days is it closed?

Posso fare foto?
[Posso pha-ray pho-to?]
May I take photos?

C'è una guida per la visita?
[Chay oona gwee-da payr la vee-see-ta?]
Is there a guide for the visit?

Quanto dura la mostra?
[Qwan-to doo-ra lay-sposee-tzyo-nay?]
How long does the exhibition last?

Quanto dura la visita?
[Qwan-to doo-ra la vee-see-ta?]
How long is the visit?

La visita/mostra dura…
[La vee-see-ta/lay-spo-see-tzyo-nay doo-ra…]
The visit/exhibition lasts…

Vorrei usufruire del guardaroba.
[Vor-ray oo-soo-froo-ee-ray dayl gwarda-roba]
I would like to take advantage of the wardrobe.

Quanto costa la guida multimediale?
[Qwan-to kos-ta la qwee-da mool-tee-may-dya-lay?]
How much does the multimedia guide cost?

Avete una cartina del museo?
[A-vay-tay oona kar-teena dayl moo-say-o?]
Do you have a plan of the museum?

Quali artisti sono in mostra?
[Kay artee-stee sono ay-spostee?]
Which artists are in exposition?

C'è un negozio di souvenir?
[Chay eel nay-go-tzyo dayl so-oo-vay-neer?]
Is there a souvenir shop?

3.9.2 At the cinema

Cosa c'è al cinema stasera?
[Ko-sa chay al chee-nay-ma sta-say-ra?]
What's at the cinema tonight?

Hai già visto questo film?
[A-ee dgya vees-to qwes-to feelm?]
Have you already seen this movie?

Guardiamo questo film insieme?
[Gwar-dyamo qway-sto feelm een-syay-may?]
Do we watch this movie together?

A che ora inizia?
[A kay ora ee-nee-tzya?]
What time does it start?

A che ora finisce?
[A kay ora phee-nee-shay?]
What time does it finish?

A che ora è l'ultima proiezione?
[A kay ora ay lool-tee-ma pro-yay-tzyo-nay?]
What time is the last screening?

Quanto dura l'intervallo?
[Qwan-to doo-ra leen-tayr-val-lo?]
How long does the break last?

Che genere di film è?
[Kay jay-nay-ray dee feelm ay?]
What's the movie genre?

È un film di…
[Ay oon feelm dee…]
It's a… movie.

Animazione [A-nee-ma-tzyo-nay] Animation

Avventura [Av-vayn-toora] Adventure

Azione [A-tzyo-nay] Action

Commedia [Kom-may-dya] Comedy

Documentario [Do-koo-mayn-taryo] Documentary

Drammatico [Dram-ma-tee-ko] Dramatic

Erotico [Ay-ro-tee-ko] Erotic

Fantascienza [Phanta-shyay-ntza] Sci-fi

Fantasy [Phan-ta-see] Fantasy

Horror [Or-or] Horror

Musical [Myoo-see-kol] Musical

Poliziesco [Polee-tzyay-sko] Detective movie

Romantico [Roman-tee-ko] Romantic

Storico [Storee-ko] Historic

Thriller [Treel-layr] Thriller

Ho prenotato dei posti.
[O pray-notato day pos-tee]
I've booked some places.

Ho prenotato due biglietti per il film…
[O pray-notato doo-ay bee-lyayt-tee payr eel feelm…]
I booked two tickets for the movie…

Vuoi dei pop-corn?
[Voo-oee day pop-korn?]
Do you want some popcorn?

Vuoi una bibita?
[Voo-oee oona bee-bee-ta?]
Do you want a drink?

Ti è piaciuto il film?
[Tee ay pya-chyoo-to eel feelm?]
Did you like the movie?

Sì, mi è piaciuto (molto).
[See, mee ay pya-chyoo-to (mol-to)]
Yes, I did like it (very much).

No, non mi è piaciuto (per niente).
[No, non mee ay pya-chyoo-to (payr nyayn-tay)]
No, I didn't like it (at all).

Mi piacerebbe rivedere questo film.
[Mee pya-chay-rayb-bay ree-vay-day-ray qway-sto feelm]
I'd like to watch this movie again.

3.9.3 At the club

Vuoi andare in discoteca?
[Voo-oee anda-ray een dee-sko-tay-ka?]
Do you want to go to the disco?

Ci sono dei locali interessanti nei dintorni?
[Chee sono day loka-lee een-tay-rays-santee nay deen-tornee?]
Are there any interesting clubs nearby?

A che ora apre?
[A kay ora a-pray?]
What time does it open?

A che ora chiude?
[A kay ora kyoo-day?]
What time does it close?

Quanto costa entrare?
[Qwan-to kos-ta ayn-tra-ray?]
How much is it to get in?

Fate musica dal vivo?
[Pha-tay moo-see-ka dal vee-vo?]
Do you have live music?

È una festa privata, mi dispiace.
[Ay oona phay-sta pree-vata, mee dees-pya-chay]
It's a private party, I'm sorry.

Il locale è pieno.
[Eel loka-lay ay pyay-no]
The club is full.

Sono sulla lista degli ospiti.
[Sono sool-la lees-ta dayl-lee os-pee-tee]
I'm on the guestlist.

La musica è molto bella!
[La moo-see-ka ay molto bayl-la!]
The music is really good!

Dov'è il bar?
[Do-vay eel bar?]
Where's the bar?

Vuoi bere qualcosa?
[Woo-ee bay-ray qwal-kosa?]
Do you want to drink something?

Ti stai divertendo?
[Tee sta-ee dee-vayr-tayn-do?]
Are you having fun?

Sì, mi sto divertendo (molto).
[See, mee sto dee-vayr-tayn-do (molto)]
Yes, I'm having fun (really much).

Questa musica è molto bella!
[Qwes-ta moo-see-ka ay molto bayl-la!]
This music is really good!

No, non mi sto divertendo/mi sto annoiando.
[No, non mee sto dee-vayr-tayn-do/mee sto an-noyan-do]
No, I'm not having fun/I'm getting bored.

Fa troppo caldo qui dentro.
[Pha troppo kal-do qwee dayn-tro]
It's too hot in here.

C'è troppo rumore qui.
[Chat troppo roo-mo-ray qwee]
It's too loud in here.

Che ne dici di tornare a casa?
[Kay nay dee-chee dee torna-ray a ka-sa?]
What about returning home?

Torno a casa.
[Torno a ka-sa]
I return home.

È stata una bella serata.
[Ay stata oona bayl-la say-rata]
It has been a good evening.

Non è stata una bella serata.
[Non ay stata oona bayl-la say-rata]
It hasn't been a good evening.

Dobbiamo rifare una serata del genere!
[Dob-bya-mo ree-pha-ray oona say-rata dayl jay-nay-ray!]
We have to have a night like this again!

3.9.4 Useful words about spare time
3.9.4.1 Sports

Io pratico…
[Ee-o pra-tee-ko…]
I practice…

Il mio sport preferito è…
[Eel myo sport pray-phay-reeto ay…]
My favourite sport is…

Vorrei praticare…
[Vor-ray pra-tee-ka-ray…]
I'd like to practice…

Arti marziali [Ar-tee mar-tzya-lee]
Martial arts

Atletica [A-tlay-tee-ka]
Athletics

Automobilismo [Aooto-mobee-lee-smo]
Motoring

Biliardo [Bee-lyar-do]
Pool

Bocce [Bo-tchay]
Bowls

Bowling [Boo-leeng]
Bowling

Caccia [Kat-chya]
Hunting

Calcio [Kal-chyo]
Soccer

Canoa [Kano-a]
Canoe

Ciclismo [Chee-clee-smo]
Cycling

Corsa [Kor-sa]
Running

Cricket [Kree-kayt]
Cricket

Danza [Dan-tza]
Dance

Equitazione [Ay-qwee-ta-tzyo-nay]
Horse riding

Ginnastica [Jeen-nastee-ka]
Gymnastics

Lotta [Lot-ta]
Battle

Motociclismo [Moto-chee-klee-smo]
Motorcycling

Nuoto [Noo-oto]
Swimming

Pallacanestro [Palla-ka-nay-stro]
Basketball

Pallavolo [Pal-la-volo]
Volleyball

Pattinaggio [Pat-tee-na-dgyo]
Skating, ice-skating

Pesca [Pays-ka]
Fishing

Rugby [Ra-gbee]
Rugby

Sci [Schee]
Skiing

Snowboard [Sno-bord]
Snowboarding

Tennis [Tayn-nees]
Tennis

3.3.4.2 Other activities

Mi piace…
[Mee pya-chay…]
I like…

Non mi piace…
[Non mee pya-chay…]
I don't like…

Amo…
[A-mo…]
I love…

Odio…
[O-dyo…]
I hate…

Ballare [Bayl-la-ray]
To dance, dancing

Cantare [Kan-ta-ray]
To sing

(Il) Canto [Kan-to]
Singing

(Il) Collezionismo [Kol-lay-tzyo-nee-smo]
Collectibles

Cucinare [Koo-chee-na-ray]
Cooking, to cook

(La) Decorazione [Day-kora-tzyo-nay]
Decoration

Dipingere [Dee-peen-jay-ray]
Painting

Disegnare [Dee-say-nya-ray]
To draw

(Il) Disegno [Dee-say-nyo]
Drawing

Fare spese [Pha-ray spay-say]
Shopping

Fare yoga [Pha-ray yo-ga]
Doing yoga

(La) Fotografia [Photo-gra-phee-a]
Photography

(Il) Giardinaggio [Dgar-dee-na-dgyo]
Gardening

(La) Lettura [Layt-too-ra]
Reading

(Il) Modellismo [Modayl-lee-smo]
Model-making

Navigare su Internet [Nay-vee-garay soo Een-tayr-nayt]
Surfing on the Internet

Passeggiare [Pas-say-dgya-ray]
Going for a walk, to go for a walk

(Il) Restauro [Ray-sta-ooro]
Restoration

(Il) Ricamo [Ree-kamo]
Embroidery

(Gli) Scacchi [Skak-kee]
Chess

(La) Scrittura [Skreet-too-ra]
Writing

Scrivere [Skree-vay-ray]
To write

(La) Scultura [Skool-too-ra]
Sculpture

Suonare uno strumento musicale [Soo-ona-ray oono stroo-mayn-to moo-see-kalay]
Playing a musical instrument

Uscire [Oo-shee-ray]
Going to, to go out

(Il) Volontariato [Volonta-ree-ato]
Voluntary work

3.10 Emergencies

In Italy, as in many other countries belonging to the European Union, the only emergency number is 112. If you have an emergency, do not hesitate to call it. This number, however, is partially active only in some regions; in others, it belongs to the Carabinieri, a type of Italian police force. The rule is the same: if you need another type of help, Carabinieri will not hesitate to pass the call and to help you out!

Ho un'emergenza.
[O oon ay-mayr-dgyayn-tza]
I have an emergency.

Ho bisogno di…
[O bee-so-nyo dee…]
I need…

Aiuto!
[A-y-ooto!]
Help!

Ho bisogno di aiuto!
[O bee-sonyo dee a-y-ooto!]
I need help!

Aiuto, non mi sento bene!
[A-y-ooto, non mee sayn-to bay-nay]
Help, I'm not feeling well!

Qualcuno faccia qualcosa!
[Qwal-koo-no pha-tchya qwal-kosa!]
Someone do something!

Vai via!
[Vada vee-a!]
Go away!

Chiamo la polizia!
[Kee-amo la po-lee-tzya!]
I'll call the police!

Bisogna chiamare la polizia!
[Bee-so-nya kya-ma-ray la po-lee-tzya!]
We must call the police!

Qualcuno chiami un'ambulanza!
[Qwal-koono kya-mee oon am-boo-lantza!]
Someone call an ambulance!

Per favore, mi aiuti.
[Payr favo-ray, mee a-yoo-tee!]
Please, help me.

Mi sono perso/persa.
[Mee sono payr-so/payr-sa]
I got lost.

Sono stato/stata derubato/derubata.
[Sono stato/stata day-roo-bato/day-roo-bata]
I've been robbed.

La mia macchina si è rotta.
[La mya mak-kee-na see ay rotta]
My car has broken down.

Ho una gomma a terra.
[O oona gomma a tayr-ra]
I have a flat tire.

La batteria della mia macchina è scarica.
[La bat-tay-rya dayl-la mya mak-keena ay ska-ree-ka]
My car battery is low.

Non so quale sia il problema.
[Non so qwa-lay see-a eel pro-blay-ma]
I don't know what the problem is.

Ho un problema.
[O oon pro-blay-ma]
I have a problem.

C'è un problema con…
[Chay oon pro-blay-ma kon…]
There's a problem with…

C'è un incendio!
[Chay oon een-chayn-dyo!]
There's a fire!

C'è stato un incidente.
[Chay stato oon een-chee-dayn-tay]
There has been an accident.

Qualcuno si è fatto male.
[Qwal-koo-no see ay phat-to ma-lay]
Someone got hurt.

Mi sono fatto/fatta male.
[Mee sono phat-to/phat-ta ma-lay]
I got hurt.

C'è bisogno di un'ambulanza!
[Chay bee-so-nyo dee oon am-boo-lantza!]
We need an ambulance!

Non trovo più…
[Non trovo py-oo…]
I can't find… anymore.

Non riesco a trovare…
[Non ree-ay-sko a trova-ray…]
I can't find…

Non trovo più i miei documenti.
[Non trovo py-oo ee myay do-koo-mayn-tee]
I can't find my documents anymore.

Non riesco a trovare la strada per l'hotel.
[Non ree-ay-sko a tro-va-ray la strada payr lo-tayl]
I can't find the way to the hotel.

Ho bisogno di fare una denuncia.
[O bee-so-nyo dee fa-ray oona day-nun-chya]
I need to make a complaint.

Vorrei contattare la mia ambasciata.
[Vor-ray kon-tatta-ray la mya amba-shee-ata]
I would like to contact my embassy.

Non riesco a contattare la mia famiglia.
[Non ree-ay-sko a kon-tatta-ray la mya pha-mee-lya]
I can not contact my family.

3.11 Asking for Internet and WiFi

C'è l'accesso a Internet qui?
[Chay lach-chays-so a Een-tayr-nayt qwee?]
Is there Internet access here?

L'accesso a Internet è a pagamento?
[Lach-chays-so a Een-tayr-nayt ay a paga-mayn-to?]
Is the Internet access for a fee?

Avete il WiFi qui?
[A-vay-tay eel WiFi qwee?]
Do you have WiFi here?

Qual è la password per Internet?
[Qwal-ay la password payr Een-tayr-nayt?]
What's the password for the internet?

C'è un Internet point nelle vicinanze?
[Chay oon Een-tayr-nay point nayl-lay vee-chee-nan-tzay?]
Is there an Internet point nearby?

C'è un WiFi pubblico qui?
[Chay oon WiFi poob-blee-ko qwee?]
Is there public WiFi here?

3.12 Making compliments

Ti sta bene!
[Tee sta bay-nay!]
That looks good on you!

Sei molto simpatico/simpatica.
[Say molto seem-patee-ko/seem-patee-la]
You're really nice.

Stai una favola!
[Sta-ee oona pha-vola!]
You look really good!

Ottimo lavoro!
[Ot-tee-mo lavoro!]
Good job!

Ben fatto!
[Bayn phat-to!]
Well done!

3.12.1 And going deeper…

Posso sedermi con te?
[Posso say-dayr-mee kon tay?]
May I sit with you?

Posso offrirti qualcosa da bere?
[Posso oph-phreer-tee qwal-kosa da bay-ray?]
May I offer you something to drink?

Vieni qui spesso?
[Vyay-neeqwee spays-so?]
Do you come here often?

Che cosa fai nella vita?
[Kay ko-sa pha-ee nayl-la vee-ta?]
What do you do for a living?

Vuoi ballare con me?
[Voo-oee bayl-la-ray kon may?]
Do you want to dance with me?

Andiamo da te/da me?
[Andee-amo da tay/da may?]
My place or yours?

Hai qualche impegno per stasera?
[A-ee qwal-kay eem-pay-nyo payr sta-sayra?]
Do you have any plans for tonight?

Andiamo a mangiare insieme qualche volta?
[Andee-amo a man-dgya-ray een-syay-may qwal-kay volta?]
Would you like to eat together sometime?

Ci prendiamo un caffè?
[Chee prayn-dyamo oon kaf-fay?]
Would you like to go get a coffee?

Posso accompagnarti a casa?
[Posso ak-kom-pa-nyar-tee a ka-sa?]
May I walk/drive you home?

Ti va di incontrarci di nuovo?
[Tee va dee een-kon-tra-rchee dee noo-ovo?]
Would you like to meet again?

Vorrei rivederti.
[Vor-ray ree-vay-dayr-tee]
I'd like to see you again.

Sei bellissimo/bellissima!
[Say bayl-lees-see-mo/bayl-lees-see-ma]
You're gorgeous!

Sei divertente!
[Say dee-vayr-tayn-tay!]
You're funny!

Hai degli occhi bellissimi!
[A-ee dayl-lee ok-kee bayl-lees-see-mee]
You have beautiful eyes!

Ho pensato a te tutto il giorno!
[O payn-sato a tay toot-to eel dgyor-no!]
I have been thinking about you all day!

È stato bello stare con te.
[Ay stato bayl-lo sta-ray kon tay]
It was nice to be with you.

Non sono interessato/interessata.
[Non sono een-tay-rays-sato/een-tay-rays-sata]
I'm not interested.

Lasciami in pace.
[La-schya-mee een pa-chay]
Leave me alone.

Toglimi le mani di dosso!
[To-lee-mee lay ma-nee dee dosso!]
Get your hands off of me!

Chapter 4 - Talking about you

4.1 Introducing yourself

Come ti chiami?
[Ko-may tee kya-may?]
What's your name?

Mi chiamo Susanna Verdi.
[Mee kee-amo Soo-sanna Vayr-dee]
My name is Susanna.

Il mio nome è Paolo.
[Eel mee-o no-may ay Paolo]
My name is Paolo.

Il mio cognome è Rossi.
[Eel mee-o ko-nee-omay ay Ros-see]
My surname is Rossi.

Quanti anni hai?
[Qwan-tee an-nee a-ee?]
How old are you?

Ho 36 anni.
[O trayn-ta-say an-nee]
I'm 36 years-old.

Da dove vieni?
[Da do-vay vyay-nee?]
Where are you from?

Dove abiti?
[Do-vay abee-tee?]
Where do you live?

Che origini hai?
[Kay oree-jee-nee a-y?]
What are your origins?

Qual è la tua nazionalità?
[Qwal-ay la too-a natzyo-nalee-ta?]
What's your nationality?

Sono inglese/americano.
[Sono een-glay-say/amay-ree-kano]
I'm English/American.

Vengo dal Regno Unito.
[Vayn-go dal Ray-neeo Oo-nee-to]
I come from the United Kingdom.

Abito in Inghilterra.
[Abee-to een Een-geel-tayrra]
I live in England.

Abito a Londra.
[Abee-to a Londra]
I live in London.

Vivo in una grande città.
[Vee-vo een oona gran-day cheet-ta]
I live in a big city.

Vivo in un piccolo paese di montagna.
[Vee-vo een oon peek-kolo pa-ay-say dee monta-nee-a]
I live in a small mountain village.

Abito in campagna.
[Abee-to een kam-pa-nee-a]
I live in the countryside.

Che lingue parli?
[Kay leen-gwe par-lee?]
What languages do you speak?

Parli…?
[Par-lee…?]
Do you speak…?

Parlo italiano e inglese.
[Parlo eeta-leea-no ay een-glay-say]
I speak Italian and English.

Non parlo spagnolo.
[Non so parla-ray spa-neeo-lo]
I don't speak Spanish.

Sei capace a…?
[Say kapa-chay a…?]
Are you able to…?

Sai…?
[Sa-ee?]
Can you…?

Qual è la tua situazione sentimentale?
[Qwal-ay la too-a see-twa-tzyo-nay sayn-tee-mayn-ta-lay?]
What is your relationship status?

Sono sposato, mia moglie si chiama Laura.
[Sono sposato, mee-a mo-lee-ay see kee-ama Laoo-ra]
I'm married, my wife's name is Laura.

Sono sposata, mio marito si chiama Nicola.
[Sono sposata, mee-o ma-ree-to see kee-ama Nee-kola]
I'm married, my husband's name is Nicola.

Sono single.
[Sono seen-gol]
I'm single.

Sono fidanzato, ho la ragazza.
[Sono fee-dantza-to, o la raga-tza]
I'm engaged, I have a girlfriend.

Sono fidanzata, ho il ragazzo.
[Sono fee-dantza-ta, o eel raga-tzo]
I'm engaged, I have a boyfriend.

Sono divorziato/divorziata.
[Sono dee-vor-tzya-to/dee-vor-tzya-ta]
I'm divorced.

Hai figli?
[A-y feel-y?]
Do you have children?

Ho un figlio/una figlia.
[O oon fee-lyo/oonafee-lya]
I have a son/a daughter.

Ho 3 figli.
[O tray fee-lee]
I have 3 children.

Non ho figli.
[Non o fee-lee]
I have no children.

Sono qui per una vacanza.
[Sono qwee payr oona vakan-tza]
I'm here on holiday.

Sono qui per lavoro.
[Sono qwee payr lavoro]
I'm here on business.

Alloggio in hotel.
[Al-lo-dgyo een o-tayl]
I lodge in a hotel.

Alloggio da parenti/amici.
[Al-lo-dgyo da pa-rayn-tee/a-mee-chee]
I lodge by relatives/friends.

4.1.1 I come from…

Io vengo da…
[Ee-o vayn-go da…]
I come from…

Africa [A-free-ka]
Africa

Albania [Alba-nya]
Albania

America [A-may-ree-ka]
America

Argentina [Ar-jayn-tee-na]
Argentina

Asia [A-see-a]
Asia

Australia [A-oo-stra-lya]
Australia

Austria [A-oo-strya]
Austria

Belgio [Bayl-gyo]
Belgium

Bielorussia [Bee-aylo-roos-sya]
Belarus

Brasile [Bra-see-lay]
Brasil

Bulgaria [Bool-gary]
Bulgaria

Canada [Kana-da]
Canada

Cina [Chee-na]
China

Croazia [Kro-a-tzya]
Croatia

Danimarca [Da-nee-mar-ka]
Denmark

Egitto [Ay-geet-to]
Egypt

Estonia [Aysto-nya]
Estonia

Europa [Ay-ooro-pa]
Europe

Filippine [Phee-leep-pee-nay]
Philippines

Finlandia [Pheen-lan-dya]
Finland

Francia [Phran-chya]
France

Germania [Dger-manya]
Germany

Giappone [Djap-pone]
Japan

Grecia [Gray-chya]
Greece

India [Een-dya]
India

Indonesia [Een-donay-sya]
Indonesia

Irlanda [Eer-landa]
Ireland

Italia [Ee-ta-lya]
Italy

Lettonia [Layt-to-nya]
Latvia

Lituania [Lee-too-anya]
Lithuania

Lussemburgo [Loos-saym-boor-go]
Luxembourg

Marocco [Marok-ko]
Morocco

Messico [Mays-see-ko]
Mexico

Moldavia [Molda-vya]
Moldova

Olanda [Olan-da]
Holland

Paesi Bassi [Pa-ay-see Bas-see]
Netherlands

Polonia [Polo-nya]
Poland

Portogallo [Porto-gal-lo]
Portugal

Regno Unito [Ray-nyo Oo-nee-to]
United Kingdom

Repubblica Ceca [Ray-poob-lee-ka Chay-ka]
Checz Republic, Czechia

Romania [Roo-ma-nya]
Romania

Russia [Roos-sya]
Russia

Serbia [Sayr-bya]
Serbia

Spagna [Spa-nya]
Spain

Stati Uniti [Sta-tee Oonee-tee]
United States

Sud Africa [Sood Afree-ka]
South Africa

Svezia [Svay-tzya]
Sweden

Tailandia [Taee-lan-dya]
Thailand

Turchia [Toor-kya]
Turkey

Ucraina [Ookra-nya]
Ucraine

Ungheria [Oon-gay-rya]
Hungary

Venezuela [Vay-nay-tzoo-ayla]
Venezuela

4.1.2 So I am…

Africano/africana [A-free-kano/a-free-kana]
African

Albanese [Alba-nay-say]
Albanian

Americano/americana [A-may-ree-ka]
America

Argentino/argentina [Ar-jayn-tee-no/ar-jayn-tee-na]
Argentinian

Asiatico/asiatica [Asya-tee-ko/Asya-tee-ka]
Asian

Australiano/australiana [Aoo-stra-lyano/aoo-stra-lyana]
Australian

Austriaco/austriaca [Aoo-strya-ko/aoo-strya-ka]
Austrian

Belga [Bayl-ga]
Belgian

Bielorusso/bielorussa [Bee-aylo-roos-so/bee-aylo-roos-sa]
Belarussian

Brasiliano/brasiliana [Bra-see-lyano/bra-see-lyana]
Brasilian

Bulgaro/bulgara [Bool-garo/bool-gara]
Bulgarian

Canadese [Kana-day-say]
Canadian

Ceco/ceca [Chay-ko, chay-ka]
Czech

In the written language, a simple "i" can make the difference! If you come from the Czech Republic, do not write that you are *cieco/cieca*, otherwise you can make it clear that your sight is inexistent!

Cinese [Chee-nay-say]
Chinese

Croato/croata [Kro-ato/kro-ata]
Croatian

Danese [Da-nay-say]
Danish

Egiziano/egiziana [Ay-gee-tzyano/ay-gee-tzyana]
Egyptian

Estone [Aysto-nay]
Estonian

Europeo/europea [Ay-ooro-pay-o/ay-ooro-pay-a]
European

Filippino/filippina [Phee-leep-pee-no/phee-leep-pee-na]
Filipino

Finlandese [Pheen-lan-day-say]
Finnish

Francese [Phran-chay-say]
French

Gallese [Gal-lay-say]
Welsh

Giapponese [Djap-ponay-say]
Japanese

Greco/greca [Gray-ko/gray-ka]
Greek

Indiano/indiana [Een-dya-no/een-dya-na]
Indian

Indonesiano/indonesiana [Een-donay-sya-no/een-donay-sya-na]
Indonesian

Inglese [Een-glay-say]
English

Irlandese [Eer-lan-day-say]
Irish

Italiano/italiana [Ee-ta-lya-no/Ee-ta-lya-na]
Italian

Lettone [Layt-to-nay]
Latvian

Lituano/lituana [Lee-too-ano/lee-too-ana]
Lithuanian

Lussemburghese [Loos-saym-boor-gay-say]
Luxembourg inhabitant

Marocchino/marocchina [Marok-keeno/marok-keena]
Moroccan

Messicano/messicana [Mays-see-kano/mays-see-kana]
Mexican

Moldavo/moldava [Molda-vo/molda-va]
Moldovan

Olandese [Olan-day-say]
Dutch

Polacco/polacca [Polak-ko/polak-ka]
Polish

Portoghese [Porto-gay-say]
Portuguese

Romeno/romena [Ro-mayno/ro-mayna]
Romanian

Russo/russa [Roos-so/roos-sa]
Russian

Scozzese [Sko-tzay-say]
Scottish

Serbo/serba [Sayr-bo/sayr-ba]
Serbian

Spagnolo/spagnola [Spa-nyolo/spa-nyola]
Spanish

Statunitense [Sta-too-nee-tayn-say]
United States Inhabitant

Sudafricano/Sudafricana [Sood-afree-kano/sood-afree-kana]
South African

Svedese [Svay-day-say]
Swedish

Tailandese [Taee-lan-day-say]
Thai

Tedesco/tedesca [Tay-days-ko/tay-day-ska]
German

Turco/turca [Toor-ko/toor-ka]
Turkish

Probably by instinct you would say that you are *turchese*, but beware: *turchese* [toor-kay-say] is a color, which corresponds to turquoise, the most common light blue.

Ucraino/ucraina [Ookra-eeno/ookra-eena]
Ucrainian

Ungherese [Oon-gay-ray-say]
Hungarian

Venezuelano/venezuelana [Vay-nay-tzoo-ayla-no/vay-nay-tzoo-ayla-na]
Venezuelan

4. 2 What's your work?

Che lavoro fai?
[Kay lavoro fa-ee?]
What's your job?

Qual è il lavoro dei tuoi sogni?
[Qwal-ay eel lavoro day too-ee so-jnee?]
What's your dream job?

Che cosa studi?
[Kay ko-sa stoo-dee?]
What do you study?

Vado a scuola, sono uno studente.
[Vado a skoo-ola, sono oono stoo-dayn-tay]
I go to school, I'm a student.

Studio legge.
[Stoo-dyo layd-jay]
I'm studying law.

Voglio diventare medico.
[Vo-lyo dee-vayn-ta-ray may-dee-ko]
I want to become a doctor.

Lavoro da casa.
[Lavoro da ka-sa]
I work from home.

Ho un lavoro in proprio.
[O oon lavoro een pro-pryo]
I have a self-employed job.

Sono disoccupato/disoccupata.
[Sono dee-sok-koo-pato/dee-sok-koo-pata]
I'm unemployed.

Sono in pensione.
[Sono een payn-syo-nay]
I am retired.

Lavoro come infermiere/infermiera.
[Lavoro ko-may een-fayr-myay-ray/een-fayr-myay-ra]
I work as a nurse.

Sono casalinga.
[Sono ka-sa-leen-ga]
I'm an housewife.

Sono direttore/direttrice.
[Sono dee-rayt-to-ray/dee-rayt-tree-chay]
I'm a manager.

4.2.1 Professions names

Agente [A-jayn-tay]
Agent

Allenatore/allenatrice [Al-laynato-ray/al-layna-tree-chay]
Trainer

Architetto [Ar-keet-taytto]
Architect

Assicuratore/assicuratrice [As-see-kurato-ray/as-see-lura-tree-chay]
Insurer

Autista [A-oo-tee-sta]
Driver

Avvocato [Avvo-kato]
Lawyer

Banchiere [Bank-yay-ray]
Banker

Bibliotecario/bibliotecaria [Bee-blyo-tay-karyo/bee-blyo-tay-karya]
Librarian

Commesso/commessa [Kom-mays-so/kom-mays-sa]
Shop assistant

Contabile [Konta-bee-lay]
Accountant

Contadino/contadina [konta-dee-no/konta-dee-na]
Farmer

Cuoco/cuoca [Koo-oko/koo-oka]
Chef, cooker

Dentista [Dayn-tee-sta]
Dentist

Ingegnere [Een-jay-nyay-ray]
Engineer

Insegnante [Een-say-nyan-tay]
Teacher

Libero professionista [Lee-bay-ro pro-phays-syo-nees-ta]
Freelance

Meccanico [Mayk-ka-nee-ko]
Mechanic

Notaio [Nota-yo]
Notary

Operaio/operaia [Opay-ra-yo/opay-ra-ya]
Worker

Segretario/Segretaria [Say-gray-tarya]
Secretary

4.3 What's your religion?

Sei religioso/religiosa?
[Say ray-lee-dgyoso/ray-lee-dgyosa?]
Are you religious?

No, sono ateo/atea.
[No, sono a-tay-o/a-tay-a]
No, I'm an atheist.

No, sono agnostico/agnostica.
[No, sono anyo-stee-ko/anyo-stee-ka]
No, I'm agnostic.

Quale religione pratichi?
[Qwa-lay ray-lee-dgyo-nay pra-tee-kee?]
What religion are you?

Qual è la tua religione?
[Qwal-ay la too-a ray-lee-dgyo-nay?]
What's your religion?

Credi in qualcosa?
[Kray-dee een qwal-kosa?]
Do you believe in something?

In che cosa credi?
[Een kay ko-sa kray-dee?]
What do you believe in?

Credi in Dio?
[Kray-dee een Dyo?]
Do you believe in God?

Credo/non credo in Dio.
[Kray-d/non kray-do een Dyo]
I believe/do not believe in God.

4.3.1 I am...

Cristiano/Cristiana [Kree-stya-no/Kree-stya-na]
Kristian

Musulmano/Musulmana [Moo-sool-mano/Moo-sool-mana]
Muslim

Buddista [Bood-dee-sta]
Buddhist

Protestante [Pro-tay-stan-tay]
Protestant

Cattolico/Cattolica [Kat-tolee-ko/Kat-tolee-ka]
Catholic

Ebreo/Ebrea [Ay-bray-o/Ay-bray-a]
Jewish

4.3.2 Religious places

Chiesa [Kyay-sa]
Church

Moschea [Mos-kay-a]
Mosque

Sinagoga [Seena-gow-ga]
Synagogue

Tempio [Taym-pyo]
Temple

4.4 Likes, dislikes, feelings

Ti piace?
[Tee pya-chay?]
Do you like it?

Mi piace.
[Mee pya-chay]
I like it.

Non mi piace.
[Non mee pya-chay]
I don't like it.

Va bene?
[Va bay-nay?]
Is it ok?

Va bene.
[Va bay-nay]
It's ok.

Non va bene.
[Non va bay-nay]
It's not ok.

Che cosa ne pensi?
[Kay ko-sa nay payn-see?]
What do you think about it?

Come lo trovi?
[Ko-may lo tro-vee?]
How do you find it?

Penso che sia molto bello/bella!
[Payn-so kay sya molto bayl-lo/bayl-la!]
I think it's very nice!

Penso che sia brutto/brutta.
[Payn-so kay sya broot-to/broot-ta]
I think it's ugly.

Non lo trovo entusiasmante.
[Non lo trovo ayn-too-syasman-tay]
I do not find it exciting.

Lo trovo fantastico!
[Lo trovo phan-tas-tee-ko!]
I find it fantastic!

È una buona idea!
[Ay oona bwo-na eed-ay-a!]
It's a good idea!

È un'idea che non mi ispira.
[Ay oon-ee-day-a kay non mee ees-pee-ra]
It's an idea that doesn't inspire me.

Non vedo l'ora!
[Non vay-do lo-ra!]
I'm looking forward to it!

Non sopporto…
[Non sop-porto…]
I can not stand…

Non sopporto aspettare a lungo.
[Non sopporto as-payt-ta-ray a loon-go]
I can not stand waiting for a long time.

Cosa ti piace fare?
[Ko-sa tee pya-chay fa-ray?]
What do you like to do?

Cosa ti piace fare nel tuo tempo libero?
[Ko-sa tee pya-chay fa-ray nayl too-o taympo lee-bay-ro?]
What do you like to do in your spare time?

Mi piace…
[Mee pya-chay…]
I like…

Non mi piace…
[Non me pya-chay…]
I don't like…

Mi piace fare passeggiate in montagna.
[Mee pya-chay fa-ray pas-say-djya-tay een monta-nya]
I like walking in the mountains.

Non mi piace guardare la televisione.
[Non mee pya-chay gwarda-ray la tay-lay-vee-syo-nay]
I don't like watching television.

Nel mio tempo libero mi piace leggere.
[Nayl myo taym-po lee-bay-ro mee pya-chay ledg-ay-ray]
In my spare time I like reading.

Amo..
[A-mo…]
I love…

Amo ballare.
[Amo bayl-la-ray]
I love dancing.

Odio…
[O-dee-o]
I hate…

Odio giocare a tennis.
[O-dee-o jyo-ka-ray a tayn-nees]
I hate playing tennis.

Qual è il tuo film preferito?
[Qwal-ay eel too-o feelm pray-fay-reeto?]
What's your favourite movie?

Qual è la tua canzone preferita?
[Qwal-ay lay too-a kan-tzonay pray-fay-reeta?]
What's your favourite song?

Il mio film preferito è "Titanic."
[Eel myo feelm pray-fay-reeto ay "Tee-taneek"]
My favourite movie is "Titanic."

La mia canzone preferita è "Greensleves."
[La mya kan-tzonay pray-fay-reeta ay "Greensleves"]
My favourite song is "Greensleves."

Come stai?
[Ko-may sta-ee?]
How are you?

Sto bene, grazie.
[Sto bay-nay, gra-tzye]
I'm fine, thank you.

Cosa mi racconti di nuovo?
[Kosa mee rak-kon-tee dee noo-ovo?]
What's new?

Non sto bene.
[Non sto bay-nay]
I'm not fine.

Sono felice!
[Sono fay-lee-chay!]
I'm happy!

Sono triste.
[Sono tree-stay]
I'm sad.

Sono eccitato/eccitata.
[Sono ay-chee-tato/ay-chee-tata]
I'm excited.

Sono annoiato/annoiata.
[Sono an-no-yato/an-no-yata]
I'm bored.

Non mi sento molto bene.
[Non mee sayn-to molto bay-nay]
I'm not feeling very well.

Mi sto annoiando.
[Mee sto an-no-yando]
I'm getting bored.

Sto (abbastanza) bene.
[Sto (abbastan-tza) bay-nay]
I'm (quite) fine.

Sto male.
[Sto ma-lay]
I'm bad.

Non mi sento bene.
[Non mee sayn-to bay-nay]
I'm not feeling well.

4.5 Talking about your daily routine

Mi sveglio alle 7.
[Mee svay-lyo al-lay o-ray sayt-tay]
I wake up at 7 o'clock.

Mi alzo alle 7.
[Mee al-tzo al-lay o-ray sayt-tay]
I get up at 7 o'clock.

Mi vesto.
[Mee vay-sto]
I get dressed.

Solitamente faccio colazione con tè e biscotti.
[Solee-tamayn-tay fa-chyo kola-tzyo-nay kon tay ay bee-skot-tee]
Usually I have breakfast with tea and biscuits.

Per colazione mangio…
[Payr kola-tzyo-nay man-dgyo…]
For breakfast I eat…

Posso fare una doccia?
[Posso pha-ray oona do-tchya?]
May I take a shower?

Vado all'università tre volte a settimana.
[Vado al-loo-nee-vayr-see-ta tray vol-tay a sayt-tee-mana]
I go to University three times a week.

Vado al lavoro/a scuola tutti i giorni.
[Vado al lavoro/a sk-wo-la toot-tee ee dgyor-nee]
I go to work/to school every day.

A che ora pranzi/ceni?
[A kay ora pran-tzee/chay-nee?]
What time do you have lunch/dinner?

Spesso pranzo alle 13.
[Spays-so pran-tzo al-lay tray-dee-chee]
Often I have lunch at 13 o'clock.

Tutte le sere ceno alle 20.
[Toot-tay lay say-ray chay-no al-lay o-ray 20]
Every evening I have dinner at 20 o'clock.

Dopo il lavoro, torno a casa.
[Dopo eel lavoro, torno a ka-sa]
After work, I return home.

Vado in palestra una volta a settimana.
[Vado een pa-lay-stra oona volta a sayt-tee-mana]
I go to the gym one time every week.

Non sempre faccio i compiti/studio.
[Non saym-pray fa-chyo ee kom-pee-tee/stoo-dyo]
I do not always do homework/study.

Nel mio tempo libero mi piace…
[Nayl myo taym-po lee-bay-ro mee pya-chay…]
In my free time I like…

Vado a dormire alle 22.
[Vado a dor-mee-ray al-lay o-ray 22]
I go to sleep at 22 o'clock.

Vado a letto molto tardi.
[Vado a layt-to molto tar-dee]
I go to bed really late.

Mi addormento sempre presto.
[Mee addor-mayn-to saym-pray pray-sto]
I always fall asleep early.

4.5.1 Adverbs of time

1 (Una) volta al mese [Oona volta al may-say]
One time a month

2 (Due) volte a settimana [Doo-ay vol-tay a sayt-tee-mana]
Two times a week

A volte [A vol-tay]
Sometimes

Ancora [An-kora]
Still

Dal 2001 [Dal doo-ay-mee-la-oono]
Since 2001

Domani [Doma-nee]
Tomorrow

Frequentemente [Fray-qwayn-tay-mayn-tay]
Frequently

Generalmente [Dgyay-nay-ral-mayn-tay]
Generally

Ieri [Ee-ay-ree]
Yesterday

Il mese scorso [Eel may-say skor-so]
Last month

L'anno scorso [Lan-no skor-so]
Last years

La settimana scorsa [La set-tee-mana skor-sa]
Last week

Mai [Ma-ee]
Never/ever

Non ancora [Non an-kora]
Yet/not yet

Normalmente [Normal-mayn-tay]
Normally

Occasionalmente [Ok-ka-syonal-mayn-tay]
Occasionally

Oggi [Od-jee]
Today

Ogni settimana/mese/anno [O-gnee sayt-tee-mana/may-say/anno]
Every week/month/year

Ora/adesso [Ora/a-days-so]
Now

Per un anno [Payr oon anno]
For a year

Più tardi [Pee-oo tar-dee]
Later

Presto [Pray-sto]
Early

Qualche volta [Qwal-kay vol-ta]
Sometimes

Raramente [Rara-mayn-tay]
Seldom/rarely

Regolarmente [Ray-golar-mayn-tay]
Regularly

Spesso [Spays-so]
Often

Tardi [Tar-dee]
Late

Tutti i giorni [Toot-tee ee dgyor-nee]
Every day

Chapter 5 - Health

5.1 Going to the doctor

Scusi, dov'è il dottore più vicino?
[Skoo-see, do-vay eel dotto-ray py-oo vee-chee-no?]
Sorry, where is the nearest doctor?

Ho bisogno di un dottore.
[O bee-so-nyo dee oon dotto-ray]
I need a doctor.

Ho bisogno di un dentista.
[O bee-so-nyo dee oon dayn-tee-sta]
I need a dentist.

Che orari fa il dottore/il dentista?
[Kay ora-ree fa eel dotto-ray/eel dayn-tee-sta?]
What timetables does the doctor/the doctor have?

È urgente.
[Ay oor-jayn-tay]
It's urgent.

Non mi sento bene, dottore, ho un forte mal di testa.
[Non mee sayn-to bay-nay, dot-to-ray, o oon phor-tay mal dee tays-ta]
I'm not feeling well, doctor, I have a strong headache.

Dove le fa male?
[Do-vay lay fa ma-lay?]
Where does it hurt?

È la prima volta che succede?
[Ay la pree-ma volta kay sooch-chay-day?]
It is the first time happening?

No, è da tanto che ho questi sintomi.
[No, ay da tanto kay o qwes-tee seen-to-mee]
No, it's been a while I have these symptoms.

Sì, è la prima volta.
[See, ay la pree-ma volta]

Mi sento così da 5 giorni.
[Mee sayn-to ko-see da cheen-qway dgyor-nee]
I've been feeling like this for 5 days.

Mi fa male qui.
[Mee fa ma-lay qwee]
It hurts here.

Mi fa male il piede.
[Mee fa ma-lay eel pyay-day]
My foot hurts.

Mi fa male un dente.
[Mee fa ma-lay oon dayn-te]
My tooth hurts.

Credo di avere una carie.
[Kray-do dee avay-ray oona ka-ryay]
I think I have a cavity.

Ho i denti sensibili, mi fanno molto male.
[O ee dayn-tee sayn-see-bee-lee, mee phan-no molto ma-lay]
I have sensitive teeth, they hurt very much.

Mi fa male tutto.
[Mee pha ma-lay toot-to]
It hurts everywhere.

Non riesco a respirare bene.
[Non ryay-sko a ray-spee-raray bay-nay]
I can not breathe well.

Non ho molta energia.
[Non o molta ay-nayr-jya]
I've got very little energy.

Non riesco a dormire.
[Non ree-ays-ko a dor-mee-ray]
I can't sleep.

Mi sono tagliato/tagliata.
[Mee sono ta-lya-to/ta-lya-ta]
I cut myself.

Mi sono scottato/scottata.
[Mee sono skot-tato/skot-tata]
I burnt myself.

Soffro di…
[Soph-phro dee…]
I suffer from…

Ho la pressione alta/bassa.
[O la prays-syo-nay alta/bassa]
I have high/low blood pressure.

Il mio gruppo sanguigno è…
[Eel myo groop-po san-gwee-nyo ay…]
My blood group is…

Che cosa posso fare?
[Kay kosa pos-so pha-ray?]
What may I do?

Che cosa posso prendere?
[Kay kosa pos-so prayn-day-ray?]
What may I take?

Può darmi una medicina per calmare il dolore?
[Pwo dar-mee oona may-dee-chee-na payr kalma-ray eel dolo-ray?]
Could you give me a medicine to calm the pain?

La visita è a pagamento?
[La vee-see-ta ay a paga-mayn-to?]
Is the visit for a fee?

Quanto costa la visita?
[Qwan-to kos-ta la vee-see-ta?]
How much is the visit?

Posso avere la ricevuta per l'assicurazione?
[Posso a-vay-ray la ree-chay-voo-ta payr las-see-kura-tzyo-nay?]
Can I have a receipt for the insurance?

Devo andare all'ospedale?
[Day-vo anda-ray al-lospay-da-lay?]
Do I have to go to the hospital?

Posso prendere delle medicine?
[Posso prayn-day-ray dayl-lay may-dee-chee-nay?]
May I take some meds?

Dove compro le medicine?
[Do-vay kom-pro lay may-dee-chee-nay?]
Where do I buy meds?

Sono incinta.
[Sono een-cheen-ta]
I'm pregnant.

Sono diabetico/diabetica.
[Sono dya-bay-tee-ko/dya-bay-tee-ka]
I'm diabetic.

Sono allergico/allergica a…
[Sono al-layr-jee-ko/al-layr-jee-ka a…]
I'm allergic to…

Vedrà che tra un paio di giorni starà molto meglio.
[Vay-drah kay tra oon payo dee jor-nee sta-rah molto me-lyo]
In a couple of days you are going to feel better.

5.1.1 Body parts

Braccio [Brat-chyo]
Arm

Caviglia [Ka-vee-lya]
Ankle

Collo [Kol-lo]
Neck

Dente [Dayn-tay]
Tooth

Gamba [Gam-ba]
Leg

Legamenti [Lay-ga-mayn-tee]
Ligaments/joints

Mano [Ma-no]
Hand

Naso [Na-so]
Nose

Occhio [Ok-kyo]
Eye

Orecchio [Orayk-kyo]
Ear

Ossa [Os-sa]
Bones

Pancia [Pan-chya]
Stomach

Piede [Pyay-day]
Foot

Schiena [Skyay-na]
Back

Sedere [Say-day-ray]
Butt

Tèndine [Tayn-dee-nay]
Tendon

5.1.2 Symptoms

Diarrea [Dee-ayr-ray-a]
Diarrhea

Mal di denti [Mal dee dayn-tee]
Toothache

Mal di pancia [Mal dee pan-chya]
Stomach ache

Mal di testa [Mal dee tay-sta]
Headache

Nausea [Naoo-say-a]
Nausea

Raffreddore [Ra-phrayd-do-ray]
Cold

Tosse [Tos-say]
Cough

Vomito [Vo-mee-to]
Vomit

5.1.3 Other words about health

Analisi del sangue [Ana-lee-see dayl san-gway]
Blood test

Analisi delle urine [Ana-lee-see dayl-lay oo-ree-nay]
Urine test

Analisi mediche [Ana-lee-see may-dee-ke]
Medical analysis

Antibiotico [Antee-byo-tee-ko]
Antibiotic

Antisettico [Antee-sayt-tee-ko]
Antiseptic

Aspirina [Aspee-ree-na]
Aspirin

Cerotto [Chay-rot-to]
Plaster

Donazione di sangue [Dona-tzyo-nay dee san-gway]
Blood donation

Fisioterapista [Phee-syo-tayra-pees-ta]
Physiotherapist

Ginecologa/ginecologo [Jee-nay-kologa]
Gynecologist

Lassativo [Lassa-tee-vo]
Laxative

Medicina [May-dee-chee-na]
Medicine

Paracetamolo [Para-chay-tamolo]
Paracetamol

Penicillina [Pay-nee-cheel-lee-na]
Penicillin

Pillola del giorno dopo [Peel-lola dayl dgyor-no dopo]
Morning after pill

Specialista [Spay-chya-lee-sta]
Specialist

Termometro [Tayr-mo-may-tro]
Thermometer

Trasfusione [Tras-phoo-syo-nay]
Transfusion

Vaccino [Vach-cheeno]
Vaccine

5.2 Buying medications

Scusi, dov'è la farmacia più vicina?
[Skoo-say, dov-ay lay phar-ma-chya py-oo vee-chee-na?]
Excuse me, where is the nearest pharmacy?

A che ora apre la farmacia?
[A kay ora ap-ray la phar-ma-chya?]
What time does the pharmacy open?

A che ora chiude la farmacia?
[A kay ora kyoo-day la phar-ma-chya?]
What time does the pharmacy close?

Qual è la farmacia di turno?
[Qwal-ay la phar-ma-chya dee toor-no?]
What is the pharmacy on duty?

Dove posso comprare delle medicine?
[Do-vay posso kompra-ray dayl-lay may-dee-chee-nay?]
Where can I buy some medicines?

Vorrei delle medicine per…
[Vor-ray dayl-lay may-dee-chee-nay payr…]
I'd like some medicines for…

Vorrei comprare delle medicine per il mal di denti.
[Vor-ray kompra-ray dayl-lay may-de-chee-nay payr eel mal dee dayn-tee]
I would like to buy some toothache medicines.

Posso comprare questa medicina?
[Pos-so kompra-ray qway-sta may-dee-chee-na?]
May I buy this medicine?

Ho la ricetta medica.
[O la ree-chayt-ta may-dee-ka]
I have the medical prescription.

Vorrei comprare un antidolorifico.
[Vor-ray kompra-ray oon antee-dolo-ree-fee-ko]
I would like to buy a painkiller.

Che cosa mi consiglia per il mal di testa?
[Kay ko-sa mee kon-see-lya payr eel mal dee tay-sta?]
What do you recommend for a headache?

Quante pillole devo prendere al giorno?
[Qwan-te pel-lo-lay day-vo prayn-day-ray al dgyor-no?]
How many pills do I have to take per day?

Questa medicina va bene per i bambini?
[Qwes-ta may-dee-chee-na va bay-nay payr ee bam-bee-nee?]
Is this medicine good for children?

Deve prendere la medicina prima/dopo i pasti.
[Day-vay prayn-day-ray la may-dee-chee-na pree-ma/dopo ee pas-tee]
You must take the medicine before/after meals.

Ci sono degli effetti collaterali?
[Chee sono dayl-lee ay-phayt-tee kol-la-tay-ralee?]
Are there any side effects?

È adatto per me?
[Ay adat-to payr may?]
Is it ok for me?

Non posso prendere questa medicina, sono allergico/allergica.
[Non pos-so prayn-day-ray qway-sta may-dee-chee-na, sono al-lay-rjee-ko/al-lay-rjee-ka]
I can't take this medicine, I'm allergic.

Chapter 6 – Education, politics, actuality

6.1 Approaching to a course

Frequento le scuole superiori.
[Phray-qwayn-to lay skoo-olay soo-payryo-ree]
I attend high school.

Vado all'università.
[Vado al-loo-nee-vayr-see-ta]
I attend university.

Sono diplomato/diplomata in…
[Sono dee-plomato/dee-plomata een…]
I graduated high school in…

Sono laureato/laureata in…
[Sono laoo-ray-ato/laoo-ray-ata een…]
I'm graduated university in…

Sto frequentando…
[Sto phray-qwayn-tando…]
I'm attending…

Sono al secondo anno.
[Sono al say-kondo anno]
I'm at the second year.

Sto studiando…
[Sto stoo-dyando…]
I'm studying…

Vorrei frequentare un corso di…
[Vor-ray fray-qwayn-ta-ray oon kor-so dee…]
I would like to attend a course of…

Dove posso trovare un corso di italiano?
[Do-vay posso trova-ray oon kor-so dee eeta-lya-no?]
Where can I find Italian language classes?

Quanto costa frequentare questo corso?
[Qwan-to kos-ta fray-qwayn-ta-ray qway-sto kor-so?]
How much does it cost to attend this course?

Posso avere dei crediti se frequento questo corso?
[Posso avay-ray day kray-dee-tee say fray-qwayn-to qway-sto kor-so?]
Can I get credits if I attend this course?

Quali materie studi?
[Qwa-lee ma-tay-ryay stoo-dee?]
What subjects do you study?

Studio…
[Stoo-dyo…]
I study…

La mia materia preferita è geografia.
[La mya ma-tay-rya pray-fay-reeta ay jay-ogra-phya]
My favourite subject is geography.

La materia che non mi piace è storia.
[La ma-tay-rya kay non mee pya-chay ay sto-rya]
The subject I don't like is history.

6.1.1 Subjects

Arte [Ar-tay]
Art

Biologia [Bee-olo-jeea]
Biology

Chimica [Kee-mee-ka]
Chemistry

Educazione fisica [Ay-doo-ka-tzyo-nay phee-see-ka]
Physical education

Filosofia [Phee-loso-phya]
Philosophy

Geografia [Jay-o-gra-phya]
Geography

Giurisprudenza [Dgyoo-ree-sproo-dayn-tza]
Law

Greco [Gray-ko]
Greek

Inglese [Een-glay-say]
English language

Italiano [Eeta-lya-no]
Italian language

Latino [La-tee-no]
Latin

Letteratura [Layt-tay-ra-toora]
Literature

Matematica [Ma-tay-ma-tee-ka]
Mathematics

Scienze [Schee-ayn-tzay]
Science

Storia [Sto-rya]
History

6.2 Talking about politics

Ti piace la politica?
[Tee pya-chay la po-lee-tee-ka?]
Do you like politics?

Qual è il tuo orientamento politico?
[Qwal-ay eel too-o oree-aynta-mayn-to polee-tee-ko?]
What's your political orientation?

Credi nella democrazia?
[Kray-dee nayl-la day-mo-kra-tzya?]
Do you believe in democracy?

Quale riforma ha il tuo Paese?
[Qwal-ay ree-phorma a eel too-o Pa-ay-say?]
What's the refor of your country?

L'Italia è una Repubblica.
[Lee-ta-lya ay oona Ray-poob-blee-ka]
Italy is a republic.

Andrai a votare?
[Andra-ee a vota-ray?]
Are you going to vote?

Che cosa voterai?
[Kay ko-sa vo-tay-raee?]
What are you going to vote?

Cosa ne pensi di queste elezioni?
[Kosa nay payn-see dee qwes-tay ay-lay-tzyo-nay?]
What do you think about these elections?

Partecipi alle manifestazioni?
[Par-tay-chee-pee al-lay manee-phay-sta-tzyo-nay?]
Do you take part in demonstrations?

Credi che gli scioperi siano efficaci?
[Kray-dee kay lee shyo-pay-ree sya-no eph-phee-ka-chee?]
Do you think strikes are effective?

Il mio orientamento politico è...
[Eel myo oryayn-tamayn-to pole-tee-ko ay...]
My political orientation is...

Credo in...
[Kray-do enn...]
I believe in...

Sono sostenitore/sostenitrice di...
[Sono sos-tay-nee-toray/sos-tay-nee-tree-chay dee...]
I'm a supporter of...

Io credo che...
[Yo kray-do kay...]
I believe that...

Io credo che gli scioperi siano/non siano efficaci.
[Yo kray-do kay lee schyo-pay-ree sya-no/non sya-no eph-phee-ka-chee]
I believe strikes are/aren't effective.

Preferisco non dire cosa voto.
[Pray-phay-rees-ko non dee-ray ko-sa voto]
I prefer not to say what I vote.

6.2.1 Useful vocabulary about politics

Assessore [As-says-so-ray]
Councilor

Campagna elettorale [Kampa-nya ay-layt-tora-lay]
Election campaign

Coalizione [Koa-lee-tzyo-nay]
Coalition

Deputato [Day-poo-tato]
Deputy

Elezioni [Ay-lay-tzyo-nay]
Elections

Governo [Go-vayr-no]
Government

Legge [Lay-dge]
Law

Ministro [Mee-nee-stro]
Minister

Parlamento [Parla-mayn-to]
Parliament

Partito [Par-tee-to]
Party

Referendum [Ray-phay-rayn-dum]
Referendum

Sciopero [Shyo-pay-ro]
Strike

Sindaco [Seen-da-ko]
Mayor

Tessera elettorale [Tays-say-ra ay-layt-tora-lay]
Electoral card

6.3 Talking about actuality

Hai letto che cosa è successo?
[A-ee layt-to kay ko-sa ay sooch-chays-so?]
Did you read what did happen?

Hai sentito cosa è successo?
[A-ee sayn-tee-to ko-sa ay sooch-chays-so?]
Did you hear what happened?

Che ne pensi di questa notizia?
[Kay nay payn-see dee qwes-ta no-tee-zya?]
What do you think about this piece of news?

Qual è la tua opinione a riguardo?
[Qwal-ay la too-a opee-nyo-nay a ree-gwar-do?]
What's your opinion about it?

Che c'è di nuovo oggi?
[Kay chay dee noo-ovo o-jee?]
What's new today?

Che cosa è successo?
[Kay kosa ay sooch-chays-so?]
What happened?

Penso che quello che è successo sia brutto.
[Payn-so kay qwel-lo kay ay sooch-chays-so sya broot-to]
I think that what happened is bad.

Penso che quello che è successo sia buono.
[Payn-so kay qwel-lo kay ay sooch-chays-so sya bwo-no]
I think that what happened is good.

6.3.1 Useful vocabulary about actuality

Alluvione [Al-loo-vyo-nay]
Flood

Ambiente [Am-bee-ayn-tay]
Environment

Articolo [Ar-tee-kolo]
Article

Attualità [At-too-alee-ta]
Current affairs

Calo [Ka-lo]
Fall, drop

Condanna [Kon-dan-na]
Conviction

Consumo [Kon-soo-mo]
Consumption

Gara [Ga-ra]
Competition

Giornale [Jor-nalay]
Newspaper

Guerra [Gwer-ra]
War

In diretta [Een dee-rayt-ta]
Live

Incendio [Een-chayn-dyo]
Fire

Incidente aereo [Een-chee-dayn-tay a-ay-ray-o]
Air crash

Incidente ferroviario [Een-chee-dayn-tay phayr-rovee-aryo]
Rail crash

Maremoto [Ma-ray-moto]
Seaquake

Notizia [Notee-zya]
Piece of news

Periodico [Pay-ryo-dee-ko]
Periodical

Prima pagina [Pree-ma pa-jee-na]
Front page

Questione [Qwes-tyo-nay]
Issue

Quotidiano [Qwo-tee-dya-no]
Daily newspaper

Recensione [Ray-chayn-syo-nay]
Review

Rubrica [Roo-bree-ka]
Column

Telegiornale [Tay-lay-jor-nalay]
Television news

Terremoto [Tayr-ray-moto]
Earthquake

Titolo [Tee-tolo]
Headline

Chapter 7 – Into the real Italian spirit

7.1 Some ways of saying

Non vedo l'ora di… [Non vay-do lora dee…]
Literally "I can't see the hour to…"
I'm looking forward to…

Che peccato! [Kay payk-kato!]
What a pity!

Costa un occhio della testa! [Kos-ta oon ok-kyo dayl-la tays-ta!]
Literally "It costs as an eye of the head!"
It costs a lot!

Chi se ne frega! [Kee say nay fray-ga!]
Who cares!

È caduto dal pero. [Ay ka-doo-to dal pay-ro]
Literally "He feel from the pear tree"
He suddenly came to reality.

Non ha peli sulla lingua. [Non a pay-lee sool-la leen-gwa]
Literally "He has no hair on his tongue"
He speaks frankly.

Oggi siamo in quattro gatti. [Od-jee sya-mo een qwat-tro gat-tee]
Literally "Today we're four cats"
Today we are very few people.

Muto come un pesce. [Moo-to ko-may oon pay-shay!]
Literally "Deaf as a fish!"
Very silent.

Acqua in bocca! [Aq-wa een bok-ka!]
Literally "Water in mouth!"
Be silent!

Mi stai prendendo in giro? [Mee sta-ee prayn-dayn-do een dgee-ro?]
Literally "Are you taking me around?"
Are you kidding me?

È permesso? [Ay payr-mays-so?]
Literally "Is it permitted?"
May I enter?

Non stare con le mani in mano! [Non stay-ray kon lay ma-nee een mano!]
Literally "Don't stay with your hands in hand!"
Don't be so a deadbeat!

Su questo non ci piove. [Soo kway-sto non chee peeo-vay]
Literally "It doesn't rain on this"
It's obvious.

Si chiama "Pietro torna indietro"! [See kya-ma "Pyay-tro torna een-dyay-tro"!]
Literally "It's name's Peter come back!"
It's mine and you have to return it.

Ho un diavolo per capello! [O oon dya-volo payr ka-payl-lo!]
Literally "I have a devil for every hair"
I'm furious!

Il mattino ha l'oro in bocca. [Eel mat-tee-no a lo-ro een bok-ka]
Literally "The morning has gold in its mouth"
Early birds catch the worth.

Non prendere lucciole per lanterne! [Non prayn-day-ray lu-chyo-lay payr lan-tay-rnay!]
Literally "Don't take fireflies for lanterns!"
Don't make obvious mistakes!

In bocca al lupo! [Een bok-ka al loo-po!]
Literally "In the wolf's mouth!"
Good luck!

Sei una frana! [Say oona phra-na!]
Literally "You're a landslide!"
You're so wimpy!

Maledizione! [Ma-lay-dee-tzyo-nay!]
Literally "Curse!"
Damn!

Sei lento come una tartaruga! [Say layn-to ko-may oona tarta-roo-ga!]
You're slow as a turtle!

Gallina vecchia fa buon brodo. [Gal-lee-na vayk-kya fa bwon brodo]
Literally "Old hen makes good broth"
Age and experience are important.

Qui gatta ci cova! [Qw-ee gatta chee ko-va!]
Literally "Here a kitty is sitting on a egg!"
Something is happening.

Si è perso in un bicchier d'acqua. [See ay payr-so een oon bik-kyer daqw-a]
Literally "He got lost in a glass of water."
He got stuck in front of a very small difficulty.

Neanche per sogno! [Nay-an-kay payr so-nyo!]
Literally "Not even for a dream!"
Never in my life!

7.2 Italian regions and towns

Italy is divided into *regioni* [ray-jyo-nee], regions, territorial bodies with their own statutes, powers and functions according to the principles established by the Constitution. They are twenty and five of these have a special status of autonomy.

The regions names are:

Abruzzo [A-broo-tzo]
Abruzzo

Basilicata [Ba-see-lee-kata]
Basilicata

Calabria [Kala-brya]
Calabria

Campania [Kampa-nya]
Campania

Emilia-Romagna [Ay-mee-lya Roma-nya]
Emilia-Romagna

Friuli-Venezia Giulia [Phree-oo-lee Vay-nay-tzya Dgyoo-lya]
Friuli-Venezia Giulia

Lazio [La-tzyo]
Lazio

Liguria [Lee-goo-rya]
Liguria

Lombardia [Lombar-dee-a]
Lombardy

Marche [Mar-kay]
Marches

Molise [Mo-lee-say]
Molise

Piemonte [Pyay-mon-tay]
Piedmont

Puglia [Poo-lya]
Apulia

Sardegna [Sar-day-nya]
Sardinia

Sicilia [See-chee-lya]
Sicily

Toscana [Tos-kana]
Tuscany

Trentino-Alto Adige [Trayn-tee-no Alto Adee-jay]
Trentino-South Tyrol

Umbria [Oom-brya]
Umbria

Valle d'Aosta [Val-lay dao-sta]
Aosta Valley

Veneto [Vay-nay-to]
Veneto

Major cities in Italy are:

Bari [Ba-ree]
Bari

Bergamo [Bayr-ga-mo]
Bergamo

Bologna [Bo-lo-nya]
Bologna

Bolzano [Bol-tzano]
Bolzano

Brescia [Bray-shya]
Brescia

Cagliari [Ka-lya-ree]
Cagliari

Catania [Ka-ta-nya]
Catania

Ferrara [Fayr-ra-ra]
Ferrara

Firenze [Fee-rayn-tzay]
Florence

Foggia [Fod-gya]
Foggia

Genova [Djay-no-va]
Genoa

Latina [La-tee-na]
Latina

Lecce [Lay-tchay]
Lecce

Livorno [Lee-vorno]
Livorno

Messina [Mays-see-na]
Messina

Milano [Mee-la-no]
Milan

Modena [Mo-day-na]
Modena

Monza [Mon-tza]
Monza

Napoli [Na-po-lee]
Naples

Padova [Pa-do-va]
Padua

Palermo [Pa-layr-mo]
Palermo

Parma [Par-ma]
Parma

Perugia [Pay-roo-dgya]
Perugia

Pescara [Pays-ka-ra]
Pescara

Prato [Pra-to]
Prato

Ravenna [Ra-vayn-na]
Ravenna

Reggio Calabria [Ray-dgyo Ka-la-brya]
Reggio Calabria

Reggio Emilia [Ray-dgyo Ay-mee-lya]
Reggio Emilia

Rimini [Ree-mee-nee]
Rimini

Roma [Ro-ma]
Rome

Salerno [Sa-layr-no]
Salerno

Sassari [Sas-sa-ree]
Sassari

Siracusa [See-ra-koo-sa]
Syracuse

Taranto [Ta-ra-nto]
Taranto

Torino [To-ree-no]
Turin

Trento [Trayn-to]
Trento

Trieste [Tree-ay-stay]
Trieste

Venezia [Vay-nay-tzya]
Venice

Verona [Vay-ro-na]
Verona

7.3 What are the public holidays?

1st of January – Capodanno
New Year's Day

This date is practically celebrated all over the world and always brings something magical with it, even if it has not been univocally celebrated in Italy for many years. The customs in Italy are different: lentils, cotechino - a kind of swine specialty, pomegranate, red colour – they always wear the underpants of this color! fireworks, throw away old things, see a man on the first day of the year. The proverb says: "Se lo fai a Capodanno, lo fai per tutto l'anno," "If you do it on New Year's Eve, you do it all year long."

6th of January – Epifania
Epiphany

Epiphany is a religious festival and its name derives from a Greek word meaning "revelation". Indeed, it is on this day that the child Jesus revealed himself as a son of God to the Magi.

A Sunday on March or April – Pasqua
Easter

It celebrates the resurrection of Jesus, which occurred, according to the Christian confessions, on the third day after his death on the cross, as narrated in the Gospels.

The Monday after – Pasquetta, Lunedì dell'Angelo
Easter Monday

This day takes its name from the fact that we remember the meeting of the Angel with the women who came to the tomb of Jesus.

25th of April – Anniversario della Liberazione
Liberation day

Symbol of the victorious struggle of military and political resistance carried out by the partisan forces during the Second World War starting from September 8, 1943 against the fascist government of the Italian Social Republic and the Nazi occupation.

1st of May – Festa del Lavoro
Labour day

It is born as a moment of international struggle for all workers, without geographical or social barriers, to assert their rights, to achieve goals, to improve their conditions.

2nd of June – Festa della Repubblica Italiana
Anniversary of the Founding of the Italian Republic

This is an Italian national commemorative day set up to commemorate the founding of the Italian Republic. June 2 was the date of the institutional referendum of 1946, with the main celebration taking place in Rome. Festa della Repubblica Italiana is one of the Italian patriotic symbols.

15th of August – Ferragosto
Assumption day

It is a popular celebration in coincidence with the religious festival of the Assumption of Mary. It was established by the Emperor Augustus in 18 BC who added it to the already existing holidays falling in the same month: it was a period of rest and festivities that originated from the tradition of the Consualia that celebrated the end of agricultural work, dedicated to Conso who, in the Roman religion, was the god of the earth and fertility.

1st of November – Ognissanti
All Saints

It is a Christian feast that celebrates together the glory and honor of all the saints, including even those that are not canonized.

8th of December – Immacolata Concezione
Immaculate Conception

The Catholic Church celebrates the Immaculate Conception of the Blessed Virgin Mary, therefore not the conception of Jesus, but the immaculate conception of her mother, who, according to the dogma of the Catholic religion, was conceived without the original sin.

25th of December – Natale
Christmas

The term Christmas means "the day of birth" and by antonomasia indicates the day of the birth of Jesus Christ. Even if the Bible does not reveal the date when Jesus was born and other sources that certify the event are non-existent, his birth is celebrated on this day.

26th of December – Santo Stefano
Saint Stephen's day

The liturgical celebration of Saint Stephen was always fixed on December 26th, just after Christmas, because in the days following the manifestation of the Son of God, the "comites Christi" were placed, that is, the closest ones on his earthly and first course to bear witness to it with martyrdom. One of these was precisely Santo Stefano.

In addition to these national holidays, every city - even the smallest village - has its own patron. The day of the calendar that corresponds to the saint becomes a day of celebration.

7.3.1 Holidays greetings

Buon Natale!
[Bwon Nata-lay!]
Merry Christmas!

Buona Pasqua!
[Bwo-na Pas-kooa!]
Happy Easter!

Buon Natale e felice anno nuovo!
[Bwon Nata-lay ay phay-lee-chay anno noo-ovo!]
Merry Christmas and a happy new year!

Buon anno nuovo!
[Bwon an-no noo-ovo!]
Happy new year!

Buone vacanze!
[Bwo-nay vakan-tzay!]
Happy holidays!

Buone feste!
[Bwo-nay phay-stay!]
Happy holidays!

I miei più cari auguri!
[Ee myay py-oo ka-ree aoo-goo-ree!]
My dearest wishes!

Auguri a te e famiglia!
[Aoo-goo-ree a tay ay a fa-mee-lya!]
Best wishes to you and to your family!

Chapter 8 – Useful terms

It is not always be possible to deal with all the words in a single foreign language. Below I will present verbs, names and anything useful in alphabetical order.

Abbigliamento [Ab-bee-lya-mayn-to] Clothes

Abbonamento [Ab-bona-mayn-to] Subscription

Abitare [A-bee-taray] To live

Abito [A-bee-to] Dress, suit

Accendere [A-chayn-dere] To turn on

Acqua [A-qwa] Water

Addormentarsi [Ad-dor-mayn-tarsee] To fall asleep

Adesso [A-days-so] Now

Aereo [A-ay-ryo] Airplane

Aeroporto [A-ayro-porto] Airport

Aiutare [A-yoo-ta-ray] To help

Albergo [Al-bayr-go] Hotel

Allarme [Al-lar-may] Alarm

Allergia [Al-layr-gya] Allergy

Alto/alta [Al-to/al-ta] Tall

Altro [Al-tro] Other, more

Amare [Ama-ray] To love

Amaro/amara [Ama-ro/ama-ra] Bitter

Amico/amica [A-mee-ko/a-mee-ka] Friend

Ammalato/ammalata [Am-malato/Am-malata] Ill

Anche [An-kay] Too, also, even

Andare [Anda-ray] To go

Anno [An-no] Year

Annuncio [An-noon-chyo] Announcement

Anticipo [An-tee-chee-po] Advance

Anziano/anziana [An-tzya-no/an-tzya-na] Senior

Appartamento [Ap-parta-mayn-to] Flat

Appuntamento [Ap-poon-ta-mayn-to] Appointment, date

Aprire [A-pree-ray] To open

Aria [A-rya] Air

Arrivare [Ar-ree-va-ray] To arrive

Asciugamano [A-shyoo-gamano] Towel

Asciugare [A-shyoo-ga-ray] To dry

Ascoltare [As-kol-ta-ray] To listen

Asma [As-ma] Asthma

Aspettare [As-payt-ta-ray] To wait

Assaggiare [As-sadgya-ray] To taste

Assistenza [As-sees-tayn-tza] Assistance

Attaccare [At-tak-ka-ray] To attach, attack, fasten

Attenzione [At-tayn-tzyo-nay] Caution

Attraverso [At-tra-vayr-so] Through

Attuale [At-too-alay] Current

Auto [A-oo-to] Car

Avere [A-vay-ray] To have

Avere bisogno [A-vay-ray bee-so-nyo] To need

Avvisare [Av-vee-saray] To inform, warn

Avviso [Av-vee-so] Warn

Bagaglio [Baga-lyo] Luggage

Bagno [Ba-nyo] Bath, bathroom

Ballare [Bal-la-ray] To dance

Bambino/bambina [Bam-bee-no/bam-bee-na] Child, kid, baby

Banca [Ban-ka] Bank

Basso/bassa [Bas-so, bas-sa] Short, low

Bene [Bay-nay] Good, fine, well, al right

Bere [Bay-ray] To drink

Bicchiere [Beek-kyay-ray] Glass

Bicicletta [Bee-chee-clayt-ta] Bicycle

Biglietto [Beel-yayt-to] Ticket

Binario [Bee-na-ryo] Platform

Birra [Beer-ra] Beer

Bollire [Bol-lee-ray] To boil

Borsa [Bor-sa] Bag

Bottiglia [Bot-tee-lya] Bottle

Bruciare [Broo-chya-ray] To burn

Brutto/brutta [Broot-to/broot-ta] Ugly, bad

Buono/buona [Bwo-no/bwo-na] Good

Cadere [Ka-day-ray] To fall

Caffè [Kaf-fay] Coffee

Calcolatrice [Kal-ko-latree-chay] Calculator

Caldo/calda [Kal-do/kal-da] Hot, warm

Calmo/calma [Kal-mo/kal-ma] Calm

Calze [Kal-tzay] Socks, stockings

Cambiare [Kam-bya-ray] To change

Camera [Ka-may-ra] Room

Cameriera [Ka-may-ryay-ra] Waitress

Cameriere [Ka-may-ryay-re] Waiter

Camminare [Kam-mee-na-ray] To walk

Campagna [Kam-pa-nya] Countryside

Campanello [Kam-panayl-lo] Bell

Cancellare [Kan-chayl-la-ray] To erase, cancel, delete

Cane [Ka-nay] Dog

Cantare [Kan-ta-ray] To sing

Capelli [Ka-payl-lee] Hair

Capire [Ka-pee-ray] To understand

Capolinea [Kapo-lee-nay-a] Terminus

Carburante [Kar-boo-rantay] Fuel

Caricare [Ka-ree-ka-ray] To charge

Carino/carina [Ka-ree-no/ka-ree-na] Nice, pretty, lovely

Carne [Kar-nay] Meat

Caro/cara [Ka-ro/ka-ra] Dear, expensive

Casa [Ka-sa] Home, house

Casco [Kas-ko] Helmet

Cassa [Kas-sa] Cash desk

Cattivo/cattiva [Kat-tee-vo/kat-tee-va] Evil, bad, nasty, naughty

Cavallo [Kaval-lo] Horse

Cellulare [Chayl-loo-la-ray] Cellphone

Cena [Chay-na] Dinner

Centro [Chayn-tro] Centre

Chiamare [Kya-ma-ray] To call

Chiave [Kya-vay] Key

Chiedere [Kyay-day-ray] To ask, ask for

Chiudere [Kyoo-day-ray] To close

Codice [Ko-dee-chay] Code

Colazione [Ko-la-tzyo-nay] Breakfast

Colore [Kolo-ray] Colour

Come [Ko-may] How

Cominciare [Ko-meen-chyay-ray] To begin, to start

Completo/completa [Kom-play-to/kom-play-ta] Full

Comprare [Kom-pra-ray] To buy

Con [Kon] With

Conoscere [Kono-shay-ray] To know

Consigliare [Kon-see-lya-ray] To advise

Consiglio [Kon-see-lyo] Advice

Continuare [Kon-tee-noo-aray] To continue

Conto [Kon-to] Account, bill

Controllare [Kon-trol-la-ray] To check, control

Coppia [Kop-pya] Couple

Correre [Kor-ray-ray] To run

Corsa [Kor-sa] Race

Costoso/costosa [Kos-toso/kos-tosa] Expensive

Costruire [Kos-troo-ee-ray] To build

Credere [Kray-day-ray] To believe

Crema [Kray-ma] Cream

Crescere [Kray-shay-ray] To grow

Cucchiaio [Kook-kyayo] Spoon, tablespoon

Cucina [Koo-chee-na] Kitchen

Cucinare [Koo-chee-na-ray] To cook

Cugino/cugina [Koo-jee-no/koo-jee-na] Cousin

Data [Da-ta] Date

Debito [Day-bee-to] Debt

Dentifricio [Dayn-tee-phree-chyo] Toothpaste

Dentro [Dayn-tro] In, inside, indoor

Descrivere [Day-skree-vay-ray] To describe

Desiderare [Day-see-day-rare] To desire

Destra [Days-tra] Right

Dieta [Dyay-ta] Diet

Difficile [Def-phee-chee-lay] Difficult

Dimenticare [Dee-mayn-te-ka-ray] To forget

Dire [Dee-ray] To say

Disponibile [Dees-po-nee-bee-lay] Available

Distanza [Dees-tan-tza] Distance

Disturbare [Dees-toor-baray] To disturb

Divano [Dee-vano] Sofa

Divertente [Dee-vayr-tayn-tay] Funny

Doccia [Do-tchya] Shower

Domanda [Do-manda] Question

Donna [Don-na] Woman

Doppio/doppia [Dop-pyo/dop-pya] Double

Dormire [Dor-mee-ray] To sleep

Duro/dura [Doo-ro/doo-ra] Hard, tough, harsh

Eccezionale [Ay-chay-tzyo-nalay] Exceptional

Economico/economica [Ay-kono-mee-ko/ay-kono-mee-ka] Economic

Elenco [Ay-layn-ko] List

Emergenza [Ay-mayr-dgen-tza] Emergency

Entrare [Ayn-tra-ray] To enter, go in

Errore [Ayr-ro-ray] Mistake, error

Esempio [Ay-saym-pyo] Example

Esperto/esperta [Ay-spayr-to/ay-spayr-ta] Expert, experienced

Evitare [Ay-vee-taray] To avoid

Fabbricare [Fab-bree-ka-ray] To manufacture

Faccia [Fat-chya] Face

Falso/falsa [Fal-so/fal-sa] False, fake

Fame [Fa-may] Hunger

Famiglia [Fa-mee-lya] Family

Fare [Pha-ray] To do, make

Felice [Phay-lee-chay] Happy

Ferie [Phay-ryay] Holidays

Ferire [Phay-ree-ray] To injure, hurt

Ferita [Pahy-ree-ta] Wound, injury

Fermare [Phayr-ma-ray] To stop

Fermata [Phayr-mata] Stop

Fermo/ferma [Phayr-mo/phayr-ma] Still

Figlia [Phee-lya] Daughter

Figlio [Phee-lyo] Son

Fila [Phee-la] Line, row, queue

Finestra [Phee-nays-tra] Window

Finire [Phee-nee-ray] To finish, end

Fiore [Phyo-ray] Flower

Firma [Pheer-ma] Signature

Firmare [Pheer-ma-ray] To sign

Forbici [For-bee-chee] Scissors

Forchetta [For-kayt-ta] Fork

Formaggio [For-madgyo] Cheese

Forno [Phor-no] Oven

Forte [Phor-tay] Strong, loud, high

Fortuna [Phor-too-na] Luck

Fotocopia [Photo-ko-pya] Photocopy

Fratello [Fra-tayl-lo] Brother

Freddo/fredda [Frayd-do/frayd-da] Cold

Friggere [Phree-dgyay-ray] To fry

Frutta [Froot-ta] Fruit

Fumare [Phoo-maray] To smoke

Furto [Foor-to] Theft

Gatto [Gat-to] Cat

Gelateria [Gyay-la-tay-rya] Ice-cream shop

Geloso/gelosa [Gyay-loso/gyay-losa] jealous

Genitori [Gyay-nee-toree] Parents

Gentile [Jayn-tee-lay] Kind

Giardino [Jar-dee-no] Garden

Giocare [Jyo-ka-ray] To play

Gioielli [Jyo-yayl-lee] Jewels

Giornale [Jyor-na-lay] Newspaper

Giorno [Jyor-no] Day

Giovane [Jyo-va-nay] Young

Girare [Jee-ra-ray] To turn

Gita [Jee-ta] Trip, excursion

Giusto [Jyoo-sto] Fair, right, correct

Grande [Gran-day] Large, big, great

Gruppo [Groop-po] Group

Guardare [Gwar-da-ray] To watch, to look at

Imparare [Eem-para-ray] To learn

Incidente [Een-chee-dayn-tay] Accident

Informare [Een-phor-ma-ray] To inform

Ingresso [Een-grays-so] Entrance, entry

Insegnare [Een-say-nya-ray] To teach

Insieme [Een-syay-may] Together

Interessante [Een-tay-rays-san-tay] Interesting

Inviare [Een-vee-aray] To send

Ladro [La-dro] Thief, robber

Lampada [Lam-pa-da] Lamp

Lana [La-na] Wool

Largo/larga [Lar-go/lar-ga] Large, wide

Lasciare [La-shya-ray] To leave, let

Lavanderia [Lavan-day-ree-a] Laundry shop

Lavatrice [Lava-tree-chay] Washing machine

Lavoro [La-voro] Work, job, occupation

Lento/lenta [Layn-to/layn-ta] Slow

Letto [Layt-to] Bed

Libero/libera [Lee-bay-ro/lee-bay-ra] Free, vacant

Linea [Lee-nay-a] Line

Liscio/liscia [Lee-shyo/lee-shya] Smooth, plain

Luce [Loo-chay] Light

Luogo [Loo-ogo] Place

Madre [Ma-dray] Mother

Magazzino [Maga-tzyno] Warehouse

Male [Ma-lay] Pain, ache

Mamma [Mam-ma] Mom

Mandare [Manda-ray] To send

Mangiare [Man-dgya-ray] To eat

Mare [Ma-ray] Seaside

Marito [Ma-ree-to] Husband

Matrimonio [Ma-tree-monyo] Wedding

Mattina/o [Mat-tee-na/o] Morning

Meglio [Me-lyo] Better, best

Messaggio [Mays-sadgyo] Message

Mettere [Mayt-tay-ray] To put, put on

Moglie [Mo-lye] Wife

Montagna [Monta-nya] Mountain

Morire [Mo-ree-ray] To die

Morto/morta [Mor-to/mor-ta] Dead

Multa [Mool-ta] Fine (sanction)

Musica [Moo-see-ka] Music

Nave [Na-vay] Boat

Negozio [Nay-go-tzyo] Shop

Nipote [Nee-po-tay] Grandson, granddaughter, niece, nephew

Nonna [Non-na] Grandmother

Nonni [Non-nee] Grandparents

Nonno [Non-no] Grandfather

Notte [Not-tay] Night

Occhiali [Ok-kya-lee] (Sight)glasses

Oggetto [O-jayt-to] Object

Ombra [Om-bra] Shadow

Ombrello [Om-brayl-lo] Umbrella

Onesto/onesta [Onays-to/onays-ta] Honest

Orologio [Oro-lodgyo] Watch, clock

Ottenere [Ot-tay-nay-ray] To obtain

Ottimo/ottima [Ot-tee-mo/ot-tee-ma] Excellent

Padre [Pa-dray] Father

Pagare [Pa-ga-ray] To pay

Pagina [Pa-jee-na] Page

Palazzo [Pala-tzo] Palace

Palla [Pal-la] Ball

Pane [Pa-nay] Bread

Papa [Pa-pa] Pope

Papà [Pa-pah] Dad

Parcheggiare [Par-kay-dgya-ray] To park

Parcheggio [Par-kay-dgyo] Parking

Parco [Par-ko] Park

Parenti [Pa-rayn-tee] Relatives

Parlare [Parla-ray] To speak, talk

Parola [Paro-la] Word

Partire [Par-tee-ray] To depart, leave

Pasto [Pas-to] Meal

Patente [Pa-tayn-tay] Driving licence

Pelle [Payl-lay] Skin

Penna [Payn-na] Pen

Perdere [Payr-day-ray] To lose, miss

Pericoloso/pericolosa [Pay-ree-koloso/pay-ree-kolosa] Dangerous

Pesante [Pay-san-tay] Heavy

Pezzo [Pay-tzo] Piece

Piangere [Pyan-jay-ray] To cry

Pianta [Pyan-ta] Map, plan, plant

Piazza [Pya-tza] Square

Piccolo/piccola [Peek-kolo/peek-kola] Small, tiny, little

Pieno/piena [Pyay-no/pyay-na] Full

Pigiama [Pee-gya-ma] Pyjamas

Piscina [Pee-shee-na] Swimming pool

Poco/poca [Po-ko/po-ka] Little, not much

Poltrona [Pol-tro-na] Armchair

Porta [Por-ta] Door

Portafoglio [Porta-folyo] Wallet

Posta [Pos-ta] Post office, mail

Potere [potay-ray] To be able, can

Premio [Pray-myo] Prize

Prenotare [Pray-nota-ray] To reserve

Preoccupato/preoccupata [Pray-ok-koo-pato/pray-ok-koo-pata] Worried

Preparare [Pray-para-ray] To prepare

Prestare [Pray-sta-ray] To lend

Promettere [Pro-mayt-tay-ray] To promise

Provare [Pro-va-ray] To try

Pulito/pulita [Poo-lee-to/poo-lee-ta] Clean

Qualcosa [Qwal-kosa] Something

Qualcuno [Qwal-koo-no] Someone

Qualità [Qwa-lee-tah] Quality

Ragazza [Raga-tza] Girl

Ragazzo [Raga-tzo] Boy

Regalare [Ray-gala-ray] To make a gift

Regalo [Ray-galo] Present, gift

Restare [Ray-sta-ray] To stay, remain

Ricetta [Ree-chayt-ta] Receipt

Ricevere [Ree-chay-vay-ray] To receive

Riconoscere [Ree-kono-shay-ray] To recognize

Ricordare [Ree-korda-ray] To remember, recall

Rimanere [Ree-manay-ray] To remain

Rispondere [Rees-pon-day-ray] To answer, reply

Risposta [Rees-posta] Answer

Ritirare [Ree-tee-ra-ray] To withdraw

Rompere [Rom-pay-ray] To break

Rossetto [Ros-sayt-to] Lipstick

Rotto/rotta [Rot-to/rot-ta] Broken

Rubare [Roo-ba-ray] To steal

Rumore [Roo-mo-ray] Noise

Sabbia [Sab-bya] Sand

Salato/salata [Sala-to/sala-ta] Salted, savory

Saltare [Salta-ray] To jump

Salute [Sa-loo-tay] Health

Sapere [Sa-pay-ray] To know

Sapore [Sapo-ray] Flavour, taste

Scala [Ska-la] Staircase

Scarpe [Skar-pay] Shoes

Scatola [Ska-tola] Box, tin

Sciarpa [Shyar-pa] Scarf

Scrivere [Skree-vay-ray] To write

Sedia [Say-dya] Chair

Semaforo [Say-ma-pho-ro] Traffic lights

Sentire [Sayn-tee-ray] To hear

Senza [Sayn-tza] Without

Serio/seria [Say-ryo/say-rya] Serious

Servire [Sayr-vee-ray] To serve

Sesso [Says-so] Sex, gender

Silenzio [See-layn-tzyo] Silence

Soldi [Sol-dee] Money

Sorella [Sorayl-la] Sister

Sorridere [Sor-ree-day-ray] To smile

Sorriso [Sor-ree-so] Smile

Sosta [Sos-ta] Stop

Spedire [Spay-dee-ray] To send

Spegnere [Spay-nyay-ray] To turn off

Sperare [Spay-ra-ray] To hope

Spiaggia [Spee-adgya] Beach, shore

Spingere [Speen-jay-ray] To push

Sporco/sporca [Spor-ko/spor-ka] Dirty

Stanco/stanca [Stan-ko/stan-ka] Tired

Strada [Stra-da] Road, street

Studiare [Stoo-dya-ray] To study, to learn

Succo [Sook-ko] Juice

Suonare [Soo-ona-ray] To play, ring

Suono [Soo-ono] Sound

Sveglia [Svay-lya] Alarm clock

Svegliarsi [Svay-lyar-see] To wake up

Tagliare [Ta-lya-ray] To cut

Tasca [Tas-ka] Pocket

Tavola [Tavo-la] Table

Tazza [Ta-tza] Mug, cup

Telefonare [Tay-lay-phona-ray] To call, phone

Tenere [Tay-nay-ray] To keep, hold

Tetto [Tayt-to] Roof

Tirare [Tee-ra-ray] To pull

Toccare [Tok-ka-ray] To touch

Togliere [To-lyay-ray] To remove

Tornare [Torna-ray] To return

Tradurre [Tra-door-ray] To translate

Traduttore [Tra-doot-toray] Translator

Triste [Tree-stay] Sad

Trovare [Trova-ray] To find

Ubriaco/ubriaca [Oobree-ako/oobree-aka] Drunk

Uguale [Oo-gwa-lay] Same, equal

Uomo [OO-omo] Man

Urlare [Oor-la-ray] To scream

Usare [Oo-sa-ray] To use

Usufruire [Oosoo-phroo-ee-ray] To take advantage of

Vacanze [Va-kan-tzay] Holidays

Vapore [Vapo-ray] Steam

Veloce [Vay-lo-chay] Fast

Vendere [Vayn-day-ray] To sell

Venire [Vay-nee-ray] To come

Verità [Vay-ree-tah] Truth

Vestirsi [Vay-steer-see] To get dressed
Viaggiare [Vyad-gya-ray] To travel
Viaggio [Vyad-gyo] Travel, journey, trip
Vincere [Veen-chay-ray] To win
Visita [Vee-see-ta] Visit
Visitare [Vee-see-taray] To visit
Vita [Vee-ta] Life, waist
Volere [Volay-ray] To want
Volere [Vo-lay-ray] To want
Zanzara [Tzan-tza-ra] Mosquito
Zia [Tzy-a] Aunt
Zio [Tzy-o] Uncle
Zona [Tzo-na] Zone
Zucchero [Tzook-kayro] Sugar
Zuppa [Tzoop-pa] Soup

Conclusion

Whether you do it in front of the mirror or in front of a flesh and blood Italian person, it is clear that now you will make a very good impression!

You can train your Italian pronunciation by watching videos or films in the original language, from which you can always learn new phrases. Write them down, otherwise you will lose the opportunity to implement your vocabulary.

If you are taking a vacation in Italy, do not be afraid to socialize. Italians do not bite! You can get help from those who really live the Italian language on a daily basis and maybe solve doubts that arise while you study.

The situations that can present in an Italian context can be innumerable: these which are in the book are obviously not all, but they are the most part. I'm sure you now have the skills to take the phrases, change them and create new ones according to your needs.

Italian is a creative language and one with many neologisms. If you create by mistake some bizarre phrases that are a bit bizaree, but sensible in the context, do not be afraid to share them around. A Checz saying says "*Imparate una nuova lingua e avrete una nuova anima,*" "Learn a new language and you'll have a new soul."

If you have enjoyed this book, can you please leave a review for it on Amazon?

Thanks for your support!

Check out more books by Language Learning University

GERMAN
LEARN GERMAN FOR BEGINNERS
Including German Grammar,
German Short Stories and
1000+
German Phrases
LANGUAGE LEARNING UNIVERSITY

PORTUGUESE
LEARN PORTUGUESE FOR BEGINNERS
Including Portuguese Grammar, Portuguese Short Stories and
1000+
Portuguese Phrases
LANGUAGE LEARNING UNIVERSITY

SPANISH PHRASE BOOK

The Ultimate Spanish Phrase Book for Travelers of Spain or South America, Including Over

> 1000 Phrases <

for Accommodations, Eating, Traveling, Shopping, and More

LANGUAGE LEARNING UNIVERSITY

SPANISH

AN ESSENTIAL GUIDE TO SPANISH LANGUAGE LEARNING

LANGUAGE LEARNING UNIVERSITY

SPANISH
SHORT STORIES
9 SIMPLE AND CAPTIVATING STORIES FOR
EFFECTIVE SPANISH
LEARNING FOR BEGINNERS
LANGUAGE LEARNING UNIVERSITY

ITALIAN
LEARN ITALIAN FOR BEGINNERS
Including Italian Grammar, Italian Short Stories and
1000+
Italian Phrases
LANGUAGE LEARNING UNIVERSITY

Go to https://www.amazon.com/Language-Learning-University/e/B074YLWYCJ to see more books by Language Learning University

Printed in Poland
by Amazon Fulfillment
Poland Sp. z o.o., Wrocław